W9-CDO-712

complete

patio & deck
BOOK

your ideal outdoor room

MAYBE YOU'RE DREAMING OF A PATIO THAT'S PERFECT FOR FAMILY GATHERINGS, or a sunny deck, or a shaded sanctuary in a corner of the yard, set amid the pleasures of your garden. Or perhaps you already have a deck, but it leaves a bit to be desired. Or maybe your patio is growing more and more dilapidated, or your pool could benefit from a new surrounding surface. Perhaps you're thinking of an overhead structure or an arbor that would make your patio more enticing by providing a touch of style and a place for climbing plants. Whatever your dream, you're ready to upgrade your outdoor living space.

This book is for you.

Lowe's Complete Patio & Deck Book is the seventh in our series of books for the homeowner, following **Complete Home Improvement**, **Complete Landscaping**, **Complete Home Decorating**, **Complete Kitchen**, **Complete Bathroom**, and **Decorating with Paint & Color**. These books express our commitment to providing everything you need for projects in and around your home. The **Complete Patio & Deck Book** will guide you in the choice of materials and designs, and provide step-by-step instructions to steer you through the building process, even if you have never attempted a construction project before. In addition, you'll find all the necessary details on more than 30 projects, such as planters and pergolas, that will make your yard and garden more beautiful and useful.

Lowe's building-materials and garden-center specialists are ready to advise you on planning your project as well as choosing the best tools and materials. If you're going to do all or some of the work yourself, our in-store classes and the wealth of information in our How-To Library on www.lowes.com can give you the guidance you need to tackle your projects with confidence.

Lowe's has been helping people beautify their yards for more than five decades. We're proud to be part of making your outdoor room everything you dreamed it could be.

Lowe's Companies, Inc.

Bob Tillman
CHAIRMAN AND CEO

Robert Niblock
PRESIDENT

Melissa S. Birdsong
DIRECTOR, TREND
FORECASTING & DESIGN

Bob Gfeller
SENIOR VP, MARKETING

Jean Melton
VP, MERCHANDISING

Mike Menser
SENIOR VP, GENERAL
MERCHANDISE MANAGER

Zach Miller
MERCHANDISER

Dale Pond
SENIOR EXECUTIVE VP,
MERCHANDISING & MARKETING

Ann Serafin
MERCHANDISING DIRECTOR

table of contents

Lowe's Series

PROJECT DIRECTOR René Klein

Staff for Lowe's Complete Patio & Deck Book

EDITOR Sally W. Smith

DESIGN AND PRODUCTION
Hespenheide Design

WRITER Steve Cory

PHOTO EDITOR Dede Lee

COPY EDITOR Carol Whiteley

PREPRESS COORDINATOR
Eligio Hernandez

PROOFREADER Alicia Eckley

INDEXER Nanette Cardon

PRODUCTION DIRECTOR
Lory Day

DIGITAL PRODUCTION
Jeff Curtis/Leisure Arts

On the cover

TOP LEFT Photo by Jamie Hadley

TOP RIGHT Photo by Karen Bussolini. Design: The KenMark Company

CENTER Photo by Jamie Hadley

BOTTOM LEFT Photo by James Frederick Housel/California Redwood
Association. Design: Mike Lervick and Vicki Mandin

BOTTOM RIGHT Photo by Michael S. Thompson. Design: Sarah and
Lance Robertson

COVER DESIGN Vasken Guiragossian

Page 1: Photograph by Thomas J. Story. Design: Gregory P. Evard,
architect; Jay Thayer, landscape architect; Nicki Moffat

Page 2: Photograph by Brian Vanden Brink. Design: Jack Silverio,
architect

10 9 8 7 6 5 4 3
First printing March 2004
Copyright © 2004
Sunset Publishing Corporation, Menlo Park, CA 94025.
First edition. All rights reserved, including the right of reproduction
in whole or in part in any form.
ISBN 0-376-00916-0
Library of Congress Control Number: 2004101497
Printed in the United States.

how to use this book

PLANNING AND BUILDING AN OUT-
door room is a journey from the dream
universe of the wish list and glossy maga-
zine photos to the reality of your world. As
you get practical, factoring in your budget,
the size of your site and its other charac-
teristics, and the architectural features of
your house, you may wonder how you will
create the space you've envisioned. This
book provides the answers.

First, look through the photos on pages
10–59 for inspiration. Then, study the construction information in the second and
third chapters, so you can build knowl-

**The photographs in the
first chapter will inspire
you as you plan.**

edgeably. The fourth chapter will help you
enhance your new outdoor setting.

a **special** space

This chapter is a photo-rich gallery that
showcases an array of successful outdoor
rooms. Mirroring the planning process, it
starts with broad concepts such as what an
ideal space might be; how to deal with
challenges that sites typically present; and
stylistic options to consider. The chapter
progresses through more practical consider-
ations, like making
sure you have
enough space for
planned activities
and working with
professionals. Then
it helps you with
specific situations:
making the most of
a small space; plan-
ning lighting; cre-
ating an outdoor
kitchen; stretching
your money; capi-
talizing on a great
view; creating a
secluded getaway;
entertaining; and
storage. The photos
also show ideas for
finishing touches,
focal points, and
well-crafted details.

decks

For decks, we include step-by-step instructions for a basic deck as well as guidance for variations such as a wraparound deck, an octagonal deck complete with a bridge, and a curved deck. The chapter walks you through the whole process, starting with detailed instructions for setting the posts and installing the joists so the basic support and structure of your deck will be solid. Then, after discussing lumber; sturdy, good-looking fasteners; and the right tools, we help you lay and secure the decking boards in a pleasing pattern. Lots of finishing touches are also detailed—for instance, railing, stair, and baluster materials.

patios

In the patios chapter, we help you prepare your site, including drainage and retaining walls. We showcase a number of attractive paving materials, from classic brick and stone to concrete pavers and tile. Directions include how to choose and install patio edg-ing and how to construct a patio on com-pacted sand and gravel or concrete. To dress up a concrete slab, explore the options shown on pages 231–39.

finishing touches

The last chapter covers amenities like mak-ing tinted concrete stepping-stones; arbors, trellises, and gazebos; lighting options for a deck or patio; and even some suggestions for furniture and built-in benches.

The book includes both general expla-nations, geared to help you understand a process and adapt it to your situation, and step-by-step instructions to guide you through a specific construction technique. Throughout, Lowe's Quick Tips offer nuggets of advice, from the best tool for the job to ideas for making the work go smoothly, as well as important safety reminders. With so many facets, *Lowe's Complete Patio & Deck Book* provides all the information you need for a successful backyard project.

How-to photos and illus-trations guide you step by step through the con-struction process.

LOWE'S QUICK TIP

Tip boxes in the mar-gins offer time-savers and helpful ideas.

a special space

A REMARKABLE EVOLUTION HAS TAKEN PLACE IN THE WAY
we think about the space just outside the door. Now we view it
as a potential room—an extension of indoor living space—that
can be developed to yield a variety of comforts and benefits.

The more comfortable and inviting the space, the more time
the family will likely spend outdoors, relieving some of the stress
and mess that accumulate indoors and channeling it to a more
carefree setting. And decks and patios can encourage casual,
spur-of-the-moment entertaining as well.

Building or improving a deck or patio is a realistic project for
a do-it-yourselfer, often requiring patience more than expertise.
The work naturally divides itself into weekend-size steps. And
the results can be dramatic, making the work a lot more fun.

In recent years, manufacturers have created a wealth of products and materials that improve the usability and comfort of
outdoor space. These products include better outdoor lighting
options; attractive deck fasteners; new railing and
baluster possibilities; tints that color concrete
more successfully; and a plethora of benches,
arbors, and other build-on products—not to
mention great new choices in outdoor sinks,
counters, and barbecue units—that give your
outdoor room just the right finishing touches.

For these special spaces, the options are
many, as are the benefits. Look through these
pages and start planning your outdoor room.

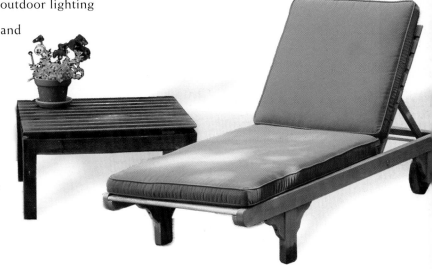

a perfect patio,
the deck of your dreams

WHETHER YOU'RE THINKING OF ADDING A NEW DECK OR PATIO OR PONDERING upgrading what you already have, chances are you're hoping for more than a simple outdoor surface. The idea of a "room" just outside the back door has a welcoming sound. And that's just what an outdoor room should be: a space that invites you out to enjoy the yard.

Right: **This small gathering space is informal and relaxed, with weathered patio furniture that's at home on crunchy gravel.**

Below: **An outdoor fireplace and generous umbrellas add a cozy touch to an airy outdoor living room.**

Like an addition to interior space, an outdoor room has many possible uses. As you consider the choices, think about the people who will be using it and what would make it more appealing to them. For instance, if you like to entertain, your priority may be expanding and upgrading your outdoor space to more comfortably accommodate a group. You might add built-in benches or spacious steps to create new conversation areas. If you enjoy evening gatherings, you'll want to check out the latest outdoor lighting products. If you find that outdoor cooking is lonely, consider adding a counter or sink, both for convenience and to attract companions to help with food preparation. If your ideal outdoor space is primarily a restful retreat, you'll want to make it as tranquil and soothing as possible—perhaps by adding a trellis to improve privacy or a shade arcade to block the sun's glare. If your family or visitors include toddlers or someone with a handicap, plan to ensure their safety and comfort.

In addition to function, consider form. A beautiful space will draw family and guests alike. If you have an old concrete slab, you can quickly dress it up by staining or painting it. Or you can pave over it with Saltillo or porcelain tiles or a more traditional material such as brick. Think about the architectural style of your home, and about incorporating art and striking color.

Whatever is on your wish list, browse the aisles of Lowe's to survey the latest products and materials. The market is ever growing. Seeing actual products helps stir the creative juices and will spark ideas. Dream a little, and then see if you can't make that dream a reality.

This overhead has a solid roof with louvered skylights, providing shelter on rainy days. It makes possible the installation of a pendant light for evening.

Left: A deck sized to fit within a circle of favorite trees provides a perch suspended above the hillside and a great perspective on the view.

Below: Pebbles of contrasting colors are artfully set in mortar to create an imaginative patio that seems like an oriental carpet.

sites and situations

A WELL-DESIGNED DECK OR PATIO MAKES THE MOST OF YOUR SITE, EMPHASIZING its assets and minimizing its problems. It can redefine the slope and shape of the yard as well as enhance your enjoyment of the garden and its surroundings.

A deck is the practical choice if your site is sloped or uneven. It will easily bridge small hills or float over swampy low spots. A raised deck that cantilevers over a slope has dramatic appeal, and often provides access to a great view. Or you can construct a series of cascading platforms to step down a slope gracefully.

A patio requires a fairly flat site, and, since it follows the yard's grade, is generally a more unassuming structure, with no railing to hinder the view from inside the house. A patio is usually the best choice if you want seclusion and privacy or if you want a flowing shape that meanders among favorite trees and flowerbeds. Patios also offer more design options than decks, since you can choose among materials such as bricks, concrete pavers, flagstones, loose gravel, tiles, and adobe.

On a sloped site, strong retaining walls make possible a patio, reached by stepping-stones and a few steps.

If you want the design features of a patio yet love the look of wood, consider a low-lying deck. Such a structure may be easier to install than a patio on a site that is swampy or has loose soil.

Often, the ideal setup is to have both a deck and a patio. Not only does this allow you to combine wood and masonry (which look great together), it increases the versatility of your outdoor space: the patio can be designed to provide solitude and the deck constructed for sociability.

Left: **On a site with a view, acrylic panels in the railings on each level allow unimpeded sight lines.**

Below: **A 3-foot-high retaining wall creates a broad flat area for entertaining, highlighted by a soaring sculpture.**

With decking, an above-ground spa is more attractive and easier to use.

The most common arrangement is to have the patio or deck abut the house, just outside a rear door. But you might want a detached patio or deck, which can be tucked behind lush plantings to form a quiet retreat. Or you may want a surface by a pool or spa. An inexpensive spa or aboveground pool can be enhanced with a deck that at least partially surrounds it. If you have a pool with a plain concrete surround, you might enhance it by covering it with skid-resistant ceramic or stone tile or flagstone.

For a city dweller, a well-landscaped patio on even a tiny lot can offer a lovely retreat. Many urban homes and apart-

Right: A fanciful railing and attractive deck furnishings draw the eye away from the nearby fence and neighboring house.

ments have back porches; if you can widen such a porch by even 4 feet or so, you'll have a deck suitable for entertaining. For the ultimate in space-saving design, think of a rooftop deck. Often this type of deck is best built using duckboards—small sections of decking that can be easily removed when the roof needs to be repaired. Consult with a contractor before attempting a rooftop deck, to make sure you will not harm the roofing or the underlying structure.

In planning for a deck or patio, think about your climate. If the site receives lots of direct sunlight, the most important factor is color: the darker the material, the more it will absorb and radiate heat. To keep the surface relatively cool in the sun, choose light-colored flagstones or wood that is stained or painted a light color. Of course, an overhead structure designed to provide plenty of shade in the afternoon will make a big difference.

Climate also affects the durability of your deck or patio. In general, the masonry materials that are typically used for a patio are easier to maintain than the wood usually found on a deck. Especially when it is exposed to direct sunlight, natural wood needs new coats of sealer and perhaps stain on a regular basis—sometimes as often as every year. However, think about composite decking materials. They are nearly as durable and as maintenance free as masonry.

In cold-weather climates, choose composite decking materials for low maintenance, or else plan to provide regular care for wood.

what's your style?

A DECK OR PATIO COHABITS MOST happily with a house and its landscaping when it is designed in a compatible style. Spend some time and brainpower customizing your design so that it blends nicely with your home.

Contemplate your home's architectural style, and do a bit of research to find the most natural way to complement it. If there are other homes in your area similar to yours, check out those with outdoor structures to see which designs work well and which are jarring to the eye.

Above: A subdued Asian theme is carried out through a gazebo with bamboo trim, simple benches and railings, and a mixture of large tiles, wood decking, and boulders.

Left: Rough decking and a log railing nicely complement a log cabin.

Above: Where the look is modern, use clear (knot-free) lumber. Aim for as few architectural lines as possible.

Left: A low deck rims an expanse of lawn that is large enough for a variety of family activities.

This "Florida-style" patio is shaded with a cloth awning and filled with comfy furniture. Potted plants and meandering vines erase the distinction between indoors and outdoors.

A traditional two-story brick home or a formal house with columns may be best complemented by a rectilinear brick patio. To suit a stretched-out ranch house, you might install a stained-wood deck. If your home is a quaint bungalow, a plant-studded flagstone patio may strike an appropriately romantic note. A deck or vertical structure next to an ornate Victorian home should have "gingerbread" features, perhaps painted trim pieces. An Arts and Crafts–style home calls for simple but elegantly geometric structures; a straightforward railing with 2-by-2 balusters may be just the ticket.

To enable your deck to achieve a look that is clean and neat, consider painting it, as well as any wood structure, such as an arbor or a trellis. If you prefer a more casual style, use stained wood. Choose lumber that is free of large knots, and install decking with hidden fasteners or carefully drive stainless-steel screws or nails in straight lines. For a very rustic look, use large, exposed timbers and leave the wood unsealed, allowing it to "go gray."

To dress up a plain deck, include vertical elements such as posts or columns with simple ornamental features. To really tie things together, purchase and add balusters that mimic the house's posts or replicate portions of the house's trim.

For a formal-looking patio, aim for crisp, distinct lines. Cut stone and ceramic tile are stylish options. Brick and concrete pavers look fairly dressy if installed neatly; mortared joints add more elegance. Edging should be precise—for instance, very carefully installed pavers or invisible edging.

An informal patio can be created from many classic paving materials, especially if they are laid in a casual manner. For instance, you can lay a flagstone patio with ragged edges (that is, with no edging) or install large paving units with wide joints to permit moss or other greenery to grow in them throughout the patio. (Large adobe blocks, bluestone slabs, and 2-foot-square concrete pavers, which have grown in popularity in recent years, are particularly suited to this kind of installation.)

Landscaping style also needs to be considered. As with architectural style, landscaping may be orderly and formal or casually structured, spare or abundant. Design your deck or patio to fit well with the landscaping style.

Another aspect of style to consider is how you and your family live. If the children are still young and like to play in the yard, keep your deck or patio small and simple. If, on

A patio in a traditional style—with a flowered tablecloth, wrought-iron furniture, and carefully tended plants—is a charming sight in dappled sunlight.

Below: A rough flagstone patio, an overhead made of hewn timbers, and bent-willow furniture combine with stars and stripes for an all-American style.

Facing page: Flagstones, set amid creeping crevice plants, lush greenery, and encircling walls, add to the secret garden aura.

the other hand, you do a lot of outdoor cooking and entertaining, go bigger, with a grill and plenty of conversation areas. If you love to garden and value the view of the landscape, design an understated project that gives you good access to the plant beds. And if you're likely to use your outdoor space in a variety of ways, keep it flexible, with movable furniture and shade-producing elements, for instance, rather than built-ins. Finally, think about your tolerance for work. If it's low, don't choose a high-maintenance design or materials.

Furnishings, of course, also do a lot to define the look of an outdoor room. Wrought iron is traditional and a bit formal; wicker and plastic are casual; and wood furniture falls in between.

spaces that work

Right: A curved patio line subtly divides cooking spaces from the dining area. Counters around the grill and the pizza oven are large enough for serious food preparation. Beyond, a lawn with a maze-like garden has its own separate space.

Below: Glass doors and patio flooring level with interior flooring create a smooth transition from the indoor room to the outdoor room.

AN OUTDOOR SETTING SHOULD NOT only look great and suit your family's life, it should also function well. A good layout avoids bottlenecks and offers appropriate space for each activity. Gardening, dining, cooking, and entertaining will all be more pleasant with the right layout, as will a well-situated sitting area. Often, a layout that functions well is also attractive because it exudes a comfortable, lived-in ambience.

Think of your outdoor living space in terms of activity-specific areas that are joined by "paths"—not literal walkways, but open routes that allow walking between areas. Although obviously each situation is unique, here are some general rules of thumb:

- A dining area includes the table plus 36 to 48 inches for chairs on all sides. A typical round or square table requires an area that is 10 to 12 feet square, and a rectangular table for eight calls for an area 10 to 12 feet by 16 to 18 feet.

- A lounge chair or hammock accompanied by a small end table for drinks will fit comfortably into an area about 4 by 8 feet.

- For a barbecue area, allow space for at least one small preparation table. A 6-by-8-foot space will hold a cook and a couple of advisers.

- Don't forget to make room for paths. A 3-foot-wide path is fine for light traffic.

Ample brick pathways amid beds of herbs are perfect for strolling alone or with a companion.

working with professionals

IF YOU ARE CONSIDERING A MAJOR OVERHAUL OF YOUR YARD, IT MAY BE WORTH the money to call in a landscape architect or designer. In addition to determining the most effective use of paving, planting, and lighting, these pros can design exterior structures, solve site problems such as ungainly slopes and poor drainage, and give advice on locating service lines, entries, and driveways. They are also familiar with landscaping and building materials as well as services and can suggest cost-saving options.

A landscape architect typically gets involved at every stage of a project, from conceptual plans to construction drawings to supervision of the installations. He or she will likely have good working relationships with several contractors. Hiring a landscape architect is pricey, but may be worth it if you have little time to devote to the project. Be sure that any landscape architect you hire is accustomed to working with residential customers; some are more used to commercial clients.

A landscape designer may not have the credentials—either academic or state issued—of a landscape architect, but will likely be less expensive. Designers often work only on the planning stages, allowing you to build the project yourself. They usually do most of their work with residential customers, so should be attuned to your needs and budget.

A deck raised higher than 6 feet, especially if it is on a slope or near water, should probably be built by a pro.

If your yard has a severe slope, serious drainage problems, or unstable soil, you may need to call in a landscape engineer.

Once the pros have helped you with planning and design, you might assume you can carry out the rest of the project yourself. However, it is often a good idea to hire a professional—a landscaping contractor, a deck builder, or a patio builder—to do at least some of the work. Look for contractors who have a record of successful installations. If you see a house with a deck or patio you like, don't hesitate to knock on the door and ask the owner about the contractor.

Interview several contractors if possible. (You may need to pay a fee for an interview at your home, while an interview at

Left: Simple acid-staining can be done by a home-owner, but creating a stained and engraved patio like this one is best tackled by an expert.

Below: Before building on a soggy site, get the advice of a landscaping professional.

the contractor's office may be free.) Ask for references—other residential clients for whom they have done similar work. Call former customers and ask if they would hire this contractor again. You should feel a rapport with your future contractor. Don't let him or her pressure you into a deal you're not comfortable with.

Be sure that you and the contractor sign a written contract. Read it carefully and negotiate any changes before you sign it. It should be very specific about which materials will be used (even specifying manufacturers' names) and drawings should be attached so that the size and shape of the project are clear. Installation methods should be described in detail. There should also be assurances that your property will not be damaged while work is progressing. The timetable for the work must be laid out clearly. It's reasonable to pay a deposit before the work begins, but structure the remaining payments so that the contractor has plenty of incentive to do a good job and do it on time.

Above: Installing a swimming pool and a spa on two different levels may require the services of both a pool installer and a landscaping engineer.

Right: Curved brick steps should be mortared onto curved concrete steps— a job for pros.

Facing page: Elaborate and precise stonework like this—especially around the fireplace—is beyond the scope of most do-it-yourselfers.

small solutions

IF THE AREA OUTSIDE YOUR BACK DOOR IS SMALL, DON'T DESPAIR. YOU HAVE A wonderful opportunity to create a cozy, charming outdoor room with a lot of visual appeal.

One advantage of working with a small space is that a few artistic touches will pack a big visual wallop. For instance, four or five handmade, one-of-a-kind tiles set into a small patio will stand out; just a few decorative elements used for the edging will make it unique. And if your deck or patio is small, you may be able to use more expensive materials since you won't need as much. Or you may be able to afford high-end products that install very easily. For instance, premade interlocking duckboards can be set on raked gravel for an almost instant, and surprisingly good-looking, low deck.

In this small, handsome patio, trellises and potted plants provide a ring of shady privacy. A raised landing with seating area increases the sense of space. During a party, the wide stairs make comfortable seats.

Left: A low deck, like a patio, needs no railing– which lessens the feeling of enclosure and opens the deck to the yard, making both feel larger.

One advantage of a small space is the opportunity to indulge in details. The artistic tile floor (below left) adds one-of-a-kind charm, while the meticulous joints and trim work in the low-lying deck below right create a memorable surface.

With small spaces, it helps to think vertically. Upright elements such as arbors, trellises, and overheads allow you to add foliage and architectural detail without taking up much yard space. Attach a trellis to the house and allow climbing plants to create a wall of foliage.

Flowerpots and planters allow you to increase the biodiversity of your setting for the cost of only a few square feet. Pots and smaller planters can be arranged on shelves and stands to create a lush, colorful backdrop that also serves as a privacy screen.

When you're building in a small space, think about the best conversations you've had. Didn't most of them take place in a cozy spot—with just a couple of chairs and a table? Arrange furniture for maximum friendliness. The two-seater arbor on pages 264–65 is a prime example of the way a small space can be turned to good advantage.

Furniture that stows away adds versatility to a small outdoor room. With the addition of a few movable pieces, your restful retreat can be transformed into a lively entertainment space.

Above: The vertical elements that outline the perimeter of this casual deck add privacy and visual appeal without reducing the usable space.

Right: A lush backdrop of potted plants makes it seem like this little patio is in the midst of a large garden.

A small space is perfect for a cozy seating area; the splash of color provided by the tulips and the portable chairs adds a cheerful touch.

The formal paving materials blend beautifully with this home's classic exterior, and the portable furniture adds versatility.

seize the night

Low-voltage lights, neatly built into the stair risers along the main traffic path on this deck, cast a downward glow that adds safety and subtle appeal.

SOFT LIGHTING MAKES A DECK OR PATIO A MAGICAL PLACE AT NIGHT, WHILE brighter lights improve safety and security. Remember the differing functions as you design your lighting system, aiming for versatility.

Low-voltage lights plug into a standard electrical outlet; the power is carried by thin cable that's easy to install. At Lowe's you will find an ever-expanding array of these types of lights, both in the aisles and in catalogs from which you can order. Among the styles available are low-voltage rope lights that can be hung from wooden structures or trees. Another type resembles pavers with little lights in the middle, which can be installed alongside standard pavers.

Many people enjoy the look of Christmas lights year-round. If you do, buy lights rated for outdoor use; since they're made to survive the winter climate, they'll certainly do well the rest of the year. A string of white (or "clear") Christmas lights is particularly suited to evening entertainment. String them overhead, or wrap them around posts and railings.

For safety, place lights along any path—they'll help prevent walkers from tripping, whether it's a guest at an evening party or you taking out the garbage at night. A well-

lit deck or patio area also serves as a deterrent to burglars.

A complete lighting system may incorporate three or four types of switches. Security and path lights should be run by a photo-cell switch, which turns them on at night and off during the day. A motion-sensor switch is ideal for a bright doorway light; it will surprise potential intruders and add welcome illumination when you go in and out. It's a good idea to place all or most of the lights on standard switches as well, so you can turn things on and off manually when needed.

Above left: **The warm glow of interior incandescent lights, plus outdoor well lights aimed at sculptures and pots, makes this setting warm and inviting.**

Twinkle lights can be used outdoors year-round. Above right, white lights climb up and over an arbor while red "grape clusters" dangle. Right, lights wrap around tree trunks and branches.

outdoor kitchens

An outdoor kitchen like this can take the stress out of a big project—like canning—by moving all of the mess and heat outdoors.

AN OUTDOOR COOKING SPACE CAN BE A FAIRLY SIMPLE AFFAIR—A GRILL UNIT and a small table in an area with enough room for several people to converse while flipping burgers. Or it can be a full-blown kitchen complete with amenities such as a sink with running water, spacious counters and cabinets, even a small refrigerator. In fact, including two cooking units in an outdoor kitchen design plus a pizza oven, a smoking chimney (for smoking meats), or a large deep-fat cooker (for frying turkeys) has become increasingly popular. Sometimes there's even a second gas-powered grill unit with a tight-fitting lid that can keep cooked food warm.

Outdoors, you can use a pizza oven, which may heat as high as 700 degrees, without fear of setting off a smoke alarm or heating up the entire house.

shoestring-budget solutions

YOU DON'T NEED TO SPEND A LOT OF money to achieve a great-looking deck or patio, especially if you appreciate a more rustic look. A tight budget can spur your creativity, encouraging you to think of new ways to use inexpensive or free objects or to reuse and reconfigure whatever you already have.

Below: On a tiny elevated deck, a touch of color and exuberant plants in containers inexpensively create a sense of lavish indulgence.

Right: This simple low-lying deck is situated where the yard is most appealing; shaded by an umbrella, it's the perfect place to read.

Left: Broken chunks of concrete form an attractive surface. Here, mortared joints are whimsically punctuated with colored pebbles.

Below: These handmade flower-patterned concrete stepping-stones, formed in a plastic mold, were tinted to resemble adobe.

Below: Imagination makes good use of inexpensive materials: a spiral of broken ceramic pieces is set in an aggregate surface.

You may be able to forage for rocks and boulders. A vacant untilled field may contain rough stones. A riverbed and its environs will likely have more rounded and smooth stones. Of course, make sure you are not removing anything from private property.

Broken chunks of concrete are surprisingly good looking both in walls and on flat surfaces. Using a broken-up old surface in your new patio is a great way to recycle. But don't overlook new concrete. It's not costly and can be shaped to suit your needs. Perhaps buy an inexpensive plastic mold or make your own to produce stepping-stones; see pages 248–51. Or pour a small concrete slab and decorate it by adding colorant, sprinkling in seeded aggregate, or staining it after it has cured (see pages 231–33).

Right: Composite decks like this one, easy to install and to clean, are a sound low-maintenance, low-budget choice.

Below: A modest-sized concrete-paver patio with invisible edging won't put much of a dent in your bank account. By taking the time to cut pavers for a curved section, you can make the patio feel more like a costly customized one.

Weathered timbers can sometimes be salvaged from junkyards or demolished buildings. The splits and cracks that make the wood unsuitable for structural use give it a rough charm that works well for edging materials or for building a planter.

Many of the arbor and trellis kits at Lowe's are remarkably inexpensive—and easy to install to boot. Plastic or vinyl ones will last nearly forever and are easy to keep clean.

Foliage can make a big impact for little cost. Buy small plants and install them in beds adjacent to the deck or patio, or put them in containers. Clay pots can look very nice, and inexpensive plastic pots do fine if they hold trailing plants whose leaves will grow down and over them.

A rectangular bed of pebbles forms an attractive surface for this seating area—an easy, inexpensive choice that works well when chairs will not be moved often.

Large rough timbers with attractive imperfections are recycled to create handsome edgings and the sturdy border for a flowerbed, the focal point of this simple brick patio.

restful retreats and open vistas

Right: This patio, tucked away among shrubs and sheltered by trees, is the next best thing to a visit to the woods.

Below: A shoreline deck has an unobstructed view of the sea, thanks to the minimalist railing.

DO YOU WANT A DECK THAT IS OPEN to the world and gives you an expansive feeling, or do you yearn for seclusion? Chances are, you want both—to revel in the outdoors and feel a part of the wider world at some times and to sit quietly in a haven at other times. With the right design, you can have it both ways: design a deck or patio that is open and free but include a nook or two where you can be alone.

A larger deck or patio obviously has a fine expansive feel, but even a small structure can provide breathing room if you open it up to the world—or, at least, to your yard. Perhaps you can lower your deck so that no railing is needed, or install low benches that take the place of a railing. Moving planters and flowerpots to the side will give you a clear view outward. Trellises and arbors should also be off to the side and, if you build an overhead, space the rafters and top pieces far apart to let in more sun.

This patio is well placed to combine a quiet chat with a panoramic view.

This deck commands both a near view of the garden and a distant view of fields and woods.

To provide privacy, a fence is a conventional solution, and it offers security as well. A more casual approach is to install just a screen—one made of lattice, perhaps—or to put up a trellis and allow plants to climb it. Trees, tall shrubs, and woody climbing plants such as wisteria, passion flower (*Passiflora*), and climbing roses can also provide shelter for a private corner of the yard.

If you'll like company in your retreat, consider the arbor with two benches on pages 264–65, or just add a second lounge chair—it will take up little more space than one. Be sure your seating is comfortable. Test lounge furniture thoroughly before buying.

If your concept of a tucked-away private spot includes indulging yourself, think about installing a hammock, for many people the ultimate in luxurious seclusion.

Left: Your own special place may consist of just a comfortable chair, a source of shade, and a pleasant view.

Above: Color and whimsy enliven a chair and table in a private patio corner, making a personalized retreat.

To enhance your yard's tranquility, wall off unattractive features such as trash cans or the air-conditioning unit with fences or trellises with tightly spaced pieces. Reduce the sun's glare by installing an arbor, overhead, or tree.

A water feature—whether a full-blown fountain or a small bubbling urn—can mask external noises and soothe with its soft flow. Or consider a small pond, with water lilies or koi.

You may also want a spa, another hallmark of luxury. Many can be installed quickly, with no special plumbing—all you need is a water hookup and access to an electrical receptacle.

Right: This narrow side yard was transformed into a tranquil bamboo garden complete with a lily pond.

Below: At the end of a gravel path, stone stairs lead to a simple patio surrounded by well-leafed-out plantings.

gathering family and friends

Right: This cheerful outdoor kitchen has a full array of amenities, including a sink and counter space generous enough to accommodate chef's helpers.

Below: A spacious deck, built into the trees, is large enough to keep the party entirely outdoors, and provides a wonderful play surface for children.

YOU CAN CUSTOMIZE YOUR OUTDOOR space to suit the ways you like to entertain and socialize. Small children will use a smooth patio surface for trikes and toys with wheels, but many kid-friendly family activities—such as badminton, bocce, croquet, running through the sprinkler, chasing lightning bugs—require plenty of lawn space. Think about where the young ones will congregate, then plan for easy sight lines so you can keep an eye on them while cooking or lounging.

There's no one layout that is best for a party. Your friends may like to congregate in a large group, in which case you will want a generous patio or deck surface—ideally with at least 15 square feet per person. If teenagers like to dance out-

doors, install a fairly smooth surface, such as a deck or paver patio, and plan how you will set speakers outdoors or in a window. Many people prefer to socialize in groups of three or four yet don't want to be shut off from the rest of the party. Deep stairs, a small patio area just off the deck, or a walkway through the foliage can be ideal for them.

For buffet dining, incorporate a space at least 7 by 10 feet to accommodate a 3-by-6-foot buffet table with diners walking along both sides. Special features of an outdoor kitchen, described on pages 34–37, all make for easier and friendlier entertaining. Several small tables scattered here and there will create a pleasant ambience.

Above: Located just outside the back door, this deck offers a safe place for children to play under the watchful eye of an adult inside.

Right: The wide doorway and level threshold assure that anyone in a wheelchair or on crutches can still enjoy the pleasures of the outdoor room.

Be sure your guests are comfortable. Provide lighting at night and shade during the afternoon. If you have friends or family members in wheelchairs or on crutches, build ramps or other alternatives to steps and make sure all the surfaces are level and smooth. Remember the extra space required by wheelchairs in doorways and for turning.

Small children, the elderly, and inattentive guests may find flagstones a tripping hazard. Similarly, flagstones and other rough surfaces make moving chairs in and out difficult; if you do a lot of dining at table, you may prefer a flatter floor surface.

Left: **This simple square surface set amongst the trees is a cozy gathering spot.**

Below: **Rafters on the overheads provide partial shade, making this open deck inviting during the sunniest times of day.**

Right: **Concrete and slate in a simple pattern make a smooth surface for furniture or dancing. The edges of the raised beds add extra seating for parties.**

storage solutions

WHEN YOU'RE MAKING PLANS FOR YOUR OUTDOOR ROOM, THINK ABOUT THE clutter that will accumulate and plan for storage to keep things looking neat and pleasant.

The area under many decks is a great resource for storage. You can install skirting with a removable panel or build an access door to make it both secure and easy to open. Or create a hatch within the decking boards, a hidden section that lifts out to provide access to a storage bin. Make sure that the site is well drained, because rainwater will come through the decking. Set anything you store under the deck on pressure-treated boards or plywood rather than directly on the ground. Better yet, purchase waterproof containers that can be easily slid in and out.

An outdoor kitchen counter with cabinet doors makes an ideal storage area for cooking-related items that need to be kept dry, such as spices or charcoal. See pages 290–97 for a counter you can build, or consider buying one of the inexpensive and easy-to-assemble storage units available at Lowe's.

Above: Hidden below the deck are doors that open to a spacious storage area.

Left and below: Molded plastic storage bins stand up to weather and are watertight and easy to clean. The unit at left serves both as a cabinet with shelves and as a countertop surface.

Benches can be built with hinged seats that open to a storage space beneath. And don't ignore the potential of wide railings and broad stairs: they may be able to accommodate attractive containers that hold entertaining or gardening supplies.

If space is tight, consider chairs that nest and other furniture that folds.

Left: The bench against the foreground planter opens to provide storage space.

Below: A built-in counter can contain plenty of storage space. In addition to cabinets in the grill area, this outdoor kitchen has wine racks opening to the outer side.

Bottom: This movable grill unit includes storage behind the cabinet doors.

focal points

OFTEN WHAT SEPARATES A MEMORABLE deck or patio from a merely good one is a plan organized around a focal point.

The natural focal point may well be the view—of the garden or out to the adjacent lake or scenic countryside. If that's the case with your deck or patio, be sure your railing, landscaping, and furniture do not interfere and that your seating plans take full advantage of your yard's best side.

Sometimes an architectural detail in a deck's design—for instance, an unusual angle or a beautiful curve—draws the eye; similarly, a paving pattern may be the focal point of a patio. Pull your outdoor room together by repeating such a detail in other areas—a cut rafter end, the shape of stairs, a counter surface.

Right: **This spacious patio is built around a favorite tree. There's a generous margin for roots that will continue to grow.**

Below: **The intricate pattern of cut bricks in this patio is centered by the gazing ball—a focal point that lends a sense of order.**

If a venerable tree graces your yard, you can showcase it by building your deck or patio around it. You might also put in a bench beneath it. Or your focal point could be a fountain, a statue, or a stunningly tiled wall.

Often you can be a bit more outlandish and whimsical outdoors than you might be indoors. Garden art abounds these days, from stained-glass butterflies and enamel dragonflies to mirrors and rusted gates. Select with care and imagination and you can set your deck or patio apart.

Lighting can train the eye on special features of a yard at night as well as create interesting drama because of the shadows. Low-voltage lights (see pages 282–89) are easy to move and adjust to achieve an effect you like.

Above: Mortared brick pavers arranged in a fan pattern spread outward from the eye-catching wall fountain.

Right: A small fragment of sculpture nestles among stones in a visual statement that is both peaceful and arresting.

making time for the details

Careful craftsmanship is on full display in this railing and gate. Joints are tight, virtually no fasteners are visible, and edges have been rounded over. Copper post caps and a thorough coat of stain and sealer complete the look.

BUILD YOUR DECK OR PATIO CAREFULLY, BECAUSE THE CUMULATIVE EFFECT OF neat work—or sloppy work—definitely affects how an outdoor room feels. Quality construction comes through subtly but surely. On a deck, make your joints nice and tight, install decking with precision, and craft railings with care. Take the time to give your patio a level surface and paver joints of strictly equal width. The quality of the understructure will show over time. Pavers set on firmly tamped soil and gravel will remain stable while a less firm base will eventually cause waves. Joists and beams that are the right size and tightly attached will keep decking straight and smooth for decades.

Round off rough edges, both for appearance and for safety, sanding or using a router on corners. Be sure to protect children from any sharp edges. Installing nails or screws—especially decking fasteners—in straight rows, perhaps using chalk lines for assistance—will give a quality feel to your deck.

Concentrate especially on the vertical elements, because they are the most noticeable. Consider buying the nicest materials for a railing. Follow a pattern for attaching to vertical elements—for instance, two bolts at all similar points of attachment.

Also take your time and work carefully when applying a finish to your structure. Even tiny gaps or flaws will show, to your project's disadvantage. Plan to refinish at least every few years, maybe as often as once per year, depending on your climate. If there are companies in your area that specialize in cleaning and refinishing decks and patios, it may be worthwhile to have them do the job.

Often a plain structure can be spruced up quickly and easily by adding a few pieces of trim. An extra piece of fascia board or some boards that wrap a planter, for instance, make a big difference in your deck's appearance. Or sprinkle your patio surface with pavers of contrasting color for variety.

Above: Paver cuts are not expected to be perfect. These cuts show the level of precision you should aim for.

Right: A mosaic project like this could be done in phases over five or six weekends. Work carefully until you lose concentration, then take a break.

making a plan

TO TURN YOUR IDEAS INTO REALITY, FIRST DRAW A BASE MAP THAT SHOWS YOUR property as it currently exists. Then draw your deck or patio plan; see pages 70–71 for drawing deck plans and pages 172–73 for patios.

Measure the primary dimensions of your property. If you have a survey or other form of property map, that will assist you. If not, you may wish to have your land surveyed, as it is important to know the exact location of your property lines.

Transfer your measurements to graph paper. Be sure to show the portion of the house that is relevant to your installations—usually, whatever parts abut the backyard. Add elements such as exterior electrical outlets, hose bibs, casement windows and French doors that open outward, major landscape features that you plan to keep, and structures such as sheds.

With the help of a compass, draw a north arrow, then note shaded and sunlit areas. If possible, indicate how these areas change, both during the day and with the seasons. Also note the microclimates—hot and cold spots. Indicate the direction of the prevailing wind and any spots that are

Facing page: The curves on either side of this patio and the pavers between them were carefully planned to create a symmetrical design.

Above: Here's a graceful way to deal with a change in levels. French doors open out onto a landing and step.

Left: Rather than cut down a beautiful tree, build around it and make it a centerpiece of your deck or patio.

Right: **This octagonal decking area is sized and oriented to take advantage of the view.**

Below: **Indicate on your base map nearby homes or unattractive views and plan for privacy elements such as this thick and tall foliage.**

especially windy, where you may require protection of some sort. In addition, note places where you will want to provide a privacy screen.

Also show high and low points with contour lines, or at least make a note of where the yard slopes. If drainage from your downspout system or from the municipality crosses your property, indicate that as well.

Make five or six photocopies of the base plan, so you can experiment with deck or patio plans. Consult pages 22-23 for guidelines on the room needed for cooking, dining, lounging, and other areas. Be sure to draw in pathways. Cut out pieces of graph paper that represent the elements you want to include—for instance, a 6-by-8-foot barbecue area and

Right: A modest-sized patio like this probably can be built without getting a permit and having it inspected, but check with your building department to make sure.

Bottom: If you have a site this hilly, make an elevation (side-view) base map as well as the plan (aerial) view map. Unless you have a large budget for excavation, plan stairs to follow the hill along a path that slopes fairly consistently; such a path will likely meander pleasantly.

a 10-by-12-foot dining area—and experiment with different locations. If your site is fairly flat, you can gain a more vivid view of a proposed layout by actually setting lawn furniture, the barbecue, and other elements on the lawn. Use a hose to outline the patio or deck, and have family members sit in chairs and walk around. To see the effect a deck and its railing will have on your view from inside the house, set up a clothesline or inexpensive plastic fencing at the proposed height, and take a gander from your kitchen or living room window. If the view is obstructed, consider lowering the deck by a step or two.

Before you go too far in planning your deck or patio, consult with your local building department about municipal requirements and restrictions. Building codes can vary greatly even from town to town in the same area, so be sure to get specific information for your municipality. Zoning ordinances may dictate where—and even if—you can build a deck or patio. Regulations may restrict the size of a deck or patio; "setback" requirements may mean that you cannot build closer than, say, 3 feet from a property line. If your plans conflict with the zoning rules, you can apply for a variance. Whatever the outcome, though, be sure you abide by the regulations; failure to meet code can get you into deep legal trouble—if not now, when you go to sell your house. See page 63 for some of the most common code requirements for decks.

Once you have an accurate base plan and a design that meets both the local regulations and your needs, you're ready to proceed.

CAP RAIL

decks

TODAY, A HOUSE HARDLY SEEMS COMPLETE WITHOUT A
deck, whether it's a slightly enlarged porch with just enough
space for cooking and eating or a sprawling rambler that can
handle large parties. Like a patio, a deck serves as an outdoor
room, extending the home into its landscape. But unlike a patio,
a deck need not be tied to the contours of the lawn. Even if
the yard slopes heavily or is difficult to access, a deck can offer
graceful entry to the outdoors.

The popularity of decks has inspired a variety of new products
that make it easier to both build decks and adorn them. For
instance, there are lumber and composite products that make for
worry-free decking and railings; concrete piers to construct footings quickly; hardware that secures framing members and decking
boards firmly and attractively; easy-to-install lighting fixtures that
attach to posts and stairs; and no-fuss finishing products.

This chapter starts with a general overview of deck
construction. Next, you'll find three representative
designs to help you design your own deck. Then
you'll learn how to choose the best lumber and hardware as well as the right tools for the job. The bulk
of the chapter walks you through all the steps
involved in building an attractive and sturdy deck with
a railing and stairs. The emphasis is on the basics,
but you'll also find techniques for adding curves and
angles. The chapter concludes with instructions for
finishing and repairing a deck.

how a deck is built

LOWE'S QUICK TIP

There is a difference between a board's nominal size (what it's called)—such as 2 by 4—and its actual size, because milling removes some of the wood. For example, 2-by lumber is really 1½ inches thick; ⁵⁄₄ boards are 1 inch thick; and 1-by boards are ¾ inch thick. A 2 by 4 is 3½ inches wide; a 2 by 6 is 5½ inches wide; and a 2 by 8 is 7¼ inches wide.

BEFORE YOU PLUNGE INTO THE SPECIFICS of planning your deck, take some time to gain a basic understanding of how a typical deck is constructed. If you're familiar with the name and purpose of each part, you'll be able to converse with the specialists at Lowe's, as well as with your local building inspector, a contractor, or an architect.

Typical deck parts are identified for you in the illustration below. (As we get into construction later in the chapter, variations on this basic design will be identified.)

In most locales, a ledger joins the deck to the house framing (in some places and situations, however, freestanding decks are preferable; see page 92). Concrete piers, often resting on wider footings below-ground, anchor the deck to the earth. Structural posts, usually made of 4 by 4s, rest on the piers and rise up to support a beam (or beams). Beams are typically made of doubled 2-by lumber.

Joists, spaced at regular intervals, support the decking. Special hardware, such as joist hangers, hurricane ties, post anchors, and beam anchors, ties framing pieces together reliably.

Decking is usually made of 2-by or ⁵⁄₄ lumber. In some cases, fascia boards made of 1-by lumber cover the outside edges. If the deck is raised, the framing may be covered with skirting (see pages 160–61).

If a deck is more than 2 feet above the ground, a railing should be installed on any side that's not protected. Railings typically consist of posts, rails, balusters, and a cap rail. A stairway is composed of treads and sometimes risers attached to stringers. The bottom of the stairway usually rests on a landing made of concrete or pavers.

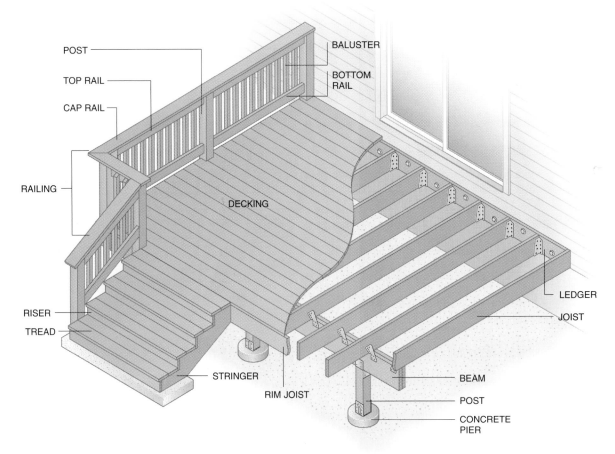

potential weak points

A deck may be buried in snow one season and baked in the sun the next, and may have to endure heavy foot traffic, deep freezes, and drenching rainfalls.

A well-designed and well-constructed deck can survive intact for decades with regular maintenance. If the deck is poorly planned and built, it may be only a couple of years before wood rots, fasteners loosen, metal rusts, and foundations heave.

The construction advice offered in this chapter will help you avoid typical deck pitfalls (see below). If you spend a little more for materials, take a little longer on the construction, and then take time to maintain and repair the deck as needed over the years, the results will be well worth your effort.

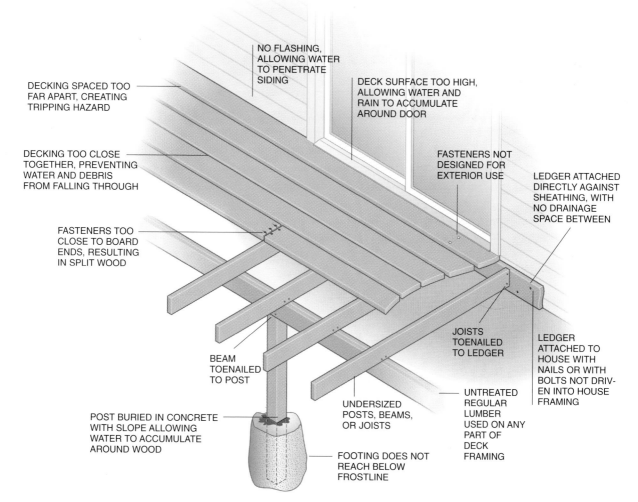

DECKING SPACED TOO FAR APART, CREATING TRIPPING HAZARD

DECKING TOO CLOSE TOGETHER, PREVENTING WATER AND DEBRIS FROM FALLING THROUGH

FASTENERS TOO CLOSE TO BOARD ENDS, RESULTING IN SPLIT WOOD

NO FLASHING, ALLOWING WATER TO PENETRATE SIDING

DECK SURFACE TOO HIGH, ALLOWING WATER AND RAIN TO ACCUMULATE AROUND DOOR

FASTENERS NOT DESIGNED FOR EXTERIOR USE

LEDGER ATTACHED DIRECTLY AGAINST SHEATHING, WITH NO DRAINAGE SPACE BETWEEN

JOISTS TOENAILED TO LEDGER

LEDGER ATTACHED TO HOUSE WITH NAILS OR WITH BOLTS NOT DRIVEN INTO HOUSE FRAMING

BEAM TOENAILED TO POST

POST BURIED IN CONCRETE WITH SLOPE ALLOWING WATER TO ACCUMULATE AROUND WOOD

UNDERSIZED POSTS, BEAMS, OR JOISTS

FOOTING DOES NOT REACH BELOW FROSTLINE

UNTREATED REGULAR LUMBER USED ON ANY PART OF DECK FRAMING

WORKING WITH YOUR BUILDING DEPARTMENT

In most locales, plans for a deck must be approved by the building department, and the deck must be inspected as it's built. The points of interest for the inspector usually include:

■ Footings and piers must be massive enough to hold the weight and must be spaced according to code. In areas with freezing weather, they may need to reach below the frostline.

■ Beams and joists must be the correct size and must span no more than the allowed distances (see pages 66–67). Code must be followed as to the method of attaching the ledger to the house.

■ Code must also be followed as to the height of the railing and the size of the openings between balusters.

design details

FOR TIPS ON DESIGNING A DECK THAT IS ATTRACTIVE AND USEFUL, SEE THE FIRST chapter. These pages discuss specific construction details that make a deck more durable and nearly maintenance free.

DECKING OVERHANG

choose attractive and strong fasteners

Nail and screw heads are highly visible on the deck surface. Screws are the most common fasteners these days, but you may not like the way the heads look. Nails have less obtrusive heads, or you might consider using "invisible" decking fasteners (see pages 132–33).

Joist hangers and other structural fasteners, such as post bases, hurricane ties, angle brackets, and post caps, are required by code because they are so strong. However, they are also a bit ugly. If they're going to be easily seen, ask your building inspector if you can use a fastening method that will be less visible. For instance, you may be allowed to drive nails or screws through the face of a rim or an end joist and into the joists, called backnailing, rather than use joist hangers.

JOIST OVERHANG

use overhangs

Overhangs, also called cantilevers, provide both visual and structural benefits. Joists and decking that extend beyond a beam partially conceal it, and also make the deck somewhat larger without additional foundation work. Decking boards that overhang perimeter joists by an inch or so make for a pleasing appearance and allow fasteners to be installed further from the board ends. This reduces the chance of splitting.

LOWE'S QUICK TIP

Consider building a deck that could be screened in later. Install footings and piers sturdy enough to support a porch roof, plan how it could connect to the house, and use a railing design that can be modified easily to provide framing for screen sections.

Attention to detail shows here in the choice of 2 by 2s for the decking boards, the varied decking patterns, and trimmed rafter ends.

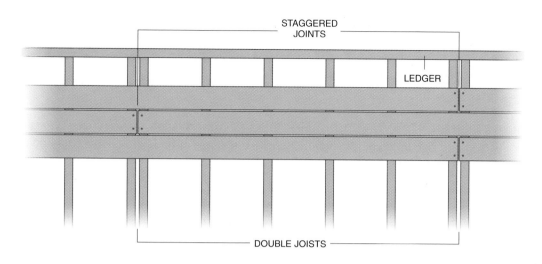

STAGGERED JOINTS

LEDGER

DOUBLE JOISTS

plan the decking **joints**

If the deck is longer than 16 feet, you will likely have to incorporate decking joints. Joints are placed over joists. Every joint will be stronger if you double the joist as shown above. A straight row of joints must be installed with great precision or it will look sloppy; staggered joints are usually more attractive. (For a variety of decking patterns, see pages 68–69.)

promote **drainage**

To keep rainwater and melted snow from causing problems, use construction techniques that encourage the water to drain away as quickly as possible. On a large decking surface, plan gaps for drainage between all rows of deck boards and plan the framing so that butt joints fall over the gaps in the double joists below.

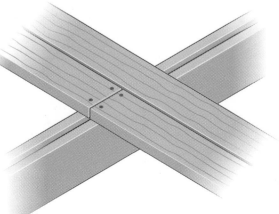

soften the edges

The edges of exposed decking, stair treads, and railing boards will look neater and be less likely to splinter if you take a little time to smooth them. Sanding by hand or by machine is effective, but using a router equipped with a round-over or chamfer bit is the quickest. However, a router or power sander will not reach edges that abut the house, so plan to round some boards prior to installing them.

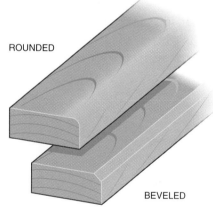

ROUNDED

BEVELED

LOWE'S QUICK TIP

With a little extra effort, decking joints can actually be attractive features. Use a power miter saw to cut the boards at precise 90-degree angles. Then use a router with a chamfer bit to produce a slight bevel at the top of each cut end. Use a nail or another spacer to create a 1/8-inch gap between the boards.

building a strong deck

TO ENSURE A STRONG AND DURABLE DECK, LOCAL CODES SPECIFY NOT ONLY the type and size of lumber for framing but also the size of foundations; see pages 92–93.

lumber types

Structural framing—the posts, beams, and joists that form the bones of a deck—is typically constructed of pressure-treated Douglas fir or Southern pine lumber. If you use other types of lumber, such as hem-fir, a lumber grading category that includes hemlock and five types of fir, check with your building department to make sure it is acceptable. See pages 80–81 for tips on selecting the right grade of lumber and choosing individual boards that are strong and straight.

understanding spans and spacing

In deck building, a span is the distance bridged by a beam, a joist, or decking—in other words, the space between two sup-

ports. Each material used has an acceptable span, shown in charts such as those on the facing page. Span charts can get very complicated, covering a wide range of wood species, sizes, and spacings. The charts here provide information for the most common lumber types.

Spacing is the distance between the centers of parallel posts, beams, and joists. Spacing is dictated by allowable spans. The distance that the chosen decking can safely span determines the joist spacing; the allowable span for the joists determines the distance from ledger to beam (or beam to beam); and the beam spacing determines the post spacing.

If you build according to the spans given in the charts shown here, you will produce a strong deck. However, your local building department may have stricter requirements, so be sure to find out.

LOWE'S QUICK TIP

Most residential decks have 4 by 4s for structural posts. However, if a deck is higher than 6 feet above the ground, you may be required to use 6 by 6s instead.

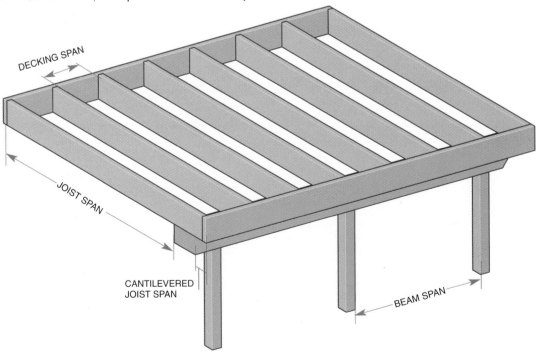

DECKING SPAN

JOIST SPAN

CANTILEVERED JOIST SPAN

BEAM SPAN

Use the following span charts to decide which materials to use for your framing. It is usually easiest to build a deck using a single beam plus the ledger (or two beams)—but you may have to use larger joists than you would need if you installed more beams. You may be able to reduce the number of postholes you need to dig if you use a larger beam. The spacing between the joists can vary depending on which material you use for the decking and the decking pattern that you choose (see pages 68–69 for decking patterns and the framing they require).

TYPICAL BEAM SPANS for Southern pine and Douglas fir, Select Structural grade

	ON-CENTER SPACING BETWEEN BEAMS OR LEDGER TO BEAM						
NOMINAL BEAM SIZE	6'	7'	8'	9'	10'	11'	12'
4 × 6	6'						
Doubled 2 × 8	7'	7'	6'	6'			
4 × 8	8'	7'	7'	6'	6'	6'	
Doubled 2 × 10	9'	8'	8'	7'	7'	6'	6'
Doubled 2 × 12	10'	10'	9'	8'	8'	7'	7'

TYPICAL JOIST SPANS for Southern pine and Douglas fir, Select Structural grade

	ON-CENTER SPACING BETWEEN BEAMS OR LEDGER TO BEAM		
NOMINAL JOIST SIZE	12"	16"	24"
2 × 6	10'3"	9'4"	8'2"
2 × 8	13'6"	12'3"	10'9"
2 × 10	17'3"	15'8"	13'8"

TYPICAL DECKING SPANS

DECKING TYPE	NOMINAL DECKING SIZE	MAXIMUM RECOMMENDED SPAN
Redwood, Western red cedar, Douglas fir	5/4 × 4	16"
	5/4 × 6	16"
	2 × 4	24"
	2 × 6	24"
Southern pine	5/4 × 4	24"
	5/4 × 6	24"
	2 × 4	24"
	2 × 6	24"
Composite	2 × 6	Varies by product; typically, 16"–24"

decking patterns

DECKING INSTALLED IN A STRAIGHTFORWARD PATTERN CAN CERTAINLY BE attractive. But you may want to add greater visual interest and appeal to your deck by installing decking in a pattern that is at least slightly unusual. In most cases, this will cost a bit more in time and materials, but will not require fine carpentry skills. Whatever pattern you choose, plan it ahead, as some require different framing layouts.

LOWE'S QUICK TIP

Most decking boards are 5½ inches wide (either 2 by 6s or ⁵⁄₄ by 6s). For a more textured look, consider alternating 2 by 6s with 2 by 4s. Alternatively, use all 2 by 4s, which look particularly handsome when installed in a herringbone pattern.

parallel to the house Most decks are constructed with decking that runs parallel to the wall of the house, and for good reasons: this style is the easiest to design, the quickest to install, and, to some, the best looking. The decking is installed over the conventional pattern of joists running perpendicular to the ledger.

PARALLEL TO THE HOUSE

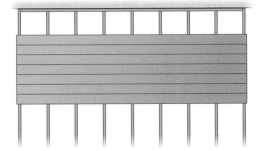

perpendicular to the house Running decking at a right angle to the house looks like a minor modification, but it actually requires that you rotate the entire frame, except the ledger, 90 degrees. This orientation may make it possible to install decking without butt joints. It also makes it easier to shovel snow off the finished deck.

PERPENDICULAR TO THE HOUSE

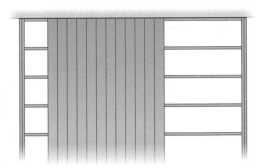

diagonal to the house Decking that runs at a 45-degree angle can be installed over conventional framing, but it requires that you measure the joist spacing (that is, the decking span) along the diagonal run of the decking. This often means that the joists must be spaced closer together, or that you need to use thicker decking. Since each board length differs, and both ends must be cut at an angle, diagonal decking takes more time to install.

DIAGONAL DECKING

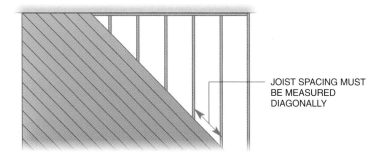

JOIST SPACING MUST BE MEASURED DIAGONALLY

V-SHAPED

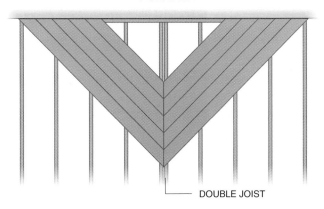

DOUBLE JOIST

V-shaped This pattern requires a doubled joist—preferably with a spacer between the two joists—running down the center of the deck or a visually pleasing place. Many of the decking boards must be cut precisely at each end, a task that is easier if you have a power miter saw and a good worktable.

herringbone This pattern is less demanding to lay than it looks, but it does require careful planning. Once the framing is correctly installed with doubled joists, you simply square-cut many of the pieces to the same length. Other pieces are square-cut at one end and can be left uncut at the other end, then trimmed all at one time.

HERRINGBONE

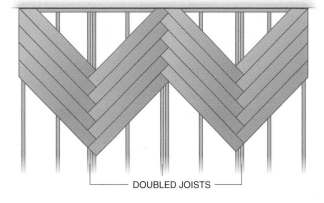

DOUBLED JOISTS

DIAMOND

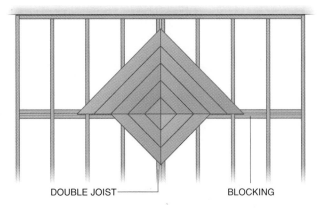

DOUBLE JOIST   BLOCKING

diamond The diamond is the most difficult pattern. However, if you install the framing accurately and have a good power miter saw and worktable, you should find it an interesting challenge rather than an overwhelming task. To install blocking, cut pieces of joist material to fit between the joists and fasten them with screws driven through the joists at a slight angle; see page 115.

drawing plans

LOWE'S QUICK TIP

Be sure to take the time to double-check your drawings and materials list for accuracy. Even professional architects rarely get them all right the first time.

ONCE YOU HAVE DETERMINED THE SITE FOR YOUR DECK, ITS BASIC CONTOURS and dimensions, and the materials you wish to use, it's time to put your ideas on paper. Consult pages 56–59 for general instructions on measuring your property and producing workable drawings. These pages show the types of deck drawings most commonly required by building departments.

We encourage you to take the time to produce careful drawings that show the location of every board. The process may seem laborious, but it will prevent mistakes and pitfalls during construction.

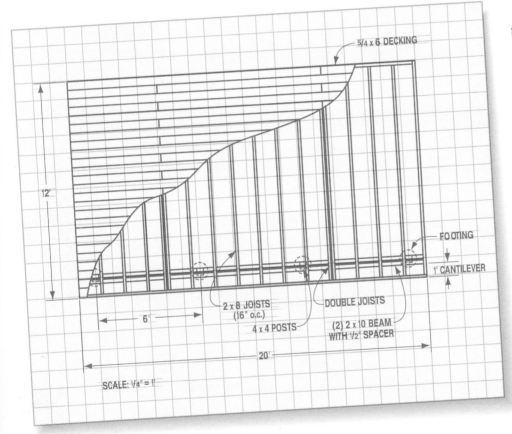

5/4 x 6 DECKING

12'

FOOTING

1' CANTILEVER

6'

2 x 8 JOISTS (16" o.c.)

4 x 4 POSTS

DOUBLE JOISTS

(2) 2 x 10 BEAM WITH 1/2" SPACER

20'

SCALE: 1/4" = 1'

the plan view

A plan view, or overhead, is drawn to scale, with accurate dimensions and structural details. Many building departments require only one plan view like the one shown at left, indicating both the decking and the framing. Others require two drawings, one that shows the decking (and perhaps the railing) and another that is devoted exclusively to the framing.

Whether you produce one drawing or two, be sure to include all of the beams, ledgers, and joists. Use dotted circles to indicate posts and footings.

JOIST CANTILEVERS

There are several advantages to designing a deck so that the joists overhang the beam (see page 64). Your local building code will tell you how far you can cantilever. Some codes say that you can safely overhang the joists by up to half of the ledger-to-beam (or beam-to-beam) distance. Thus, if the joists travel 8 feet from the ledger to the beam, the deck can overhang the beam by up to 4 feet. However, some local codes simply limit the cantilever to a specific distance—often, no more than 2 feet. If you plan to install skirting (see pages 160–61), you may want to limit the cantilever to only 1 foot.

LEDGER-TO-BEAM SPAN

2/3

1/3

2'

MAXIMUM OVERHANG EQUALS HALF OF THE LEDGER-TO-BEAM SPAN

CODES MAY RESTRICT THE OVERHANG TO 2' MAXIMUM

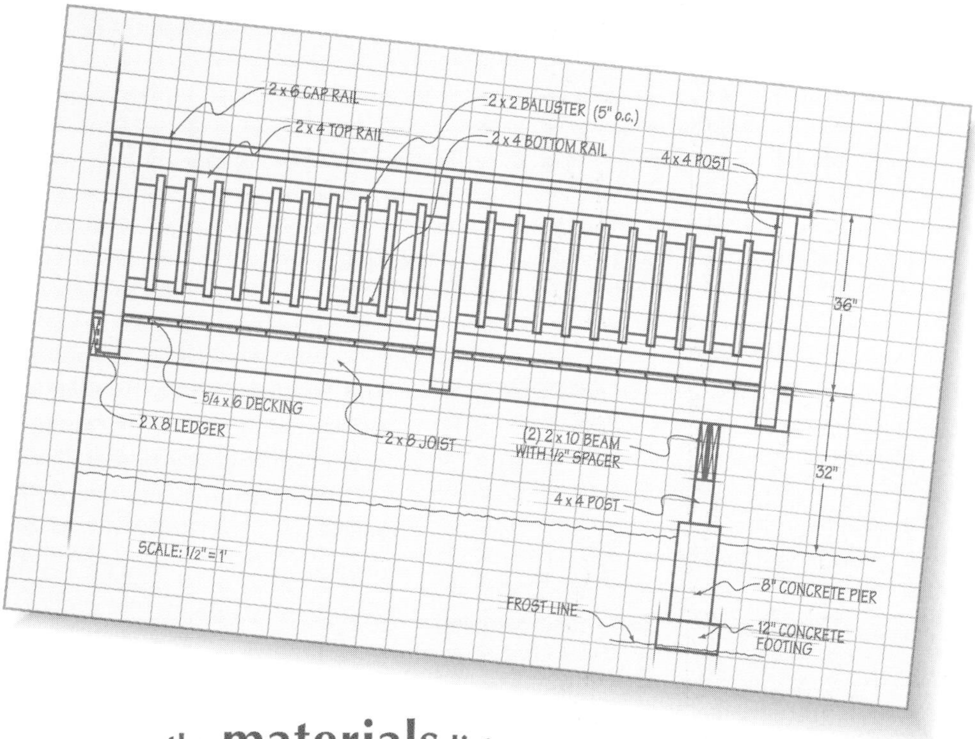

The elevation drawing (top right):

2 x 6 CAP RAIL
2 x 4 TOP RAIL
2 x 2 BALUSTER (5" o.c.)
2 x 4 BOTTOM RAIL
4 x 4 POST
36"
5/4 x 6 DECKING
2 x 8 LEDGER
2 x 8 JOIST
(2) 2 x 10 BEAM WITH 1/2" SPACER
4 x 4 POST
32"
SCALE: 1/2" = 1'
8" CONCRETE PIER
FROST LINE
12" CONCRETE FOOTING

elevations
and detail drawings

An elevation drawing (right) is a side view. It typically presents important information about footings, posts, and railings. A single elevation drawing may suffice, but it's a good idea to draw elevations showing at least two sides of the deck and at least one that shows the stairway.

Detail drawings present close-ups of particular features of a deck, such as stairs, a railing, or a bench. Even if your building department does not require close-ups, you'll thank yourself later if you produce detail drawings showing any part of the deck that is at all unusual.

the materials list

Use your drawings to generate a complete list of all the materials you will need. The lumber list should include ledgers, posts, beams, joists, decking, and materials for railings and stairways. Also list hardware, such as joist hangers and hurricane ties, as well as concrete and concrete tube forms.

LOWE'S QUICK TIP

The drawing process may reveal several ways you can save money. If, for instance, your plan calls for joists that are 12 feet 3 inches long, you will need to buy 14-foot joists. Reduce the width of the deck by 3 inches and you can use less expensive 12-footers.

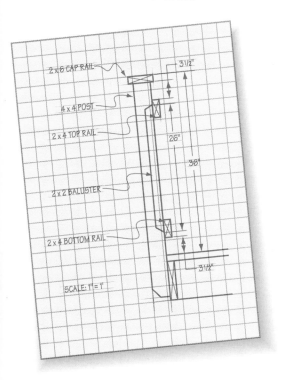

2 x 6 CAP RAIL
3 1/2"
4 x 4 POST
2 x 4 TOP RAIL
26"
36"
2 x 2 BALUSTER
2 x 4 BOTTOM RAIL
3 1/2"
SCALE: 1" = 1'

GET ENHANCED DRAWINGS AT LOWE'S

To better visualize your future deck, take your drawings to Lowe's and ask for a session with a computer design expert. You need supply only the outside dimensions and contours of your deck, as well as the height and type of railing you want. Equipped with this information, the Lowe's expert can generate not only plan views and elevations, but also perspective drawings.

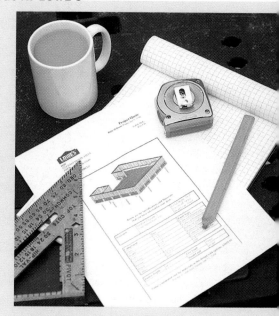

your basic deck plan, with a few twists

Above: Though compact, this deck will comfortably hold a dining table for four and a barbecue.

THIS DECK IS A STRAIGHTFORWARD RECTANGLE WITH A popular railing style. It is easy to design and build, but has subtle design elements that raise it above the ordinary.

To keep maintenance at a minimum, the plan calls for solid composite materials for the decking, fascia, balusters, rails, treads, and risers. The gate, however, is made partly of wood, since hinges can't be screwed securely to composite material.

the framing

This deck uses the most common deck-framing configuration: a ledger attaches to the house and a single beam rests on posts that are supported by concrete piers. Joists attach to the ledger via joist hangers at one end; they rest on top of the beam at the other end, cantilevering over the beam by 2 feet.

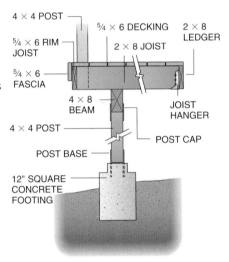

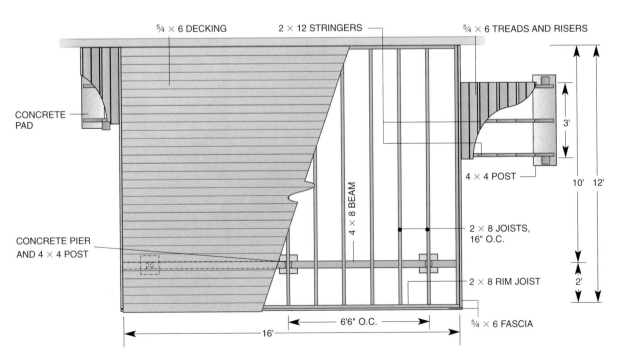

the railing, decking, and stairs

After the basic framing is complete, build the railing. The system shown here—4-by-4 posts, 2-by-4 bottom and top rails, 2-by-2 balusters, and a ⁵⁄₄-by-6 cap rail—is most commonly used. Install the railing posts after the framing and before the decking, attached to the insides of the joists. Then lay the decking, frame the stairs, and add treads and risers. Finish building the railing, adding the gate if small children or pets are a concern.

As a final touch, install a ⁵⁄₄-by-6 fascia around the perimeter that reaches partway down the joists, and paint the joists to match it. The result is a pleasing banded look. You may choose to build the fascia out of several pieces of 1 by 3 or 1 by 2 stacked on top of each other for an even more interesting appearance.

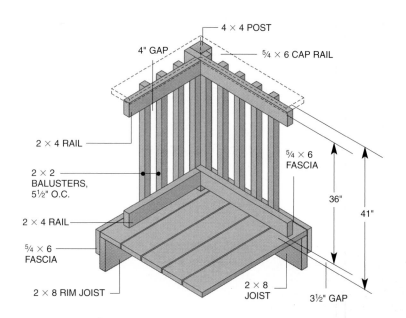

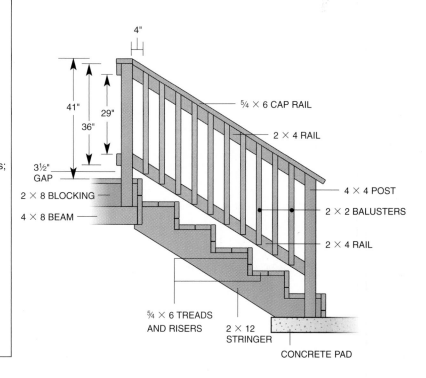

MATERIALS LIST

Designed for pressure-treated structural members and composite decking, railing, and fascia.

Posts	4 by 4
Beams	4 by 8 or doubled 2 by 8s
Joists and ledgers	2 by 8
Fascia and borders	⁵⁄₄ by 6
Decking	⁵⁄₄ by 6
Stairs	2-by-12 stringers; ⁵⁄₄-by-6 treads and risers
Railings	4-by-4 posts; 2-by-4 rails; 2-by-2 balusters; ⁵⁄₄-by-6 cap rails
Gates	2-by-4 frames; 2-by-2 balusters, nailers, and braces; composite cladding
Concrete	Piers, footing
Nails	16d, as appropriate for connectors
Bolts and screws	2½" stainless-steel screws (decking); ½" lag screws (ledger)
Connectors	Post connectors; joist hangers
Other	Gate hardware

LOWE'S QUICK TIP

The beam shown in the drawing below is a single 4 by 8, but you can use doubled 2 by 8s instead. In fact, doubled (or laminated) beams are stronger and less prone to crack than 4-by lumber.

an overlook
deck on a sloping site

THIS DECK FEATURES AN OCTAGONAL LOOKOUT THAT'S IDEAL FOR SITES WITH a fine view. The location shown is a severe slope. To build a large deck on such a site, a structural engineer must approve the plans, and special construction techniques must be used, particularly in an earthquake-prone location.

the foundation
and framing

The concrete work for this deck is extensive: not only is the footing very large and deep, but massive concrete tie beams join all the footings. In some cases, the tie beams must reach back to the house's foundation. Concrete professionals should handle this part of the construction.

A deck this large calls for two beams. Extra-large members—such as 6-by-8 beams, 6-by-6 posts, and 3-by-8 ledgers— are used to increase strength. The joists,

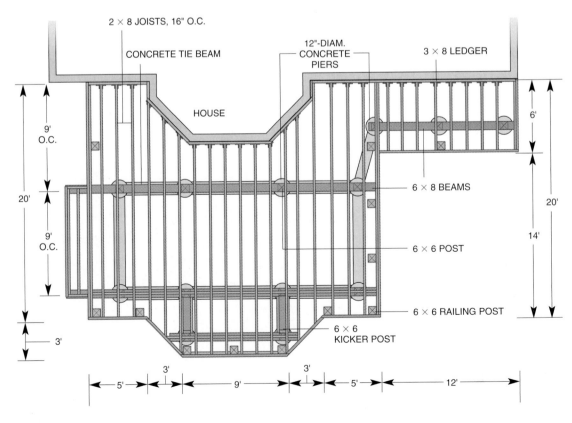

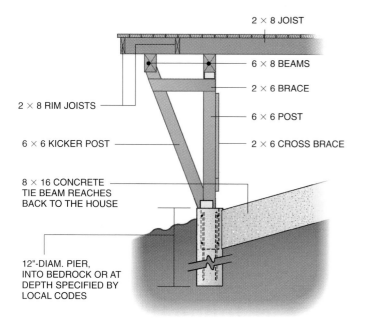

2 × 8 JOIST

6 × 8 BEAMS

2 × 6 BRACE

2 × 8 RIM JOISTS

6 × 6 POST

6 × 6 KICKER POST

2 × 6 CROSS BRACE

8 × 16 CONCRETE
TIE BEAM REACHES
BACK TO THE HOUSE

12"-DIAM. PIER,
INTO BEDROCK OR AT
DEPTH SPECIFIED BY
LOCAL CODES

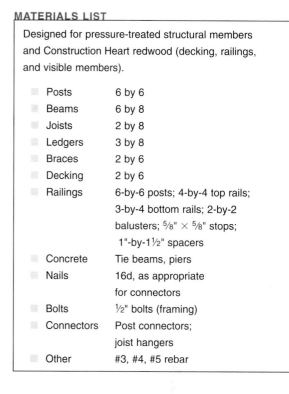

MATERIALS LIST

Designed for pressure-treated structural members
and Construction Heart redwood (decking, railings,
and visible members).

Posts	6 by 6	
Beams	6 by 8	
Joists	2 by 8	
Ledgers	3 by 8	
Braces	2 by 6	
Decking	2 by 6	
Railings	6-by-6 posts; 4-by-4 top rails; 3-by-4 bottom rails; 2-by-2 balusters; $\frac{5}{8}$" × $\frac{5}{8}$" stops; 1"-by-1$\frac{1}{2}$" spacers	
Concrete	Tie beams, piers	
Nails	16d, as appropriate for connectors	
Bolts	$\frac{1}{2}$" bolts (framing)	
Connectors	Post connectors; joist hangers	
Other	#3, #4, #5 rebar	

however, are standard 2 by 8s. On a slop-
ing site, a "kicker" post (see above) is
sometimes used to extend the support
outward.

the **railing**

Railing posts are made of 6 by 6s, not only
for extra strength but also because they
create an attractive picket-fence appearance. The posts are attached to the framing
before the decking is installed. Railing sections, sized to fit between the posts, are
constructed ladder-style and then attached
to the posts (see page 153).

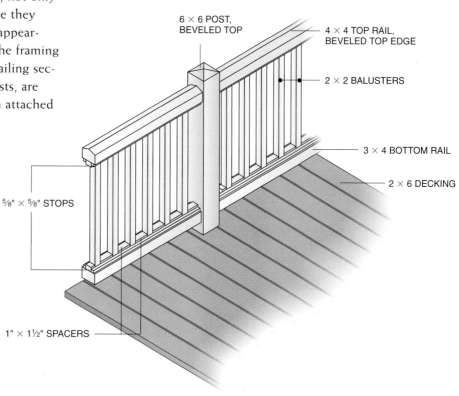

6 × 6 POST,
BEVELED TOP

4 × 4 TOP RAIL,
BEVELED TOP EDGE

2 × 2 BALUSTERS

3 × 4 BOTTOM RAIL

2 × 6 DECKING

$\frac{5}{8}$" × $\frac{5}{8}$" STOPS

1" × 1$\frac{1}{2}$" SPACERS

LOWE'S QUICK TIP

A painted railing such
as the one shown
here contrasts nicely
with redwood decking.
It is also easy to wipe
clean, and you will not
have to worry that
water rings will be left
by drinks placed on
the cap rail.

an octagonal
deck with a pathway

A DECK THAT IS LOW TO THE GROUND SEEMS TO FLOAT OVER THE YARD. THE benches, emphasizing the deck's outline, serve as tables for potted plants. Low-voltage lighting (see pages 282–89) positioned under the seats adds subtle illumination.

On a deck this low, railings are not required. Here, the deck steps down to a low bridge that crosses a small pool; such a bridge could also function as a graceful entry to the lawn.

A low deck near water gives the feel of a wharf. For the framing, be sure to use pressure-treated lumber rated for ground contact.

LOWE'S QUICK TIP

Built-in benches may force a seated person to look at the house rather than the view. One solution: position patio chairs looking outward, and use the benches as footrests.

the foundation
and framing

This deck was built in an area where frost is rare; in your area, codes may require that footings be sunk below the frostline.

When a deck is very low to the ground, the beams rest directly on the footings, which must be poured at the correct level. If the site slopes down, short posts are placed on top of the footings.

The walkway section shown here spans a 16-foot-wide pool. Standard 2-by-8 joists are not strong enough to carry the load. Instead, three beams made of 4 by 8s

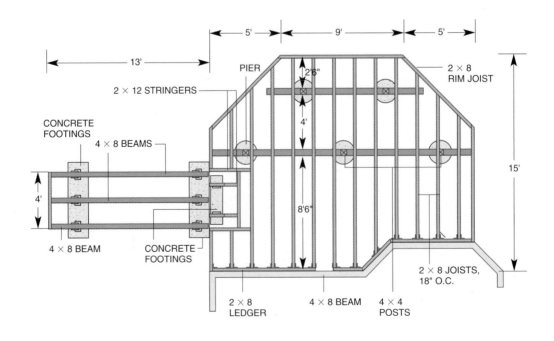

(or doubled 2 by 8s) act as joists, with the decking resting directly on top of them.

The main portion of the deck uses a standard ledger-and-beam configuration, like the basic deck shown on pages 72–73. However, the octagonal front section, which cantilevers out over 5 feet, needs an additional beam for support.

the **benches**

Once the framing is complete, the 4-by-12 bench posts (or doubled 2-by-12 posts) are attached via pieces of blocking. Wire for the low-voltage lights is then roughed in. After the decking is installed, the benches are finished and the lighting is installed.

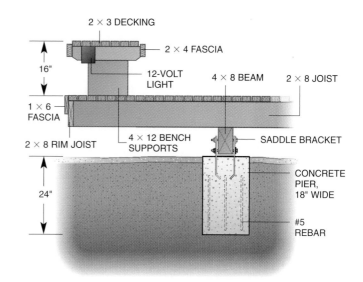

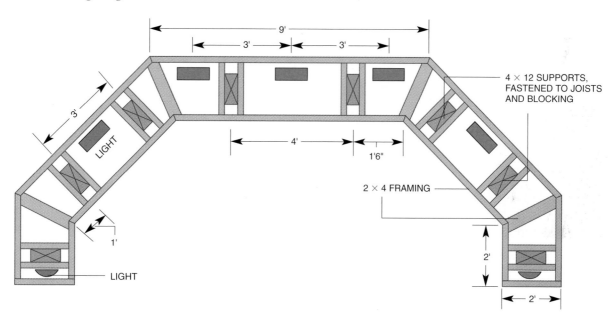

MATERIALS LIST

Designed for pressure-treated structural members and Construction Heart redwood (decking, railings, and visible members).

Posts	4 by 4	
Beams	4 by 8, or doubled 2 by 8s	
Joists and ledgers	2 by 8 joists and blocking; 2 by 12 stringers	
Decking	2 by 3	
Bench	4 by 12, or doubled 2 by 12 supports; 2 by 4 framing; 2 by 3 seating	
Fascias	1 by 6 deck fascia; 2 by 4 bench fascia	

Concrete	Piers, footings	
Nails	16d; 10d finish (decking and fascia); as appropriate for connectors	
Bolts and screws	½" lag screws to attach the ledger	
Connectors	Beam-to-footing connectors; joist hangers; post connectors	
Other	#5 rebar	
Surface-mount low-voltage lights (under bench)		

LOWE'S QUICK TIP

The 2-by-3 decking shown here produces twice the between-board lines that standard 2 by 6s would—an attractive look, especially for a small deck.

lumber choices

DECKS, BY THEIR VERY NATURE, ARE EXPOSED TO THE ELEMENTS—NOT ONLY TO rain (and possibly snow), but also to temperature changes, ultraviolet rays, mildew, and wood-boring insects. Choose lumber with a proven track record of durability in your area.

Even boards that are nowhere near the ground often remain moist for prolonged periods, so use lumber rated "ground contact" for all the structural deck members.

LOWE'S QUICK TIP

"Brown-treated" wood is not only treated with a preservative, it is also stained an attractive color. This type of lumber will likely need to be restained every two or so years.

treated lumber

Wood that has been factory-treated with preservatives will survive the elements much longer than untreated wood. Pressure-treated lumber is only marginally more expensive than untreated lumber, making it the logical choice for all structural members.

For years most wood has been treated with the preservative chromated copper arsenate (CCA). CCA-treated lumber rated for "ground contact" or with a treatment content of 40 or greater is nearly indestructible. However, because of concerns about its arsenic content, CCA is being banned from use. Newer, more environmentally friendly treatments include ammoniacal copper quaternary (ACQ) and copper boron azole (CBA). Consult with a lumber specialist at Lowe's to find the type of pressure-treated lumber that lasts longest in your area.

Also check that your fasteners—hardware as well as screws and nails—are compatible with the treated lumber you choose. For instance, some treatments can cause zinc (an ingredient in many joist hangers and other hardware pieces) to corrode.

Treated Douglas fir is typically the strongest and most stable structural lumber you can buy, but it may not be available or it may be expensive. Southern pine absorbs liquid treatment readily, and so is often an inexpensive option. However, though it's strong, it is also somewhat brittle and prone to cracking.

Hem-fir is an umbrella category that includes hemlock and five types of fir. This means that in some locales it may be strong and resistant to warping, while in other places it may be much less satisfactory. Ask your Lowe's lumber specialist whether hem-fir performs well where you live. If you use it, be sure to apply water repellent to any cut ends.

REDWOOD

BROWN-TREATED DOUGLAS FIR

CEDAR

IPÉ

CAMBARA

MERANTI

IRONWOODS

Often, the liquid treatment does not penetrate all the way through a board's thickness; this is almost always the case with 4-by lumber. Soak all cut ends of the boards in preservative before installing them.

Most treated lumber is a greenish color, which will fade in time to gray. You can buy stains designed to beautify green or graying pressure-treated lumber. However, if the lumber has slits from the treatment process, they will never disappear.

redwood and cedar

Both redwood and cedar are naturally resistant to rot. However, only the heartwood of these species—which is usually darker in color—is strongly rot resistant; the lighter-colored sapwood may rot within a year if not sealed. In addition, cedar and redwood have many different grades, which can be confusing. Your Lowe's lumber specialist can help you select boards that will last. For best wear, regularly apply sealer to any redwood or any cedar lumber that is exposed to the weather (see pages 162–65).

tropical hardwoods

Several varieties of tropical hardwoods are available. Beautiful and extremely durable, these woods are also expensive and difficult to work with; you will have to drill pilot holes for each fastener (see page 87).

composite and vinyl

Composite decking and railing components are made from recycled plastic and wood chips. Some types mimic wood grain while others present a smooth face. Solid vinyl products are also increasingly popular; they typically have a shinier surface. Composite and vinyl materials are easy to work with and are completely resistant to rot. See pages 134–37 and 158–59 for a variety of composite and vinyl options that are available at Lowe's.

LOWE'S QUICK TIP

Use pressure-treated lumber for all structural pieces—posts, beams, stringers, and joists—that will not be visible. You can also use it for the decking and railing, but you may want to invest in higher-end products, such as composite, redwood, or cedar, for these visible parts of the deck.

VINYL

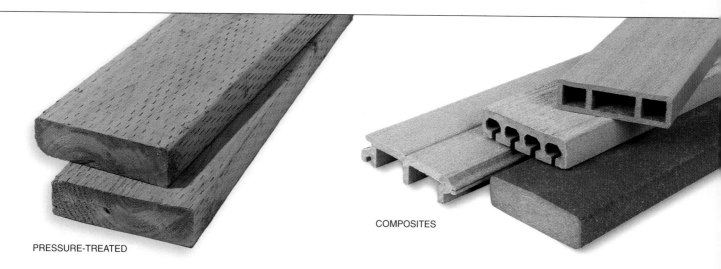

PRESSURE-TREATED

COMPOSITES

selecting boards

IT'S NOT ENOUGH TO CHOOSE THE SPECIES AND TYPE OF LUMBER YOU WANT.
You must also select individual boards that best suit your purposes.

lumber grading

LOWE'S QUICK TIP

If you're unable to sort through boards yourself, order about 20 percent more lumber than you need. That way, you can set aside any defective boards and keep working; you can return the bad boards at the end of the project.

Most boards display a grading stamp or sticker that gives important information about the board's quality. Grading systems vary dramatically from one species of wood to another, but here are some of the most common designations.

- To indicate strength, lumber is often rated Select (or Select Structural), No. 1, No. 2, or No. 3. Another system uses the terms Construction, Standard (or Standard and Better), and Utility. Avoid using lumber labeled No. 3 or Utility. No. 2 or Standard boards are strong enough for most structural work, but your building department may require a higher grade.

- Cedar and redwood are graded for appearance and heartwood content. When buying redwood, either buy boards with a label that contains the word "heart," or plan on applying sealer to the sapwood, the softer part of the wood that is otherwise liable to rot. If cedar board labels don't contain information about heartwood content, choose the darker-colored boards.

- A board with a high moisture content is more likely to warp and shrink; the drier the board, the more stable it will be. If a board is labeled S-DRY or its moisture content is 20 percent or less, shrinkage and warping should not be a problem. Pressure-treated lumber labeled KDAT (kiln dried after treatment) is the driest and most stable; you may want to buy KDAT boards for the cap rail of a railing or for other very visible parts.

decking and fascia boards

Cedar decking, typically ⁵⁄₄ by 6, is a popular choice. The edges are usually rounded to minimize splintering, and the cedar has a pleasing appearance. However, most cedar decking is not very resistant to rot. To ensure that you will not have to replace boards in a few years, apply a liberal coat of sealer (the wood will readily soak it up) to both sides of the boards before you install them, and seal the decking again after the deck is built. Be aware that cedar is fairly soft, and so may be unsuitable for a deck where chairs are often scooted or where children play.

For the fascia, you may choose cedar or redwood that has a rough side, which has a pleasant woody appearance. Avoid using rough-textured lumber wherever it will be handled or walked on, though, because the rough texture is easily dented and difficult to keep clean.

VERTICAL AND FLAT GRAIN

Depending on how it was cut at the sawmill, a board may have either vertical grain—narrow, parallel grain lines—or flat grain—wide grain lines that form wavy V shapes. Many boards contain both vertical and flat grain. Vertical-grain lumber is less likely to cup or twist, and is stronger than flat-grain lumber. Whenever possible, choose boards with primarily vertical grain.

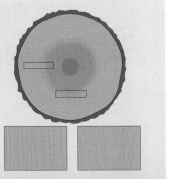

checking for defects

Pick up and examine each board to make sure it will suit your purpose. Check the surfaces for defects, then pick up one end and sight along the board's length to see that it is straight. All the boards won't be perfect, but make sure none are damaged in a way that will harm the deck's structure.

Here are the major defects to watch for:

■ CROOK a severe warp (more than an inch on an 8-foot-long piece) along the edge line. If the warp is not severe, it is called a crown, and can be straightened out on decking boards. Joists are installed with the crown side up.

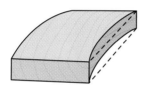

■ BOW a warp on the face of a board from end to end. Unless the bow is extremely pronounced, it usually can be straightened during installation.

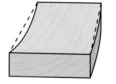

■ CUP a hollow across the face of a board. This is difficult to straighten out, so reject a board with a severe cup.

■ TWIST multiple bends in a board. Twists are usually difficult to straighten.

■ KNOT a circular, cross-grain area. Knots smaller than 1½ inches across and tightly in place are no problem, but you may prefer not to have them visible. A large knot, or one that is already loose, will almost certainly fall out in time, but the resulting hole is just a cosmetic problem that will not affect the strength of the board.

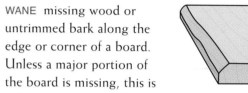

■ WANE missing wood or untrimmed bark along the edge or corner of a board. Unless a major portion of the board is missing, this is only a cosmetic problem.

■ CHECKING cracks that run along the length of a board but do not go all the way through. If the check is wider than $\frac{1}{16}$ inch or deeper than half the board's thickness, the checked portion must be cut off.

■ SPLIT a crack that goes all the way through the board. This usually occurs at one of the board's ends. Plan to cut off the split portion.

LOWE'S QUICK TIP

Save the straightest and best-looking boards for those places that are most visible. In particular, the cap rail should be made of the best boards you can find.

deck fasteners

EVEN THE BEST-QUALITY FASTENERS ACCOUNT FOR ONLY A SMALL PORTION OF the cost of a new deck, and they are well worth the modest investment. Choose fasteners that not only hold firmly but also resist corrosion. To ensure a strong deck, purchase fasteners that exceed the requirements of your local code.

nails

Nails are commonly used for fastening deck structures because they install quickly. Common nails with smooth shanks have the least holding capability, and can come loose when the wood shrinks over time. Cement-coated nails are easy to drive and hold firmly but will rust if exposed to moisture. Hot-dipped galvanized nails are a better choice. The somewhat chunky galvanized surface not only inhibits rust, but also adds to the nail's grabbing power. Spiral-shank galvanized nails have even greater holding ability and are a good choice for decking. Deck nails are the most resistant to rust, and also grab firmly.

Many people automatically choose screws to install decking. But you may prefer the less obtrusive appearance of nail heads. However, it takes patience and practice to drive nails without marring the decking surface.

screws

Equipped with a strong drill and a screwdriver bit, you can drive screws just as quickly as you can hand-drive nails. If you rent a screw gun and buy screws that come in long clips, you can move even faster.

Stainless-steel screws are classy looking and impervious to corrosion, but they are also very expensive. Galvanized screws are an option, but decking screws are more resistant to rust. Standard Phillips-head screws can be stripped easily. Instead, buy screws that use a square drive bit or a special deck-screw bit.

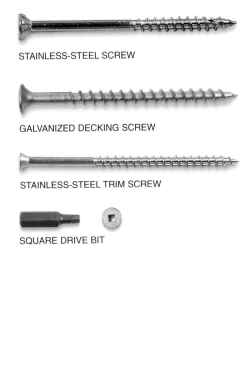

STAINLESS-STEEL SCREW

GALVANIZED DECKING SCREW

STAINLESS-STEEL TRIM SCREW

SQUARE DRIVE BIT

LOWE'S QUICK TIP

For large nailing jobs, you may choose to rent a power nailer, which drives nails with machine-gun speed. If you use a nailer to install decking, be careful to set the depth just right; a sunken nail head creates a little pool when it rains.

JOIST HANGER NAIL

COMMON NAIL

RING-SHANK NAIL

SPIRAL-GROOVE NAIL

FINISH NAIL

STAINLESS-STEEL SPIRAL-GROOVE NAIL

hidden fasteners

Many people dislike seeing nail or screw heads all over the surface of a deck, especially if the decking itself is topnotch. In response to that concern, several types of hidden fasteners have been developed. They cost more and take longer to install, but the results can be worth it. See pages 132–33 for more information.

BISCUIT FASTENERS

DECK CLIP

METAL TRACK
FASTENERS

bolts and lag screws

Bolts are heavy-duty fasteners intended to carry bigger loads than standard nails and screws. Carriage bolts and lag screws are used to connect ledgers, railing posts, and other critical framing members; your building code will likely specify the exact size and number of such fasteners. Carriage bolts, which require a nut and washer, are usually stronger than lag screws, but cannot be used for very thick connections or if the back side of the fastener is not accessible. Carriage bolts and lag screws both require pilot holes. Anchor bolts (or J-bolts) are used to secure post anchors to concrete piers. Use a washer whenever driving a lag screw or a bolt.

To fasten a ledger or other board to masonry, options include expanding anchors, masonry screws, and lag screws with masonry shields (see page 240).

ANCHOR
BOLT

MASONRY
SCREW

LAG
SCREW

SCREW WITH
SHIELD

CARRIAGE
BOLT

framing hardware

A variety of items, including joist hangers and metal straps, are made specifically for connecting the various components of a deck. Be sure to buy connectors that are coated for exterior use; uncoated hardware will quickly rust.

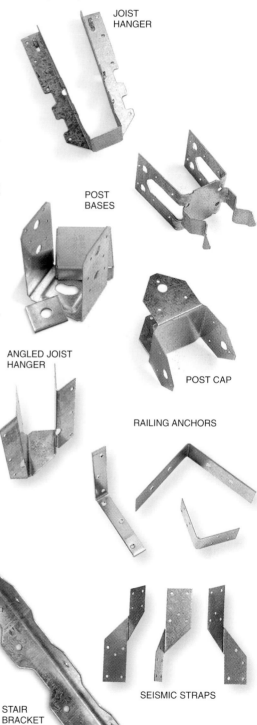

JOIST
HANGER

POST
BASES

ANGLED JOIST
HANGER

POST CAP

RAILING ANCHORS

STAIR
BRACKET

SEISMIC STRAPS

hand tools

LOWE'S QUICK TIP

Most homeowners prefer a 16-ounce hammer, which is light enough for those not used to construction work. If you are strong and have some experience, however, you may choose a 20-ounce hammer, which can drive 16d nails in as few as two blows.

YOU DO NOT NEED A LOT OF TOOLS TO BUILD A DECK. THOSE YOU DO NEED are all standard construction tools, so you will likely use them again for other home-improvement projects. Basic hand tools are discussed here; power tools are covered on pages 86–89. One accessory you will want to have at just about every step of the way is a tool belt.

tools for **measuring** and laying out

A 25- or 30-foot tape measure will probably handle all your measuring needs. If your deck is very large, you may also want to have a 50- or 100-foot model. A framing square allows you to quickly check corners for square and is ideal for marking stair stringers. A smaller angle square is handy for marking cut lines on lumber, guiding the base of a circular saw, and marking precise angle cuts. You may also need a T bevel to duplicate unusual angles. Colored mason's line is superior to standard string for laying out your deck. Use a chalk line to quickly mark a long, straight line.

To check structures for level and plumb, a carpenter's level will usually do the job. On a large site, you may want to use a water level. A post level lets you check a post for plumb in both directions at once while leaving your hands free.

fastening and cutting tools

A curved-claw hammer will come in for constant use, so buy one that is comfortable to work with. Use a nail set to drive nails below a surface without marring it. A hand-

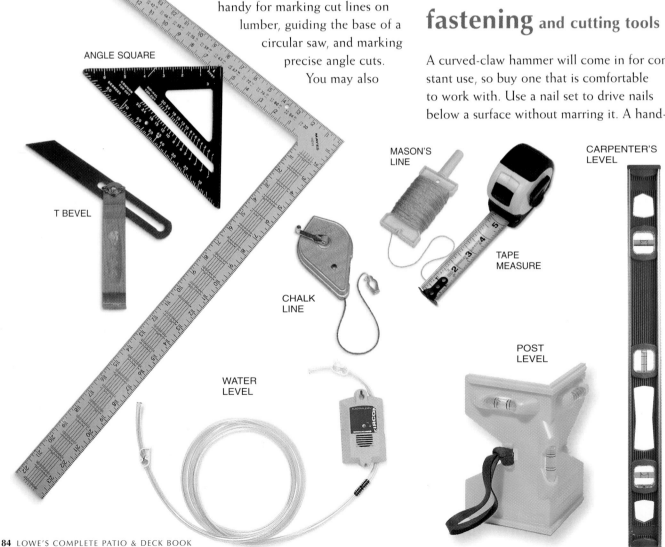

FRAMING SQUARE

ANGLE SQUARE

T BEVEL

CHALK LINE

WATER LEVEL

MASON'S LINE

TAPE MEASURE

POST LEVEL

CARPENTER'S LEVEL

saw is occasionally handy for quick cuts. Wood chisels clean out notches, complete cuts at inside corners, and can be used to pry crooked deck boards into place, as can a flat pry bar. A caulking gun is needed for sealing joints with caulk. For securing nuts, bolts, and lag screws, use an adjustable wrench plus a socket wrench with suitable sockets. A variety of clamps will come in handy. You may need tin snips to cut metal flashing. A hand sander quickly rounds off wooden edges.

excavation and concrete tools

Even if you use a power auger to dig holes for footings, you'll need a hand posthole digger to clean out the dirt. Mix concrete in a mortar tub or a wheelbarrow; a mortar hoe is the best tool for mixing the dry ingredients with water.

NAIL SET

ADJUSTABLE WRENCH

SOCKET WRENCH

HAND SANDER

FLAT PRY BAR

POSTHOLE DIGGER

BAR CLAMP

SQUEEZE CLAMP

HANDSAW

CURVED CLAW HAMMER

MORTAR HOE

MORTAR TUB

C-CLAMP

TIN SNIPS

WOOD CHISEL

power tools

A DECK BUILDER MUST HAVE A CIRCULAR SAW AND A DRILL. THOSE TWO essential tools are discussed here; other helpful power tools are covered on the two pages that follow.

To build a deck, and for occasional work around the house, you do not need top-of-the-line professional-grade tools. At the same time, stay away from low-cost power tools, which are frequently underpowered and may be poorly constructed. At Lowe's you'll find a great selection of mid-priced products aimed at experienced and demanding do-it-yourselfers. Before you buy, read reviews in consumer or construction-related publications and consult with a tool specialist at Lowe's.

circular saw

In deck building and most carpentry tasks, no power tool sees more action than a circular saw. The most common style takes a 7¼-inch blade, which will cut to a depth of about 2½ inches.

Choose a saw that feels comfortable and is easy to operate. Check that you can easily sight along the notch in the base as you cut. It should also be easy to adjust the base, both for cut depth and to produce bevel cuts. Read the fine print in the saw's manual: a quality saw will be rated at more than 12 amps and will use ball or roller bearings rather than sleeve bearings.

Purchase at least one carbide-tipped blade with at least 24 teeth. Such a blade will last longer and produce smoother cuts than less expensive blades. When the blade starts to labor rather than glide during cutting, replace it.

One important note: a circular saw is a serious tool that demands your respect. Always follow the manufacturer's safety recommendations. Practice on scrap pieces of wood until you are skilled at making straight cuts.

LOWE'S QUICK TIP

A heavy-duty cordless drill can work well for building a deck, but cordless circular saws are usually not powerful enough; use a standard corded circular saw.

Before making a cut, unplug the saw and adjust the saw depth to about ¼ inch below the bottom of the board. This adjustment is easiest to make with the blade alongside the bottom of **the board (see left). Use an angle square to mark a board for cutting. You can also use the angle square as a guide for making accurate 90- and 45-degree cuts (see below).**

drill

You will need a drill to make pilot holes for screws and bolts. Add a screwdriver bit, and you can also use the drill to drive screws. You may appreciate having two or more drills available as your deck-building project moves along. A corded drill is handy for heavy-duty use, while a cordless drill is often more convenient. Choose a cordless drill rated at 12 volts or more; an 18-volt cordless drill is as powerful as many corded drills. If you need to drill holes in concrete, you will enjoy having a hammer drill, which can also serve as your regular corded drill.

To make a professional-looking butt joint in decking, cut both pieces perfectly square. Drill pilot holes at slight angles before driving fasteners.

CORDLESS DRILL

MAGNETIC SLEEVE

HAMMER DRILL

LOWE'S QUICK TIP

If you use a cordless drill, be sure to have an extra battery, and set up the battery charger in a convenient location. That way, one battery can always be charging while the other is being used.

THE IMPORTANCE OF PILOT HOLES

When driving nails or screws near the ends of boards, you stand a good chance of splitting a board, and thus weakening the connection to other boards. To prevent that, whenever driving a fastener within 2 inches of a board end, first drill a pilot hole (see above) using a drill bit slightly smaller in diameter than the screw or nail. Then drive the fastener.

When installing carriage bolts, first drill a pilot hole all the way through the lumber, using a bit that is the same size as the bolt's shaft. Lag screws, which are often used to attach a ledger, require two drilling steps, as shown at right. For ½-inch lag screws, first drill a ½-inch-diameter pilot hole completely through the first board. Then change to a smaller drill bit—about 5/16 inch—and drill a second hole into the second board. Put a washer on the lag screw and drive it using an adjustable wrench or a socket wrench.

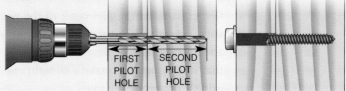

FIRST PILOT HOLE SECOND PILOT HOLE

staying safe while you work

A CONSTRUCTION SITE CAN HOLD A NUMBER OF SAFETY CONCERNS. MINIMIZE THE dangers by learning how to operate power tools safely, wearing appropriate safety gear, and using common sense. Keep the area around the site clean of lumber scraps and other debris. If you are working under a hot sun, drink plenty of water and take frequent breaks.

You are usually safer if you work with a helper. A helper can carry part of a heavy load, hold a board firmly while you work on it, and spot potential mistakes before you make them.

safety gear

Whenever there is a danger that particles of wood or other materials will fly around, wear long clothing, safety goggles, and gloves. However, while cutting with a power tool, do not wear gloves, for a better grip, and either wear short sleeves or firmly roll up your long sleeves so the fabric cannot get caught in the teeth of the blade.

If you will be creating dust, wear a dust mask. When working with solvents and solutions that create toxic fumes, be sure the area is well ventilated, and consider wearing a ventilating mask.

working
with power tools

- If you are using a power tool for the first time, read the owner's manual and practice on scrap lumber or masonry units.

- Always keep the tool unplugged when it is not in use for an extended period, or when you are making an adjustment or changing a blade.

- To guard against shocks, make sure all power tools are connected to a GFCI-protected outlet.

EAR PLUGS: WEAR WHEN USING POWER SAWS, ROUTERS, OR OTHER LOUD TOOLS

SAFETY GOGGLES: WEAR WHEN USING POWER TOOLS, HAMMERING, CHISELING, SANDING, MIXING CONCRETE, OR APPLYING FINISH

DUST MASK: WEAR WHEN CUTTING TREATED WOOD, SANDING, OR MIXING CONCRETE

WORK GLOVES: WEAR WHEN MIXING CONCRETE OR HANDLING TREATED LUMBER—BUT NOT WHEN USING POWER TOOLS

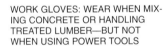

- When you leave the work site, put power tools away so that children cannot reach them.

working high

If you are building over a steep slope or at the second-story level, take extra precautions. In most cases, a couple of stepladders and a helper or two will be all you need. To reach higher locations, use an extension ladder.

If the job requires that you work aboveground for much of the project or if you need to lift a heavy beam over your head, consider renting some scaffolding. Installed correctly, scaffolding offers the easiest and safest way to work off the ground.

before you dig

Utility lines that can be damaged by digging may lurk below your yard. Check with your utility companies to learn the routes of electrical lines, plumbing pipes, telephone cables, and gas pipes.

working with
pressure-treated lumber

Although newer, safer products are increasingly available, assume that any treated lumber contains some toxic ingredients. When working with it, take the following precautions:

- Use only treated wood that is dry to the touch, visibly clean, and free of surface residue.

- When cutting or sanding, wear a dust mask and eye goggles.

- Wear gloves when handling the wood. Wash your hands before eating or drinking.

- Clean up all sawdust and construction debris from the work site.

- Do not burn any lumber scraps. Instead, dispose of them with the trash.

- Seal the wood with a water-repellent finish at least every two years.

lifting and carrying

When handling heavy or medium-weight objects, take it easy. Stand up and stretch every few minutes. Take plenty of breaks. Employ a high school student or two for at least some of the grunt work. For a large excavation, hire workers or rent a small earth-moving machine. Insist that heavy materials be delivered close to the job site, even if it means paying a bit extra.

Lift with your legs: joints and muscles in the lower back are the most susceptible to long-term damage. When lifting a moderately heavy object, keep your back straight and bend your knees, rather than bending your back. A lifting belt can help prevent strain.

To transport large stones or boulders across a lawn, rent or buy a heavy-duty hand truck, with air-filled tires and a strap that can be ratcheted tight. Lay a path of 2-by-4 or plywood planks on the lawn. Work with a helper to load the stones and strap them on tight before transporting.

LOWE'S QUICK TIP

Avoid not only lifting heavy loads, but also repeatedly lifting medium-size loads; both can cause serious lower-back injury, even if you do not feel a strain while you are doing the work.

deciding on the right foundations

DECK-BUILDING MISTAKES ABOVE ground can be corrected as needed, but the foundation will be hard to access once the structure is in place. Therefore, plan your foundation carefully.

Factor in any heavy accessories—such as a built-in grill or a spa—that you may want to incorporate as these could require you to beef up the foundation. Follow the steps on pages 100–105 carefully, and double-check for correct positioning before you pour any concrete.

The curved arrows indicate how the load is carried through joists, beams, and posts from the deck to the earth. Additional load is carried through the ledger to the house and its foundation.

distributing the load

There are two kinds of weight, or load, on a deck. The "dead load" is the weight of the structure itself plus all of its permanent components, such as railings, overheads, and built-in benches. The "live load" consists of variable factors, such as people, portable furniture, and snow. The typical code requirement is that decks be able to support a dead load of 10 pounds per square foot and a live load of 40 pounds per square foot, for a total maximum load of pounds per square foot. These requirements apply to decks that will be used for normal purposes and that are built on undisturbed soil. If you want to include any particularly heavy features, such as a spa or a large planter, or if the soil is loose or contains a lot of clay, discuss your plans with the local building department or a construction professional.

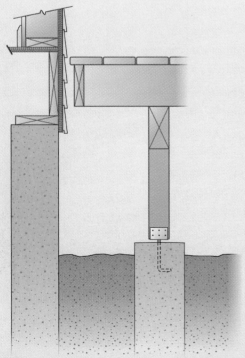

SUPPORTING A FREESTANDING DECK

An alternative to the ledger-mounted decks shown on the following pages is a freestanding deck, one that is not connected to the house at all. Instead of being bolted to a ledger, the part of the deck alongside the house rests on an extra row of posts and an additional beam. This approach eliminates the need to attach a ledger, which can sometimes be complicated (see pages 94–97). However, freestanding decks generally require extra work: adding more posts and footings, which may need to be dug very deep to reach undisturbed soil; the area near the house was probably deeply excavated when the house was built. If the deck is more than 3 feet above the ground, extra bracing may be required.

footing types

In a deck, as in a house, the foundation anchors the structure to prevent settling and shifting. It also distributes the weight of the deck and everything on it onto the earth. But while most house foundations are composed of a masonry wall around the entire perimeter, most deck foundations consist of a series of individual concrete piers and footings.

Local building codes govern the size and spacing of foundations, and specify how deep into the ground they must go. Typical codes call for 16-inch-square or 18-inch-diameter footings that are 8 inches thick.

In cold climates, codes often also require that the bottom of the footing extend below the frostline. If it does not go this deep, ice can form beneath it and push up the deck an inch or more, a process called "frost heave." In some circumstances this movement can seriously weaken the deck. However, if the deck is not attached to the house, codes may allow the deck to "float" independent of the house; in that case, footings can be above the frostline.

Codes provide detailed specifications for several types of foundations. One common configuration (see above right) is a cylindrical pier supported by a footing. In another type, the post is embedded in the footing while the concrete is wet; the upper portion of the posthole is later filled with gravel or compacted soil (see above left). Where frost heave is not a concern, you can use precast piers that are simply set on tamped soil, a concrete footing, or a tamped gravel bed (right).

POST ON SOLID CONCRETE PIER

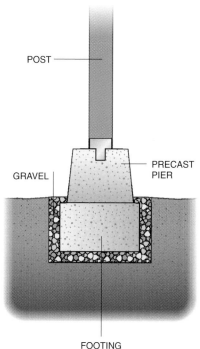

POST IN CONCRETE FOOTING

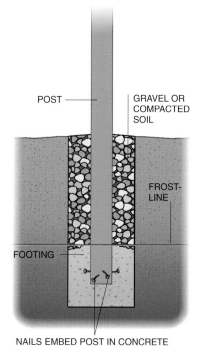

NAILS EMBED POST IN CONCRETE

POST ON PRECAST PIER

LOWE'S QUICK TIP

In the parlance of most building departments, a "pier" is the vertical portion of a foundation; a "footing" is a horizontal piece, often located at the bottom of a pier; and "foundation" refers to all the concrete parts that support a post.

starting with the ledger

THE LEDGER BOARD IS ANCHORED TO THE HOUSE TO SUPPORT ONE END OF THE deck joists. Installing it is usually the first construction task in deck building. Once the ledger is cut to the correct length and firmly and properly in place, it becomes the reference point for laying out the rest of the deck.

Installing a ledger can be simple or complicated, depending on your plan, the type of siding on your house, and local codes. Check with your building department to make sure you attach the ledger in a way that will be approved. The next four pages show the most common fastening methods.

LOWE'S QUICK TIP

If the deck will go around corners, you may need to install more than one ledger. All additional boards need to be aligned at precisely the same height, or the deck surface will be wavy. Take the time to draw accurate level lines on the house and double-check the boards for correct position before you drive the fasteners.

getting the **length** right

In most cases, you should use the same size board for the ledger as you will for the joists. You can use a wider board, however, if it will permit a stronger connection to the house's framing. Figure the size of the overall framing, remembering to allow for any decking overhangs and any fascia boards. The length of the ledger should be 3 inches less than the width of the deck framing (this takes into account the thickness of the end joists on either side).

getting the **height** right

When determining the height at which to install the ledger, take into account how much below the interior floor it needs to be, as well as the thickness of the decking.

To keep snow and water out of the house, the finished surface of the deck should be lower than the interior floor of any room leading onto it. To avoid creating a tripping hazard, locate the deck ¾ inch to 1 inch below the interior floor. Where snow is a concern, locate the deck surface 6 to 8 inches below the interior floor. This distance will produce a safe, clearly visible step from the deck up to the house. Local building codes may offer more specific guidelines on this issue.

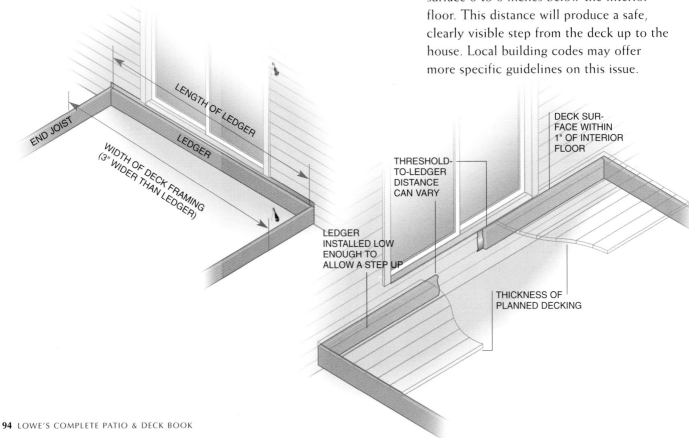

END JOIST

LENGTH OF LEDGER

LEDGER

WIDTH OF DECK FRAMING (3" WIDER THAN LEDGER)

LEDGER INSTALLED LOW ENOUGH TO ALLOW A STEP UP

THRESHOLD-TO-LEDGER DISTANCE CAN VARY

DECK SUR-FACE WITHIN 1" OF INTERIOR FLOOR

THICKNESS OF PLANNED DECKING

anchoring to the house

The correct way to attach a ledger to siding is a matter of debate among deck builders and inspectors. Some say that the ledger should simply be attached firmly up against the siding; others prefer to use spacers to hold the ledger away from the house so that water can drain through; and still others believe that siding (especially beveled siding) should be cut away and the ledger installed in the cutout. All these approaches have pluses and minuses. The best course is to find out your inspector's preferred method and follow it. The following pages cover all three approaches.

making it strong A ledger will not only be stressed in a downward direction; in many cases weight on the deck will pull the ledger outward as well. Therefore, ledgers should never be merely nailed to the house, and they must always be connected securely to the house framing or foundation—never just to the sheathing, which cannot support a deck.

Regardless of the type of siding the ledger is attached to, the strongest ledger connection relies on bolts that run through the ledger, the house sheathing, and the rim joist, with nuts and washers attached in the basement or crawlspace. If you cannot gain access to the other side of the fasteners, use lag screws instead of bolts. It may be necessary to use both types of fasteners, as shown at right.

The size and spacing of the bolts or lag screws should be spelled out in your building code. If not, install pairs of ½-inch bolts:

- every 14 inches on decks with joist spans of up to 10 feet

- every 10 inches for joist spans of up to 14 feet

- every 8 inches for longer spans

Position the bolts about 2 inches from the bottom and top edges of the ledger.

Drill test holes to determine how long the fasteners need to be. A lag screw should penetrate through the 1½-inch-thick ledger and the house's siding and sheathing and nearly all the way through the rim joist. A carriage bolt should extend about 1½ inches past the rim joist.

If the floors in your house are framed with something other than solid wood, such as wood I-joists or another kind of manufactured joist system, you will probably need to take extra steps to secure the ledger. Or, you may opt for a freestanding deck (see page 92). Discuss your options with the building department or a construction professional.

the hold-away method This technique leaves a space behind the ledger to allow for drainage. On flat siding, placing three or four washers (preferably stainless steel) on each bolt, as shown below, will do the trick. Alternatively, wood spacers can be cut out of pressure-treated plywood and placed behind the ledger, as shown at right. For added protection against moisture infiltration, squirt some caulk into the holes

LOWE'S QUICK TIP

If a fastener head ends up right where you want a joist to tie into the ledger, you will have a real headache. To avoid this problem, draw layout lines on the ledger (see page 112) before you fasten it, and drive fasteners where the joists won't be.

CONNECTING TO SMOOTH SIDING

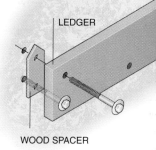

LEDGER

WOOD SPACER

TYING THE DECK TO THE HOUSE

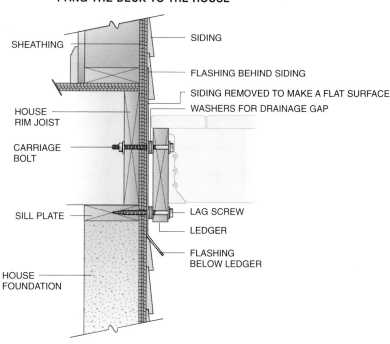

SHEATHING

SIDING

FLASHING BEHIND SIDING

SIDING REMOVED TO MAKE A FLAT SURFACE

WASHERS FOR DRAINAGE GAP

HOUSE RIM JOIST

CARRIAGE BOLT

SILL PLATE

LAG SCREW

LEDGER

FLASHING BELOW LEDGER

HOUSE FOUNDATION

before inserting bolts or lag screws. When you're installing on beveled siding, it's a good idea to add flashing, as shown in the illustration below. Your local building department may require such flashing no matter what sort of siding you have.

snugging up to the siding
Some deck builders simply mash the ledger up against the siding (see right). This is certainly the easiest method, but detractors point out that moisture will be trapped, especially in the case of beveled siding. The method seems to work fine, however, for building in a dry climate or when both the ledger and the siding are made of extremely rot-resistant materials.

setting into the siding
Some building departments require that you cut out a section of siding to accommodate the ledger. To do so, cut away what's needed for the ledger plus 1½ inches to each side to allow for the end joists. Remove enough siding

so that flashing can be tucked behind the siding above the ledger and also overhang the siding below the ledger, as shown below. (Metal flashing is often installed to cover the top edge of the ledger, but extending it below the ledger is better.) You may need to have flashing fabricated at a sheet-metal shop. It is important that it cover all places; one gap could lead to serious moisture damage to your house.

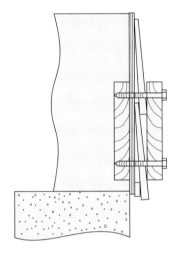

LOWE'S QUICK TIP

To ensure a straight horizontal cut in the siding, tack a straight guide board to the house and rest the side of the circular saw's base on it as you make the cut.

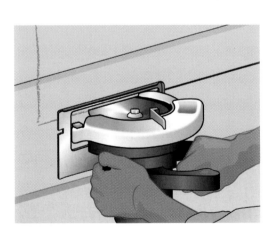

1 You can cut vinyl siding with a utility knife. For other materials, adjust the circular saw blade so it cuts just to the depth of the siding and not into the sheathing underneath. Cut with the circular saw just up to the corners and no more; finish the corners of the cut with a chisel.

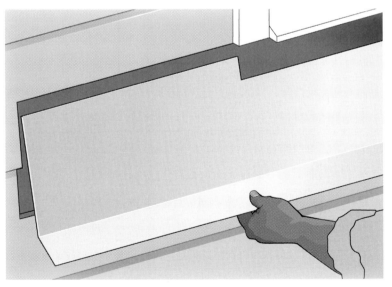

2 Cut the flashing to fit around the door threshold, as shown. Slide the flashing beneath the siding at the top of the cutout—you may need to temporarily remove some siding nails first. Apply caulk to the joint between the threshold and the flashing.

attaching to masonry Ledgers can also be attached to solid concrete or to brick walls. If your walls are concrete block, fill the hollow cores with grout where the ledger will attach; if that is not possible, you'll need to consult a professional. For solid concrete and grout-filled concrete block, use ½-inch lag screws with masonry shields, or use expanding anchors (see page 83). For other types of masonry walls, epoxy anchors are best (see page 240).

LOWE'S QUICK TIP

You can also anchor a ledger to masonry using injectable epoxy and threaded rods; see page 240.

1 Drill holes in the ledger for the bolts. Temporarily brace the ledger in place against the wall. Mark the bolt hole locations on the wall with a nail.

2 Using a hammer drill and masonry bit, drill holes to the necessary depth. If the bit starts to heat up, squirt some oil on it or allow it to cool off.

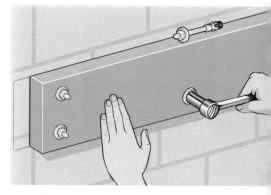

3 Vacuum out the holes. If you are using masonry shields or expansion anchors, tap them in before repositioning the ledger, then drive the screws.

attaching to stucco Drill test holes to locate framing members behind the stucco. Attach the ledger using carriage bolts or lag screws, as shown on page 95. Purchase special preformed flashing meant for use on stucco walls. Such flashing has an extra lip on the top that can be inserted in a saw kerf—a slot the width of the saw blade.

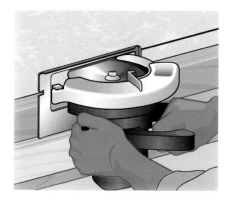

1 After the ledger is firmly anchored, attach a temporary cutting guide on it and put a masonry blade on your circular saw. Cut a ⅜-inch-deep kerf into the stucco.

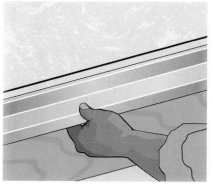

2 Vacuum out the kerf thoroughly, removing all dust. Cut the flashing to length and test to see that it will fit. Squirt silicone caulk into the kerf and insert the flashing.

3 With the flashing sealed firmly in the kerf and along the ledger, add a bead of caulk along the top edge of the flashing. You may need to temporarily brace the flashing until the caulk dries.

laying out the deck

LAYING OUT A DECK INVOLVES ESTABLISHING THE EDGES OF THE PROPOSED DECK framing with string lines, then using those lines to locate the planned foundation holes.

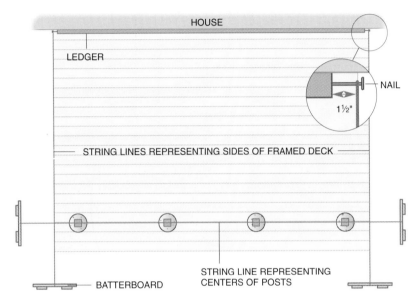

HOUSE

LEDGER

NAIL

1½"

STRING LINES REPRESENTING SIDES OF FRAMED DECK

BATTERBOARD

STRING LINE REPRESENTING CENTERS OF POSTS

laying out
rectangular decks

For a rectangular deck, position the batterboards (see below right) a few feet beyond the edges of the planned deck. You can use string lines to mark the perimeter of the deck framing on all sides, the position of all foundation holes, or, as in the drawing at left, a combination of the two.

basic layout method

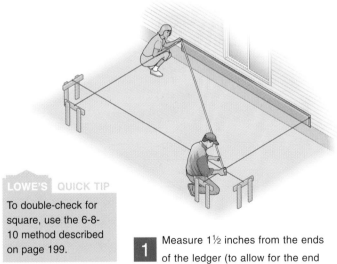

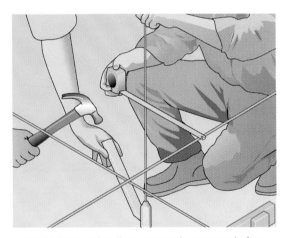

LOWE'S QUICK TIP

To double-check for square, use the 6-8-10 method described on page 199.

1 Measure 1½ inches from the ends of the ledger (to allow for the end joists) and run string lines for the sides of the framing. Set up another line to represent the center line of the footings. Carefully measure the diagonals. Adjust the strings until the measurements are identical. Secure the strings with screws driven into the batterboard crosspieces.

2 With the string lines squared, measure in from the side strings to find the center of the outside footing holes. The exact distance depends on your plans, including how far the beam will overhang the posts. Drop a plumb bob (you can use a chalk line) from the correct location, then have your helper drive a small stake into the ground marking the center of the foundation hole. Continue measuring along the string line to find the other hole locations.

laying out
irregular shapes

Lay out an irregularly shaped deck with the same approach as for a rectangular deck. If you are building a deck that wraps around a corner, run a single corner string line out from one of the ledgers, as shown (see right), creating two rectangles. Check each rectangle for square.

If the deck has mitered corners (see right), first establish a rectangular layout. Then measure back from the end string line an equal distance on each side and run another string line. For more complicated decks, follow the same basic principle: divide the deck into a series of rectangles and check each for square.

laying out with a
raised ledger

If you are building an elevated deck, attach a plumb bob to each outside edge of the ledger and drop it to near ground level. Install batterboards and mark them, using the plumb lines for reference. If you cannot drive batterboards this close to the house, fasten nails to the siding and attach the layout lines to the nails.

using batterboards

Batterboards will make your layout more accurate and save you time in the long run. Make batterboards out of scrap 2-by or 1-by lumber (see page 198). The stakes should be pointed, but their length depends on how high they need to be and how soft your soil is. The crosspiece should be about 2 feet long. Build two batterboards for each outside corner of the deck.

LAYING OUT A WRAPAROUND DECK

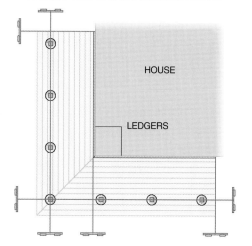

HOUSE

LEDGERS

LOWE'S QUICK TIP

Because you may need to remove and replace layout lines several times during the course of layout and construction, be sure the batterboards are securely anchored. Also be sure to clearly mark the crosspieces with the precise locations for the lines.

LAYING OUT A DECK WITH MITERED CORNERS

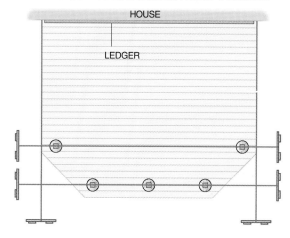

HOUSE

LEDGER

LAYING OUT A HIGH LEDGER

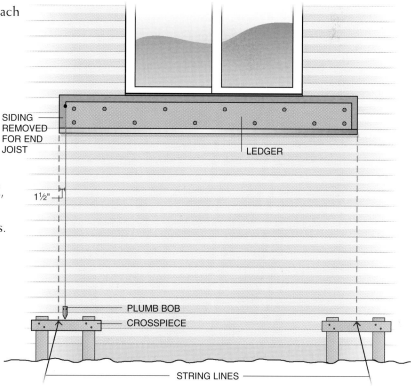

SIDING REMOVED FOR END JOIST

LEDGER

1½"

PLUMB BOB

CROSSPIECE

STRING LINES

digging foundation holes

BEGIN BY MOVING THE LAYOUT LINES OUT OF THE WAY. LEAVE THE BATTERBOARDS in place and mark their crosspieces so you can reinstall the lines to double-check your foundations later.

If your soil is soft and you do not have to dig deep, this part of the job can be fairly easy. In most cases, however, digging holes large enough and deep enough to satisfy codes is demanding work. Consult with your inspector or a contractor to see how holes are usually dug in your area.

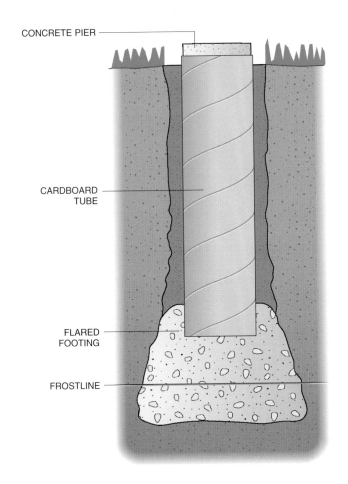

CONCRETE PIER

CARDBOARD TUBE

FLARED FOOTING

FROSTLINE

If your soil has rocks or roots, you may need to pry or jab with a breaker bar before you can use the clamshell digger.

the right size and shape

See pages 92–93 for basic foundation options. Cardboard tube forms ensure that the pier is the right diameter to meet codes. Dig each hole just wide enough for the tube form to fit. If you are using 4-by-4 posts to support your deck, 8-inch-wide tubes are usually sufficient. For 6-by-6 posts, use 10- or 12-inch-wide tubes. If you plan to bury the posts in concrete, dig each hole wide enough so that there will be at least 2 inches of concrete around the post at all points. Codes may require that the bottom of the hole be "flared," or widened, to form a more massive footing.

manual digging

A garden spade may be the only tool you need to dig holes up to 2 feet deep. For deeper holes, you will need a posthole digger. A clamshell digger like the one shown at left is effective for most types of soil. Use a spade to carefully dig around the stake that marks the center of the hole (see page 98, Step 2). Remove the stake and dig away all sod. Grasp the digger with the handles held together. Stab the digger into the ground, spread the handles apart, and lift out the dirt. If you encounter large rocks or need to loosen hard soil, use a breaker bar, also called a digging bar. Cut tree roots with a pruning saw.

Left: A hand-held power auger works quickly if the soil is fairly easy to dig.

Below: A pro with a tractor-mounted auger can dig clean, precise holes quickly.

power auger options

A rented power auger can remove dirt much faster than a manual digger can. But that does not mean that it will make the job easy. Choose an auger bit that matches the hole width you want to dig. Rent a two-person auger like the one shown above; a one-person hand-held auger can do serious damage to your shoulders and arms.

Even the best two-person power auger, however, should be used by two strong people who are ready for a tough physical workout. Digging can be a wrenching experience, especially if you encounter a large stone or root. If you are working alone, rent a flexible-shaft auger. The engine is separated from the auger, rather than sitting on top of it, which makes the tool lighter and easier to handle.

CONTROLLING WEEDS AND PUDDLES

In a dry climate, you may be able to simply build a deck on the lawn, allowing the grass to die over a year or so. However, if you get plenty of rain, water may puddle under the deck and take a long time to dry out. In lush areas, weeds may grow up through a low-lying deck. The usual solution is to remove sod, install landscaping fabric, and cover the fabric with gravel. For tips on removing sod, see pages 200–201. Consult with a Lowe's gardening expert for the best type of landscaping fabric and gravel to use in your area.

pouring foundations

WAXED CONCRETE TUBE FORMS ARE CONVENIENT AND PRACTICAL, AND ARE required by many codes. They create smooth-sided piers that resist the uplift caused by frost. They also make it easier to estimate how much concrete you will need. And they hold moisture in the curing concrete longer, resulting in stronger piers.

Before getting started, make sure you understand the inspection process for foundations. Under some codes, you may be required to have footings inspected before making the piers. Sometimes you may need to add several inches of gravel to the bottom of each footing before adding concrete.

using tube forms

LOWE'S QUICK TIP

Special posthole concrete, which is available at Lowe's, is the easiest to install—you just pour the dry mix directly from the bag into the hole, squirt in some water, and mix by stirring with a piece of rebar or a 1 by 2. Check to see if this type of concrete is allowed by your building department.

1 To measure for a tube, set it in the hole and mark it at the correct height—about 2 inches above grade. Remove the tube and cut it square. Tubes can be cut with a handsaw, but the job will go faster if you use a reciprocating saw.

2 Put the layout strings back in place, insert a cut-to-length tube form in each hole, and check that each is centered and aligned properly. You may need to scrape the holes to realign a form or two. If you have already poured footings and the concrete is still wet, push the tubes an inch or two into the footings. Use a level to ensure that the tubes are close to level at the top, then shovel 6 to 8 inches of dirt into the hole around the outside of the tube. Tamp the dirt with a board so that it is fairly firm. Continue until the hole is filled, checking the tube periodically with a level.

SUSPENDING THE FORMS

If you are pouring footings and piers simultaneously, or if you need to raise the top of the piers to a precise height, you will need to suspend the tubes with braces made of 1-by lumber. Anchor the braces in the ground on either side of the form. Raise the tube into position and drive two screws to hold it in place.

estimating the
amount of concrete

Concrete is a mix of Portland cement, sand, gravel, and water. You can buy pre-mixed bags of the dry ingredients and add your own water. A 60-pound bag of dry-mix concrete produces ½ cubic foot of concrete, which will fill about 20 inches of an 8-inch tube form, 13 inches of a 10-inch form, or 9 inches of a 12-inch form. An 80-pound bag contains .6 cubic feet and will therefore fill a few more inches. To esti-mate what you'll need for other sizes or shapes, show your drawings to a Lowe's sales associate, or see page 227.

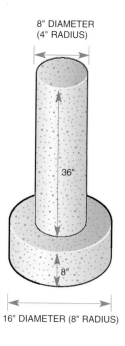

8" DIAMETER
(4" RADIUS)

36"

8"

16" DIAMETER (8" RADIUS)

mixing by **hand**

To mix your own concrete, you will need a plastic mortar tub or a wheelbarrow, a mortar hoe (a shovel or garden hoe works almost as well), and a source of water. Squirt an inch or so of water into the con-tainer and pour in a full bag of dry mix. Slowly add more water, mixing and scrap-ing along the bottom and sides of the container. Avoid adding too much water; a runny mixture makes for weak concrete. Aim for a mix that is just barely pourable and that holds its shape when you pick some up with a tool (see above right).

Top right: **A good con-crete mix will stick to a trowel for at least a second.**

Left: **Mix the concrete right next to where you want to pour it.**

ordering
ready-mix concrete

If you need more than half a yard of con-crete (27 cubic feet), it is probably most cost effective to have it delivered in a ready-mix truck—and it will certainly save labor. Some companies have special trucks for delivering amounts less than a yard. Call around for the best price.

pouring into **forms**

LOWE'S QUICK TIP

To prevent your reciprocating saw blade from overheating, which will cause it to dull quickly, periodically squirt a bit of oil on it.

1 Before you mix or pour concrete, cut lengths of concrete reinforcing bar, called rebar, to be inserted into the piers. Required by some codes, rebar adds strength, so include it even if your code doesn't call for it. Use either #4 rebar, which is ½ inch thick, or #3, which is ⅜ inch thick. Unless your piers are unusually large, plan two pieces of #4 rebar, 2 to 3 inches shorter than the form, for each pier. Cutting with a reciprocating saw with a metal-cutting blade is easiest. Clamp the rebar firmly before cutting.

2 A narrow shovel or spade makes filling the forms easier. Fill the bottom 2 feet of the tube with concrete and work it as shown in Step 3; then continue to fill the tube. If you are having the concrete delivered, ask the company if they offer the option of having the concrete pumped directly into the tubes through a hose. Such a service is well worth the additional cost. Otherwise, have a couple of helpers on hand, along with two or more wheelbarrows, and be prepared to pour concrete without interruption.

3 After filling a tube with about 2 feet of concrete, use a piece of 1 by 2 or a length of rebar to stir and agitate the mix. Work the board or rebar up and down in several places. This removes air pockets, which weaken a foundation. Add more concrete and agitate again, continuing until the tube is just slightly overfilled.

4 Immediately add the rebar as specified by code. Position the rods about 2 inches from the tube so that they won't interfere with the anchor bolt or post base (Step 6). Push them all the way into the wet mix by hand, then use a scrap piece of lumber to push them 2 to 3 inches below the surface of the concrete.

5 Use a short 2 by 4 to level and smooth the surface, a process called screeding. Move it from side to side in a sawing motion as you pull it toward you. Fill any low spots with additional concrete. (For clarity, the tubes shown here and in Step 6 are shown without bracing; both this step and Step 6, however, apply to braced tubes, and the bracing should be left in place for both steps.)

6 Before the concrete starts to harden, insert an anchor bolt (also called a J-bolt) into each pier. Later, after the concrete has cured, you will attach post bases to the anchor bolts. The bases can be adjusted an inch or so, but align the anchor bolts as precisely as possible now. If your batterboards are still in place, set up the string lines again to guide you. Otherwise, use a long straight board as a guide. Insert the bent end of the anchor bolt into the concrete, allowing 1 inch of the threaded end to rest above the surface. Check that the bolt is plumb.

7 With all the anchor bolts in place, it is time to take a break. Allow the concrete to cure for at least two days. For greatest strength, keep the concrete damp while it cures; cover it with plastic sheeting if the air is dry. If you have suspended tubes, backfill the holes as shown on page 102. Once the concrete has cured, cut away the exposed portion of the cardboard tubing. Reattach your layout line or use a straight board to guide you as you attach the post bases to the anchor bolts, making sure they all line up perfectly.

NON-ADJUSTABLE POST BASES
Local codes may require a one-piece post base with fins, as shown. This type of base is the strongest, but it is not adjustable, so take extra care with alignment if you use it.

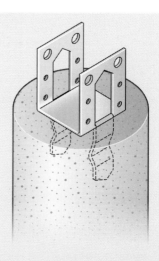

setting posts

DECK POSTS RARELY TURN OUT TO BE ALL THE SAME LENGTH, SINCE PIERS ARE usually not perfectly level with each other. Therefore, don't try to measure and cut posts before setting them in place—it is too easy to make mistakes that way. The safer method is presented in the steps on the facing page.

post-and-beam options

LOWE'S QUICK TIP

Decks are sometimes built with posts that extend above the deck surface to serve double duty as railing posts. To have this work, the posts must be positioned precisely and be very straight.

The strongest and most secure way to install a beam is to seat it directly on top of the posts. The beam can be held in place by angle-driven screws or nails, but a post cap makes the strongest connection and is usually the easiest solution. Post caps are available to fit most typical post-and-beam configurations, even where the beam is narrower than the post.

If you are using a 6-by-6 post, you can notch it on either side to accommodate a

beam that consists of two 2-by pieces (see below center). If you are using 4-by-4 posts, bolt the two 2-by beam pieces to either side, and further support them with 2-by-4 cleats, as shown (see below right). The cleats, which are made from framing lumber, should be screwed or nailed to the post. This method requires more work, but most people prefer the look of wood and bolt heads to post caps, so consider this method if the connection will be visible.

BEAM ON POST

NOTCHED POST

6 × 6 POST
(MINIMUM)

CLEAT SUPPORTS

staying aligned

To be sure that all of your posts are aligned, reattach the string lines to your batterboards, or use stakes and string as a

guide. Either way, be absolutely certain that the string is parallel with the ledger or the house. If you are using adjustable post bases, check them for alignment, then tighten them in place.

setting and **cutting** posts

1 Cut posts longer than they need to be. Check the bottom of each post for square. If you have to cut it, apply a coat of sealer. Set the post in the post base and drive one nail through the base and partway into the post, just far enough to hold the post in place; you may have to remove and reposition the nail later. Plumb the post by checking it with a carpenter's level on two sides; better yet, use a post level (at right). With the post plumb, attach temporary braces to two adjacent sides. Use one or two clamps to hold the post in position while you check for plumb. Once you are sure all the posts are plumb and aligned, drive nails or screws through the post bases to anchor them. Then drive nails or screws into the posts.

LOWE'S QUICK TIP

A post level, a handy (and inexpensive) tool, lets you check for plumb in two directions at once, and leaves both your hands free.

2 Follow this and the next step to mark posts at either end of a row of posts. First, place a carpenter's level atop a long straight board. Rest one end of the board on top of the ledger, then raise or lower the other end against the post until it is level. (It helps if you have a helper check the level while you adjust the board.) Mark the post at the bottom of the board to represent the top of the joists.

3 Place a short piece of joist stock under the mark and mark its bottom edge on the post. If the joists will attach on the side of the beam (see page 112), this will be the cutting line for the post. If the joists will attach on top of the beam, position the top edge of a piece of beam stock flush with this line and mark its bottom edge on the post, then cut the post on this line.

4 Once the posts at either end are marked for cutting, use a long straight board or a chalk line to mark the middle posts. On each post, use a square to transfer the cut line to all four sides. Set the blade of your circular saw to cut as deeply as possible. Cut a 4-by-4 post twice, on opposite sides. For a 6-by-6 post, cut on all four sides, then finish the cut with a reciprocating saw or handsaw.

beam options

A BEAM, ALSO CALLED A GIRDER, SPANS FROM POST TO POST AND SUPPORTS the joists. In most cases, joists rest on top of the beam, but if a deck is low you can save height by tying the joists into the beam via joist hangers. Modest-sized decks typically are built with a single beam, but larger decks may require two or more. Consult local codes for approved ways to build and mount a beam. Regardless of the beam style you use, you can be sure the beam will be heavy. Have a helper or two available when you need to lift a beam into place.

solid beams

You can purchase 4-by lumber and use it as a beam. Then there will be just a one-piece beam to be cut, saving you plenty of work. And a 4-by piece will fit perfectly on top of a 4-by-4 or 4-by-6 post. If you can find good boards, and if the piece will not be too heavy, this may be the easiest way to construct your deck.

It can be difficult, however, to find massive boards like this that do not have large cracks, and any cracks that are already visible will likely enlarge over time. Any twists or other warping problems are also likely to worsen over time, and there will be no way to straighten the beam out.

built-up beams

Constructing a beam by laminating two or more pieces together requires extra time and effort, but the result is a beam that is stronger and more stable than one of a single piece.

When the deck's design calls for placing a beam made of two 2-by boards over 4-by-4 posts—a very common arrangement—many builders construct the beam with ½-inch spacers between the boards (see center right). This produces a beam that fits perfectly on top of the post, since 2-by lumber is 1½ inches thick. Additionally, the spacers permit water to drain through the boards, which prolongs

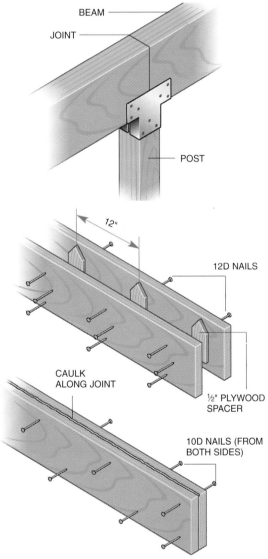

the life of the beam. You can also make a built-up beam without spacers. If you are not using spacers, apply a bead of silicone caulk to the joint between the boards to keep moisture from penetrating.

attaching beams

Beams are often attached to posts simply by angle-driving screws or nails through the beam and into the post. If you do this, drill pilot holes first, or you are likely to crack the beam. A post cap makes a surer connection.

If the beam is a doubled 2-by, it will be only 3 inches thick, so ½ inch of the post top will be exposed. That is not a problem, as long as the post is pressure-treated.

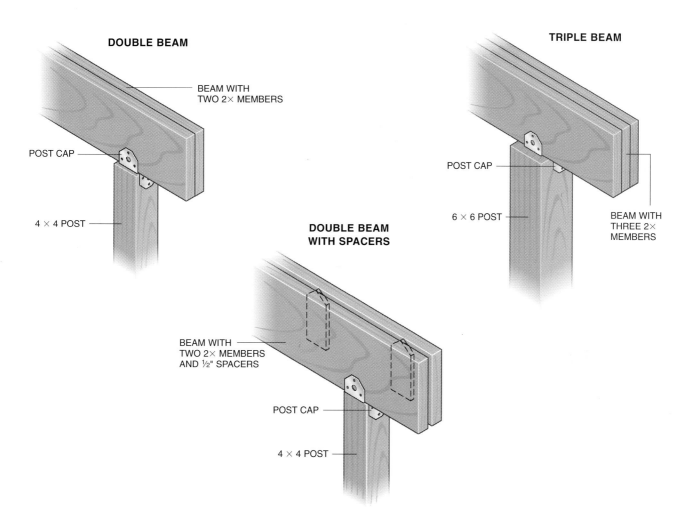

DOUBLE BEAM

BEAM WITH TWO 2× MEMBERS

POST CAP

4 × 4 POST

TRIPLE BEAM

POST CAP

6 × 6 POST

BEAM WITH THREE 2× MEMBERS

DOUBLE BEAM WITH SPACERS

BEAM WITH TWO 2× MEMBERS AND ½" SPACERS

POST CAP

4 × 4 POST

INSTALLING WITH THE CROWN SIDE UP

Structural lumber nearly always has a visible crown, or arch, as shown below. Install both beams and joists with the crown facing up. That way, when the deck load bears down on the crown, the board will level out. You can usually see where the crown is by sighting down the edges of the board. Alternatively, set the board on edge on a flat surface, such as a driveway or a garage floor. Mark an arrow on every board to indicate the direction of the crown.

building and installing a beam

1 Begin by checking the ends of the lumber for square—typically, one in ten or so will be out of square—and also for cracks. Cut off any out-of-square or cracked ends. Locate and mark the crown for each piece, and be sure to install all the boards crown side up.

2 It is smart to start with your beam a bit longer than needed, so that, if necessary, you can shift the joists slightly to square up the frame. Once that is done, the beam can be cut to finished length. If you're making a built-up beam, assemble it on a pair of sawhorses. If you're using spacers, make them of ½-inch pressure-treated plywood. Screw or nail the spacers to one board every 12 inches, then set the other board on top and drive three 16d nails or 3-inch screws at each spacer location. Flip the two boards over and repeat the fastening pattern.

3 Attach post caps to the tops of the posts. Position or reattach string lines representing the sides of the deck framing (see pages 98–99). With a helper or two, lift the beam—crown side up—onto the posts, slipping it carefully into each post cap.

4 Align the beam with the string lines at each end. If you made the beam a bit longer than needed, overlap the string an equal distance on each end. If the beam feels a bit wobbly, temporarily brace it by attaching several pieces of long 2-by lumber to the ledger at one end and to the beam at the other end. Check that the beam is plumb along its face and that it is squared up with the ledger. Drive nails or screws through the post caps to anchor the beam to the posts.

LOWE'S QUICK TIP

If you're building a raised deck, you may need post-to-post bracing. Check with your inspector for the materials and configurations that will meet code.

BRACING POSSIBILITIES

Even if bracing is not required by local codes, you may want to add it for extra strength to decks that feature 4-by-4 posts more than 4 feet high or 6-by-6 posts more than 8 feet high. Freestanding decks over 3 feet high should also be braced. The most common type of bracing forms a Y shape between the post and the beam. The simplest Y bracing has one 2 by 4 on each side of the post and beam (below left). Carriage bolts

secure the connections. Cut the ends of the 2 by 4s plumb, as shown, so that water and dirt will not have a place to accumulate.

Many people prefer the look of solid 4-by-4 braces (below right), which can be used with solid beams. The ends must be cut at 45-degree angles, and lag screws secure the braces at either end.

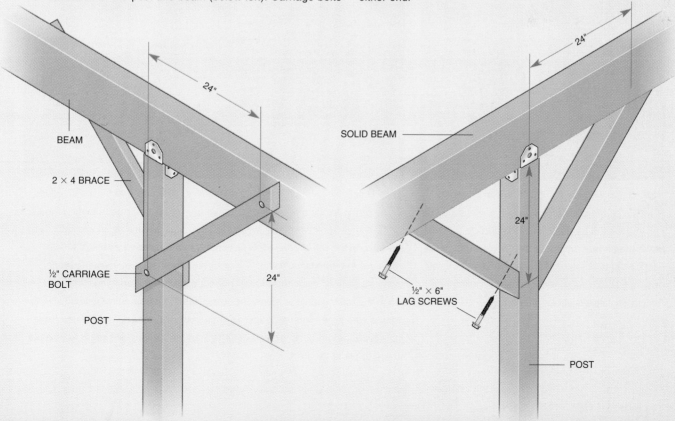

BEAM

2 × 4 BRACE

½" CARRIAGE BOLT

POST

24"

24"

SOLID BEAM

24"

24"

½" × 6" LAG SCREWS

POST

installing joists

LOWE'S QUICK TIP

Always use the joist hangers specifically made for the size joists you are using. Attach them with the type and quantity of fasteners specified by the manufacturer. Joist-hanging nails are thicker than most nails and screws, because the pressure on them is primarily downward. Purchase angled joist hangers for use where joists attach at a 45-degree angle.

THE SIZE OF THE JOISTS, AS WELL AS THEIR SPAN AND SPACING, SHOULD BE determined in the planning stage (see pages 66–69). Joist spacing is commonly given as "on center" (o.c.), which means the spacing is measured from the center of one joist to the center of the next. The most common joist spacings are 12, 16, and 24 inches on center. The spacing from the end joist to the next joist is often less than the normal spacing.

Where joists tie into a ledger or beam at the same height, joist hangers are used. Where joists rest atop and overhang a beam, they are attached by toenailing or with metal fasteners known as hurricane or seismic ties.

Choose joist stock carefully. Look for straight boards, and plan to cut off any cracked ends. Always install joists with the crown side up (see page 109). Check the ends that you will insert into joist hangers for square, and cut them square if necessary. You won't cut the other ends until after all the joists are installed.

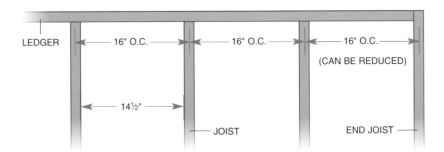

LEDGER — 16" O.C. — 16" O.C. — 16" O.C.
(CAN BE REDUCED)
14½"
JOIST   END JOIST

1 Begin with the end joists, which typically cover the ends of the ledger and rest on the outside ends of the beam. On the outside (not visible in the photo), drill three pilot holes through the joist end and into the ledger, and drive in 16d nails or 3-inch deck screws. On the inside, attach reinforcing angle brackets as shown.

2 Before installing the intermediary joists, measure and mark the ledger for the location of each one. Begin the layout from the outside edge of the framing—hook your tape measure to the outside face of an end joist and mark along the top of the ledger according to the planned spacing: if your joists are to be installed 16 inches on center, for instance, mark the ledger every 16 inches. You can reduce—but not expand—the spacing when you reach the other end joist. Once the ledger is marked, use an angle square to draw a vertical line on the ledger at each mark, as shown. These lines represent the edge of a joist, so you need to mark an X alongside them to indicate where to place the joist.

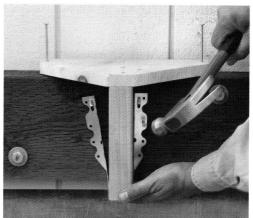

LOWE'S QUICK TIP

If your ledger is perfectly straight (use a string line to check), you can cut all of the joists to length before installing them. That way, you can skip Steps 7 and 8 (page 114).

3 The rim joist (also called the header joist) covers the ends of the other joists. Usually, you'll save time and avoid mistakes later if you mark the rim joist at this time. On a basic rectangular deck, the rim joist is the same length as the ledger, plus 3 inches. (The outside joists, which are each 1½ inches thick, butt into it rather than attach to the sides, as they do with the ledger.) Use the straightest board you can find and cut it to length. Hook your tape measure over one edge and mark the joist spacing along the inside face. Mark vertical lines and Xs, as in Step 2.

4 To create a flat surface for decking, the tops of the joists must be level with the top of the ledger. The key to success here is to install joist hangers in just the right positions. Build a jig following the directions below. Align the 2 by 4 in the jig with the layout line on the ledger, then tap the two 12d nails on top into the ledger just deep enough to hold the jig in place. Slide a joist hanger onto the 2 by 4, fasten one side to the ledger, then fasten the other side.

5 Rest one end of a joist on the beam and set the other end into the first joist hanger. Use a framing square to see that the joist is perpendicular to the ledger. If it sits too high in its hanger, trim a bit off the bottom with a chisel. If it is too low, shim the bottom. When you are satisfied with the fit, drive joist-hanger nails through the joist hanger into the joist on both sides. Repeat across the ledger.

PROJECT CONTINUES ➡

MAKING A JOIST JIG

Especially if you do not have a helper available, a joist jig (shown in Step 4, above) will ease the job and produce reliable results. To make it, cut a 2 by 4 to the precise size of the joists and fasten it to a 12-by-5-inch piece of plywood or 1-by lumber cut as shown. Since 2-by lumber can vary slightly in thickness, make sure the 2 by 4 is at least as thick as the joist stock.

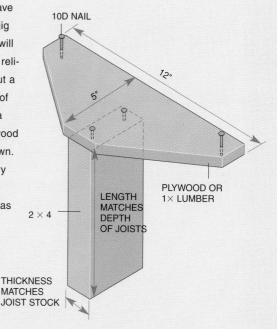

10D NAIL

12"

5"

2 × 4

LENGTH MATCHES DEPTH OF JOISTS

PLYWOOD OR 1× LUMBER

THICKNESS MATCHES JOIST STOCK

6 Check the alignment of the joists by laying the rim joist on top of them, with the layout marks on the rim joist lined up with the joists. When you are sure the joists are square and correctly spaced, attach them to the beam. Building codes often permit you to do this with three 8d or 10d nails driven at an angle (that is, toenailed). However, for added strength, use seismic or hurricane ties.

7 The cut ends of the joists must form a straight line. Measure out from the ledger along each end joist and mark the desired length. Snap a chalk line on these marks across the tops of the joists. Use a square and a pencil to transfer the chalk marks to the face of each joist. If you have already cut the joists to length, use the chalk line to see that the joists line up properly. If they do not, trim those that are too long.

8 Use a circular saw to cut each joist to length. Cut carefully so that the ends are straight and plumb.

9 To position the rim joist accurately, tack pieces of scrap lumber to the bottoms of a couple of joists and rest the rim joist on them. Make sure the top of the rim joist is flush with the tops of the joists. Have a helper apply pressure while you drive three fasteners into each joist.

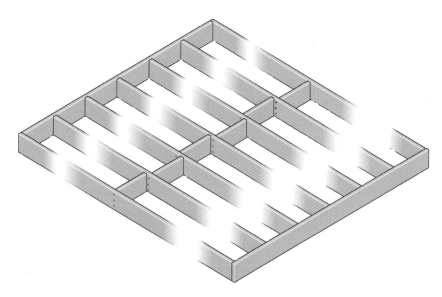

blocking

Some building codes require the use of blocking (also called bracing) between the joists. Blocking can strengthen a deck, especially if it has joists with spans of 10 feet or more. Blocking also minimizes warping of joists. Cut blocking pieces out of joist stock. Snap a chalk line across the tops of joists, then install blocking on alternating sides of the line. Drive three nails or screws into each joint.

LOWE'S QUICK TIP

Use a string line to check the joists for straightness every third or fourth piece of blocking that you install. You may need to cut one or two blocking pieces a bit longer or shorter in order to maintain straight joists.

10 If you need to cut a beam to length, use a square to mark the vertical cut line, then start the cut with a circular saw. Finish the cut with a reciprocating saw. Trim the bottom corner at an angle, as shown, for a cleaner look.

overlapping joists

On a large deck with two beams, you'll probably need to use two joists to span the distance from the ledger to the rim joist. The best way to handle this is to overlap the joists at the middle beam, as shown below. Allow at least 12 inches of overlap, and secure the joists to each other with 16d nails or 3-inch deck screws. Note that this will cause the joists at the rim joist to be offset by 1½ inches from the joists at the ledger.

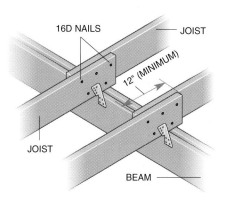

16D NAILS — JOIST

12" (MINIMUM)

JOIST

BEAM

ALIGNING TWISTED BOARDS

If a board is severely twisted, you may have difficulty aligning it with the lay-out line. Driving nails or screws at angles can move a board over slightly. For more serious problems, use a pipe clamp as shown.

building a low deck

A LOW DECK IS A NECESSITY IF THE FLOOR OF YOUR HOUSE IS CLOSE TO THE ground. But you may also choose to make your deck low. A deck that is raised only inches above the ground has the feel of a patio. There's no need for a railing, so the structure blends unobtrusively with the yard, and since a low deck is usually freestanding, you probably don't need to install a ledger.

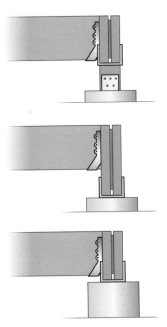

ways to keep it low

You can usually lower the height of a deck by using smaller-width joists and beams. However, this change may require you to reduce the beam and joist spans, which in turn may mean pouring more footings. Another strategy is to attach the joists to the side, not the top, of the beam.

Decks built close to the ground often employ short posts (top left). But posts less than 10 inches in length, with nails securing fasteners at the top and bottom, are prone to splitting. You can usually design your way around short posts by increasing the beam size (center left) or by raising the height of concrete piers (bottom left). Either way you'll need piers that are at precisely the same height, so make sure the tops of cardboard tube forms are level with each other.

A low deck with rough decking and randomly protruding joists is at home in this setting.

LOWE'S QUICK TIP

If a low deck will be very close to the ground, or if decking will be in contact with foliage, apply two or more coats of sealer to the cut ends, which are otherwise particularly vulnerable to rot.

constructing
without posts

To build a low deck with no posts, plan to install at least two rows of piers (more for a larger deck) with identical beams installed along each row. Construct the beams with double 2-by members. The inside board should be shorter by 1½ inches at both ends, to create a place for the end joist to fit (see middle right). Attach joists with joist hangers on the inside faces of each beam.

a deck with no footings

The small platform deck shown below right requires no poured concrete and does not even use precast piers. The foundation consists of two 4-by-6 timbers partially buried belowground. Timbers used this way must be pressure treated and rated for ground contact. Joists rest on top of the timbers.

Dig two parallel trenches that are about 6 inches deep for the timbers, then add about 4 inches of sand to each trench. Set the timbers on the sand and make sure they are perfectly parallel. Level the timbers by adding or removing sand, then fill in the trenches by adding sand to the sides of the timbers.

Mark a joist layout on each timber. Install the joists on top of the timbers with two 12d toenails or 2½-inch angle-driven deck screws driven through each side into the beam. Trim the joist ends, if necessary, and attach the rim joists. Install the decking (see pages 128–37).

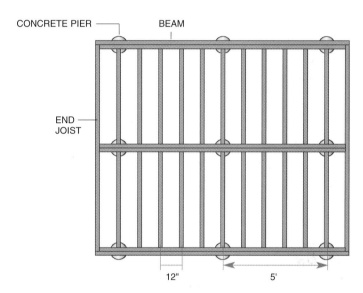

CONCRETE PIER · BEAM · END JOIST · 12" · 5'

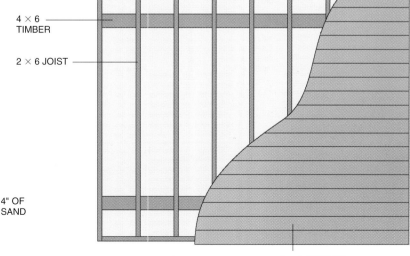

2 × 6 RIM JOIST · 4 × 6 TIMBER · 2 × 6 JOIST · 2 × 6 DECKING

4 × 6 TIMBER · SOD REMOVED BENEATH DECK · 4" OF SAND

a floating-foundation deck

LOWE'S QUICK TIP

For stability, install precast piers as you would stepping-stones (see pages 246–47).

This octagonal deck is built on piers that simply rest on firm soil. The posts for the overhead are sunk in deep post-holes for lateral strength.

PRECAST PIERS MAKE IT POSSIBLE TO BUILD A DECK WITHOUT DIGGING AND pouring footings. You will need to install quite a few piers, but they are not difficult to set. While several types of precast piers are available, those shown here—part of the Dek-Block system, sold at Lowe's—are shaped to firmly hold either 2-by-6 joists or 4-by-4 posts.

A deck built on precast piers must be freestanding; do not attach it to the house. The reason for this is that the deck needs to be free to move—to float. In an area with freezing winters, a deck can rise and fall as much as an inch when the ground freezes and thaws. Even in areas without frost, piers may settle a bit, causing the deck to lower slightly over time. Check with your building department to make sure this type of construction is allowed in your area. If it is, you may not need a permit for a deck that is modest in size, low to the ground, and unattached. In a typical deck of this type, joists are placed on 24-inch centers—close enough so you can install 2-by-6 decking. The piers must be spaced no farther than 5 feet apart.

a low deck on a **flat site**

If the yard is level and the deck will be low to the ground, you will not need posts. However, the piers must all be level with one another.

Excavate all sod and organic material from the deck area, digging just deep enough to reach bare dirt. Check that the area is roughly level with a carpenter's level set atop a long straight board. Plan the locations of the piers, and set piers in place at the four outside corners. Place the four outside joists in the piers and check them for square, then for level. Adjust pier heights as needed by removing or adding soil. Drive screws or nails to fasten the outside joists to each other.

With the outside frame installed, cut the interior joists to fit. Set each joist in place, supported by piers as needed. Adjust the height of the piers so each supports its joist firmly, then fasten the joists. Once the framing is completed, install the decking (see pages 128–37).

a **raised** deck on a sloping site

If the site is sloped, making it necessary to have posts, use joists or string lines to position all the piers. Cut posts longer than they need to be and set one in each pier. Set a carpenter's level atop a long straight board and mark all the outside posts at the appropriate height. Cut the posts with a circular saw (see page 107). Set the joists on top of the cut posts and anchor them using hurricane or seismic ties. Then hold the inside joists in position to mark the inside posts for cutting. Cut the posts and attach the joists.

Top: Using a level and a straight board, you can quickly mark posts for cutting.

Above: When constructing without posts, the trick is to get all the piers level with each other.

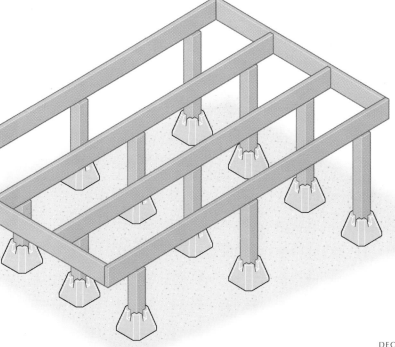

special framing techniques

SINGLE-LEVEL RECTANGULAR DECKS ARE THE EASIEST AND QUICKEST TO BUILD. However, this basic design can be humdrum. Fortunately, it usually doesn't take a lot of effort to add some variety. Basic plans may also need to be changed to suit a site—some decks almost demand to be built with multiple levels, around a corner, or shaped to accommodate a favorite tree. The next four pages show how to build decks with angles, multiple levels, and openings. To add curves to your deck, see pages 124–27.

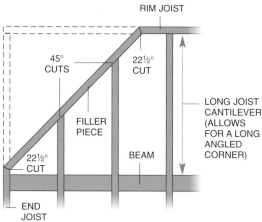

Lopping off a corner softens the line of this deck—and makes it easier to walk around the deck.

RIM JOIST

45° CUTS

22½° CUT

FILLER PIECE

LONG JOIST CANTILEVER (ALLOWS FOR A LONG ANGLED CORNER)

BEAM

22½° CUT

END JOIST

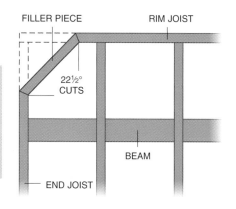

FILLER PIECE

RIM JOIST

22½° CUTS

BEAM

END JOIST

LOWE'S QUICK TIP

A partial octagon creates a pleasant bay window effect. To build one, start with a rectangular deck and lop off equal-sized corners at either end.

angling a corner

This is an easy way to add interest and avoid a boxy look. You can use any angle you choose, but 45-degree angles are the least complicated. Plan ahead for this detail, cantilevering the joists enough that the beam will not interfere with the angled corner. If the angled corner will run more than 2 feet beyond the beam, you may need to insert an additional beam.

To add a small 45-degree corner, build the framing as though it were a normal rectangle, then cut off the corner of the framing. The corner shown at bottom left requires only two cuts in the framing. Set your circular saw at a 22½-degree angle and cut the rim and end joists plumb. Cut a short filler piece with a 22½-degree angle on each end, then attach it with nails.

A larger angled corner requires cutting several joists. The more the joists overhang the beam, the bigger the cutoff can be (check your building code for restrictions). In the example at middle left, the end and rim joists are cut at 22½-degree angles. A chalk line is then snapped across the top of the joists to mark them for cutting. Cut them plumb at 45-degree angles. Cut a filler piece, with 22½-degree angles at either end, and fasten it to the rim and end joists. The intermediary joists can be attached to the filler piece with 45-degree joist hangers (right).

wrapping around

A deck that turns around the corner of a house offers many benefits. It can allow you to take advantage of different views or microclimates, create a private area, or reach the deck from more than one house door. And usually it requires only minimal added effort.

Early in the planning process, decide how you want to install the decking boards, as this will affect the framing (see illustrations below). Parallel and diagonal decking can be framed the same way, with three parallel beams. If you will cut off a corner, however, you need to install a short diagonal beam. Perpendicular decking calls for the easiest framing, essentially two conventionally framed rectangular decks that meet at the corner of the house (one ledger extends under the decking). The mitered decking pattern requires more time and effort, but it produces a particularly attractive deck.

The outside corner of a wraparound deck makes a nice space for dining.

PARALLEL DECKING

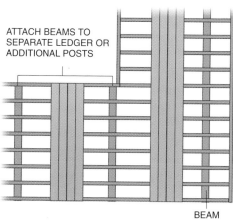

ATTACH BEAMS TO SEPARATE LEDGER OR ADDITIONAL POSTS

BEAM

DIAGONAL DECKING

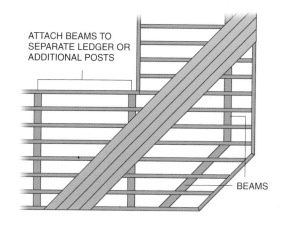

ATTACH BEAMS TO SEPARATE LEDGER OR ADDITIONAL POSTS

BEAMS

MITERED DECKING

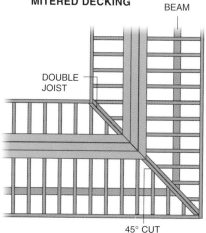

BEAM

DOUBLE JOIST

45° CUT

PERPENDICULAR DECKING

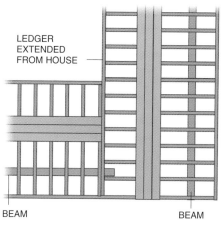

LEDGER EXTENDED FROM HOUSE

BEAM

BEAM

Strong 2-by decking can cantilever as much as 4 inches beyond the framing, making curves like this possible.

making deck **openings**

building around trees The most common need for an opening is to incorporate a tree. Build a basic rectangle as described below. Then, if you wish, cut angled framing pieces to fit as closely as possible around the tree.

For a rectangular opening, first double the joists on the sides. Then insert header joists on the other two sides, using two pieces of joist stock. Use joist hangers or angle brackets at all connections. Attach joists to the headers, maintaining your regular on-center spacing. Cut and install the decking so that it overhangs the framing by 1 to 4 inches, depending on the strength of the decking.

To round the opening, cut and install diagonal joists across the corners. Cut and install decking so that it covers as much of the opening as possible, then mark and cut a circle in the decking.

gaining access to utilities If your deck will cover a water faucet or an electrical outlet, you may need to build a small access panel. Attach 2-by-4 cleats to facing joists, 3½ inches below the top edges of the joists. Build a frame with 2 by 4s, about ½ inch narrower than the space between the joists. Cut and attach decking pieces to the frame, then drill two finger holes.

LOWE'S QUICK TIP

When making an opening for a tree, remember that the tree will keep growing, and make the opening larger than is immediately needed.

RECTANGULAR OPENING

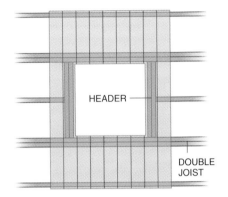

HEADER

DOUBLE JOIST

ROUND OPENING

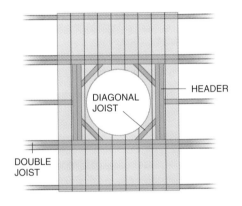

HEADER

DIAGONAL JOIST

DOUBLE JOIST

ACCESS PANEL

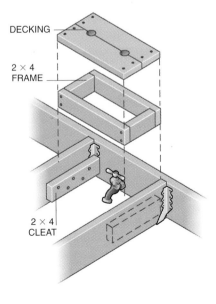

DECKING

2 × 4 FRAME

2 × 4 CLEAT

stepping down

Level changes can dramatically boost the visual appeal of a deck. It's possible to build separate decks next to each other, but the most efficient and cost-effective approach is to use one foundation to support adjacent levels. The transition between levels, no matter how wide, constitutes a step, and so should be somewhere between 5 and 8 inches high; anything less or more will be a tripping hazard. If your deck will have multiple levels, make sure they all have the same rise.

sharing a beam The most common technique for building multiple levels utilizes one beam to support two levels. The rim joist for the upper level falls directly over the lower rim joist, and the two are joined with tie plates. This style of level change can also be built by attaching the lower joists to the side of the beam with joist hangers and resting the upper joists on top of the beam. With 2-by-6 or 2-by-8 joists, the shared-beam technique creates a comfortable step between levels.

stacking a frame This method is less efficient in its use of materials, but offers an easy way to frame a small raised area, such as a step up to the house. Simply construct a separate deck frame and set it on top of the main one. Use tie plates to hold the top frame in place. On either side, attach short nailers to the lower joists to provide nailing surfaces for the decking.

sharing posts If you want to create a difference in height between two levels greater than a single step, the technique of shared posts is preferred. Codes may require that you use 6-by-6 posts. The upper beam rests on top of the posts, with joists either overlapping, as shown above,

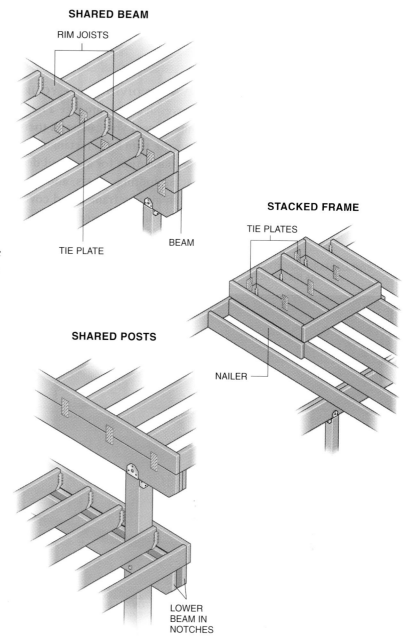

SHARED BEAM

RIM JOISTS

TIE PLATE

BEAM

STACKED FRAME

TIE PLATES

NAILER

SHARED POSTS

LOWER BEAM IN NOTCHES

or hung from the side of the beam. The lower beam is attached to the sides of the posts. Stairs are required to bridge the gap between the two levels.

FRAMING FOR A SPA

Supporting a spa may be a job for pros. If you decide to tackle it yourself, be sure to consult closely with your inspector. There are two basic methods. If you want the spa at the same level as the decking, pour a concrete slab for it to rest on, then construct the deck around the spa. If you want the spa to be raised above the decking, add a beam and additional joists to beef up the framing where you will place the spa.

framing a curve

LOWE'S QUICK TIP

When cutting joists for a curved section, you may need to make some cuts at an angle that exceeds the range of your circular saw. Make these cuts using a reciprocating saw.

1 With an angle square, extend the cut marks (see page 114) down both sides of each joist. Set your circular saw for the angle of the cut, then cut the joist as shown. Note that each joist will probably have to be cut at a different angle, requiring you to readjust the saw for each one. The angles of the cuts do not have to be perfect, but they should be fairly close.

2 Blocking between the joists will keep them from flexing as you bend the fascia around the ends. It will also provide a solid nailing surface for the skirting and may support railing posts. Cut the blocking pieces individually. Again, you will need to adjust your circular saw to produce different angles for nearly every cut. Once you have a blocking piece that fits fairly well, install it by drilling pilot holes and driving nails or screws.

3 There are several ways to create fascia material. Match your other deck materials as much as possible. You can use strips of ¼- or ⅜-inch exterior plywood. If you have a band saw or a table saw, cut thin strips out of the decking material. A standard 2-by rim joist can be turned into a bendable fascia by cutting a series of 1⅜-inch-deep kerfs, or slots, spaced 1 inch apart, across the back side of the board. Soak the board for a couple of hours to make it easier to bend. Perhaps the easiest approach is to use composite fascia boards. Many manufacturers now offer matching 10- or 12-inch-wide composite boards that are ½ inch thick or even less, making them extremely easy to bend.

Use clamps to hold the fascia material in place and attach it by driving at least two nails or screws into the end of each joist.

curved **railings**

If your deck is high enough to require a railing, follow the instructions for posts on pages 150–53, spacing them no farther than 4 feet apart. Because of the extra pressure that bent rails can exert on the posts, posts need maximum strength, so do not notch them but secure them to the joists with blocking on all sides.

The easiest way to install top and bottom rails is to attach thin composite wood or boards to the insides of the posts. Alternatively, several layers of ¼-inch-thick wood can be laminated together with polyurethane glue and many wood clamps to form a strong, bendable rail. For best results, clamp the rail to the post temporarily before fastening with screws. Install balusters on the outside faces of the rails.

If you choose to install a flat cap rail, cut segments of 2-by lumber at angles that roughly correspond to the curve of the deck. Glue the segments together, then mark the exact curve and cut the cap rail with a jigsaw. Attach it to a double top rail, as shown below.

curved **decking**

Once the posts are installed, you can lay the decking, as directed on pages 128–37. Start by laying the decking in place above the curved framing, making sure the boards are spaced properly. If necessary, install temporary fasteners, as few as possible. Trace along the fascia on the underside of the decking to mark the line of the curve. Turn the decking over, cut all of the curves with a jigsaw, then turn the decking right side up and install it.

These curved top and bottom rails are each made of two 1 by 4s laminated together using many wood clamps and polyurethane glue.

LOWE'S QUICK TIP

Soaking a board in a trough of water for a day or two will make it more flexible.

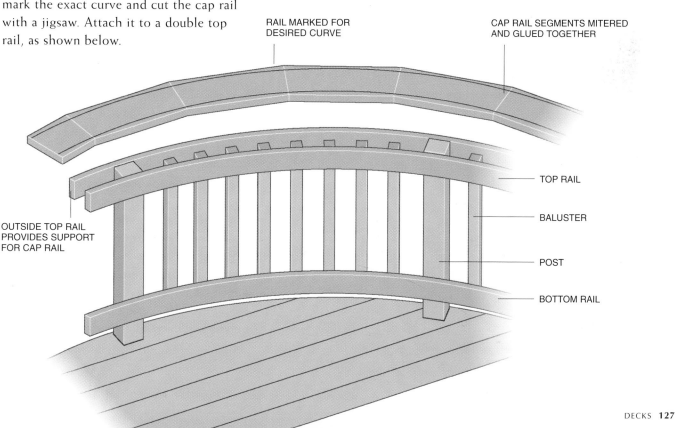

RAIL MARKED FOR
DESIRED CURVE

CAP RAIL SEGMENTS MITERED
AND GLUED TOGETHER

TOP RAIL

BALUSTER

POST

BOTTOM RAIL

OUTSIDE TOP RAIL
PROVIDES SUPPORT
FOR CAP RAIL

installing decking

EVEN A SIMPLE DECK WILL BENEFIT FROM CARE IN INSTALLING THE DECKING.
Check the boards for defects, and plan to return those that are unsightly or badly twisted.
If the deck will have butt joints, firmly attach 2-by-4 nailers alongside the joists where
they will occur so you can have twice the nailing surface.

edging possibilities

The most common approach is to leave decking board edges exposed, overhanging the perimeter joists by an inch or so. This is also the easiest technique, allowing you to install slightly oversized boards, then cut them to length all at one time.

If your joists are not pretty, cover them with a 1-by fascia board (above right) that matches your decking material. Install the decking so it will overhang the fascia by about an inch on all sides.

If you do not like the look of the decking's end grain, consider installing a fascia board that covers it (right). To do this, trim the decking flush with the joist faces. Use 2-by boards for the fascia, choosing a width that can span from the top of the decking to a bit below the joist. Choose high-quality boards that are unlikely to shrink or twist (see pages 80–81). Miter the corners for the neatest appearance.

(see pages 80–81)

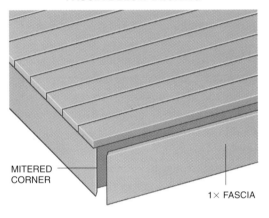

FASCIA BELOW DECKING

MITERED CORNER

1× FASCIA

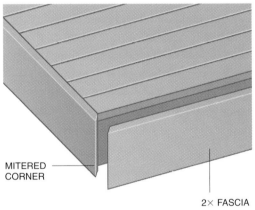

FASCIA FLUSH WITH DECKING

MITERED CORNER

2× FASCIA

Another option is to install breadboard edging (left), using material the same width as the decking's thickness, for a finished appearance. With this option, the decking need not be cut flush with the joists. Instead, cut the decking straight, then attach a 2 by 2 or a ripped piece of $\frac{5}{4}$ lumber to the edge. Again, buy high-quality lumber and miter the corners.

> **LOWE'S QUICK TIP**
>
> Examine each board for cosmetic flaws, and install the best-looking side up. If a board has splits near an end, either cut off the flawed area or install the board in a way that you can cut the end off later.

You can rip-cut decking material to make bread-board edging. Fasten it into each decking board.

getting **started**

With most decking patterns (see pages 68–69), the first installed board becomes a reference for the rest of the boards. If it is not perfectly aligned, the rest of the pattern will suffer accordingly.

parallel decking For decking that runs parallel to the house, measure out from the house on each side of the deck the width of a decking board plus an additional ½ inch. Mark the location on each end joist. Snap a chalk line between the marks. Using the straightest board you can find for this first row, install it so the outer edge is aligned with the line.

diagonal decking If you are installing diagonal decking, determine the distance from the house to the end of the deck. Measure an equal distance along the rim joist from the corner toward the center and make a mark. Snap a chalk line between that mark and the outside corner of the end joist at the house. Install the first decking board in alignment with the chalk line.

choosing fasteners Be sure to choose a fastener that's right for the decking you are installing, particularly with pressure-treated lumber. Stainless steel is a good choice for redwood, cedar, and tropical hardwoods; it should also be used near salt water. See page 82 for more information on screws and nails.

In terms of strength, use 3-inch screws or 16d nails for 2-by-4 or 2-by-6 decking, and 2½-inch screws or 12d nails for ¾ decking.

board **spacing**

A ⅛-inch gap between decking boards is ideal, but since wood decking often shrinks after it has been installed, shrinkage must be taken into account during installation. Boards that are wet and heavy will likely shrink the most. These boards can usually be installed tight against each other and, over the course of a year, will shrink enough to create a satisfactory gap. Dry, kiln-dried boards may not shrink much at all, and so should be installed with a ⅛-inch gap. A Lowe's lumber specialist can help you predict how much particular boards will shrink. An 8d common nail makes a useful spacer, but an inexpensive deck-spacing tool (right) is handier.

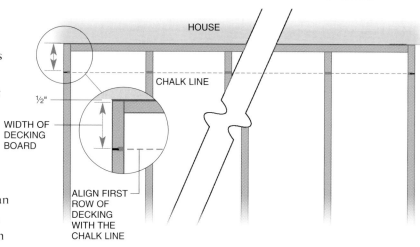

GETTING STARTED: DECKING PARALLEL TO HOUSE

HOUSE

CHALK LINE

½"

WIDTH OF DECKING BOARD

ALIGN FIRST ROW OF DECKING WITH THE CHALK LINE

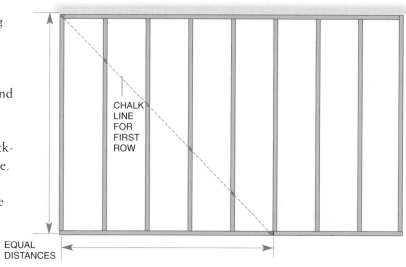

GETTING STARTED: DIAGONAL DECKING

CHALK LINE FOR FIRST ROW

EQUAL DISTANCES

This deck-spacing tool is easy to insert and to remove.

fastening the decking

The job will go quicker if you first scatter boards for 10 to 15 rows of decking across the joists; you'll have easy access to the boards as you work. This is particularly important if you have to deal with butt joints; arrange the decking so the joints will be staggered before you start driving fasteners. Also check that the ends that will be butted together will meet in a crisp joint, and that they are free of splits. You may choose to cut all the flawed ends before you start.

When driving screws or nails at board ends, drill pilot holes first to avoid splitting the wood. Install the screws or nails 1 inch from each edge of the decking, and try to keep the pattern as straight as possible along each joist.

nailing Drive nails as straight as possible into each board. Try to avoid mis-hits, to prevent creating a line of smile- or frown-shaped indentations on the decking. To be safe, you may want to use a nail set when delivering the last blow, to drive the nail just flush with the top of the decking.

driving screws For best results, drive screws with a variable-speed drill-driver with an adjustable clutch. If you're using a standard drill, buy an attachment (left) that will allow you to adjust the screw depth. Experiment with scrap pieces of decking until you are proficient at driving screws without marring the wood.

LOWE'S QUICK TIP

To achieve a reasonably straight row of decking fasteners, initially install only as many fasteners as are needed to keep the boards straight. Once all the decking is in place, snap chalk lines (using blue chalk, which will wash away) as guides for the fasteners.

THE LAST ROW

As you approach the last several rows of decking, give some thought to the width of the last row. If full-sized boards are not going to fit perfectly, plan to rip small amounts off boards in the final three or four rows (see larger illustration), rather than leave yourself with a single narrow row at the edge of your deck (inset). In some cases it may help to double the thickness of the fascia.

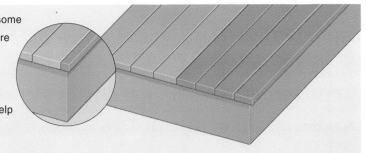

aligning decking boards

Every five or six decking boards, stretch a string line to check for straightness, and adjust as needed. Some boards will be strongly bowed or even twisted. Here are some ways to persuade unruly decking boards:

■ A flat pry bar or utility chisel can be used to straighten most boards. Start the fasteners before you start straightening. Knock the sharp end of the bar or chisel into the joist on an angle, as shown above left, then pull the board toward you.

■ If prying by hand does not do the trick, hook one end of a pipe clamp against a pry bar stuck between two boards and the other end over the edge of the problem board. Tighten the clamp until the board is properly aligned.

■ If a board needs to move only ¼ inch or so, angle-drill a pilot hole through the edge of the decking board and drive a screw in the direction that you want the board to move.

Above left: Pry with a chisel to tame a modestly curved board.

Above right: Use a bar clamp to straighten a tougher curve.

notching for posts

Some deck designs call for railing posts to be installed before the decking. Take your time notching the decking neatly around the posts, because all of these joints will be very visible.

1 Set the decking board in place against the post. Measure for the depth of the cut—the distance between the new board and the installed board, minus the amount of spacing you want between the boards (typically, ⅛ inch). Mark the cutout with an angle square.

2 Cut the notch with a jigsaw. Cut a little to the outside of the lines so that the notch will not be too tight. Hold the jigsaw firmly so it does not wobble, and cut carefully, blowing away the sawdust as you go so you can always see the cut line.

3 If necessary, add cleats so that you have a nailing surface all around the post. Drill pilot holes and drive fasteners through the decking and into the cleats. A joint can be left open for water to drain through, or it can be caulked to keep water out.

tongue-and-groove decking Tongue-and-groove composite decking is installed much like hardwood flooring in your house. Fasteners are driven through the grooves, which are then covered with the tongues of subsequent boards.

1 Install the starter strip at the far end of the deck with screws driven into the rim joist. It must be straight and parallel with the house.

2 To install the decking, slide the tongue of the first board into the groove of the starter strip. The decking is designed to create a ¼-inch gap between the boards. Drive screws through the tongue of the board and into the joist. Continue sliding tongues into the grooves of previously installed boards.

3 If a full board fits comfortably in the row next to the house, drive screws vertically through the groove section. Otherwise, rip the board to fit and attach it to a 1-inch-square block of wood. Allow a ¼-inch gap between the decking and the house. Attach fascia boards to cover the edges of the decking.

THE VINYL OPTION

Vinyl decking is another low-maintenance option, although one that produces a particularly non-traditional-looking deck. Installation differs as well. In general, first an aluminum or a vinyl track is installed across the joists, and then top pieces are snapped into place. One of several available products is shown here.

Th
called
requir
run, b
Work
choos
togeth
a shor
a deep
better
is that
the ri

Sta
36 inc
at leas
a strin

Sta
have a
railing
above
ing po
5 feet
than 4
quentl
filling
but co
people
risers.
be att
at the

finishing composite decking

Cutting or drilling composite lumber may produce a burr. This can be quickly eliminated with a rasp (below right) or sandpaper.

Unlike wood, composite decking does not have to be coated with a protective finish. If you desire a different color, however, most products can be stained or painted. Keep in mind that if you do apply a finish, you will have to recoat the surface regularly. Use the type of paint or stain recommended by the manufacturer.

Perpendicular center decking strips not only add visual interest, they limit the length of the other decking boards, so you do not need to make butt joints.

building stairs

THE CRUCIAL ELEMENT IN MAKING SAFE STAIRS IS THE STRINGERS. THEY MUST BE strong, accurately sized, and well secured at the top and bottom. The decking at the top and the landing pad at the bottom should be in place before you begin planning the stringers.

To start, purchase a pair of stair gauges. You'll also need a framing square. Attach the stair gauges to the outside edges of the framing square, on the long blade for the run and the short blade for the rise (see pages 140–41 for how to establish rise and run).

making cut stringers

Stairs with cut stringers are usually designed so that the top tread is on the same level as the deck surface, rather than one step down. That makes it easier to attach the stringers to the deck, since they will be resting against a rim joist or an end joist. If you need to build stairs with the first tread resting below the deck surface, use a hangerboard—an extra board that provides a solid nailing surface for stringers—as discussed on page 144.

Position the board for the first stringer across a pair of sawhorses. Plan your cuts so that its crown side will be up when the board is installed.

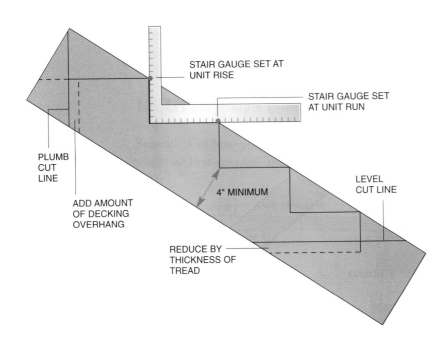

STAIR GAUGE SET AT UNIT RISE

STAIR GAUGE SET AT UNIT RUN

PLUMB CUT LINE

ADD AMOUNT OF DECKING OVERHANG

4" MINIMUM

LEVEL CUT LINE

REDUCE BY THICKNESS OF TREAD

1 Begin by laying out and cutting one stringer to use as a template to mark the others. Place the framing square along the crown side of the stringer with the corner resting on the board and the stair gauges flush against the edge. Leave enough room to make the bottom riser (see next step). Run a pencil along the outside of the square. Slide the framing square along the board until it meets the previous mark perfectly, then mark again. Continue marking all the riser and tread cuts.

LOWE'S QUICK TIP

If one of the stringer's "teeth" breaks off, don't despair. A stringer handles little side-to-side pressure, so it's safe to reattach it. Drill pilot holes through the tread surface and drive screws at an angle into the stringer.

att

If y

inst

the

narr

of a

driv

into

for

drai

rise

are

a co

each

at le

scre

trea

one

the

2 After laying out the stringer for all the risers and treads, extend the top riser line for the plumb cut. If the stringers will be installed one step below the surface of the decking, increase the length of the top tread by the amount the decking overhangs it. You also need to shorten the bottom rise of the stringer by the thickness of one tread: set a piece of tread stock along the bottom line and draw another line (the level cut line) across the stringer. Double-check your measurements.

3 Clamp the stringer to your sawhorses. With a circular saw, cut the top along the plumb cut line and the bottom along the level cut line. Set it in position against the deck. Check that the tread cut lines are level and that the riser heights will all be identical after the treads are installed. When everything is right, clamp it back on the sawhorses and start cutting the "teeth." Run the saw blade only up to the spot where the lines meet. With a jigsaw or a handsaw, finish all the cuts.

4 Set the stringer in place and check the fit one more time. It should rest flat on the landing pad and against the deck joist, with the tread cuts fairly level and the riser cuts fairly plumb. Once you're satisfied with its fit, clamp it on top of another piece of stringer stock, making sure that the new piece is crown side up and that the edges are perfectly aligned. Mark the bottom piece by tracing along the cuts with a pencil.

making **solid** stringers

Mark solid stringers as for a cut stringer (Steps 1 and 2). Cut the plumb line and the level line as described in Step 3 above. Align stair brackets with the tread lines. Drive screws to attach the brackets to the stringers.

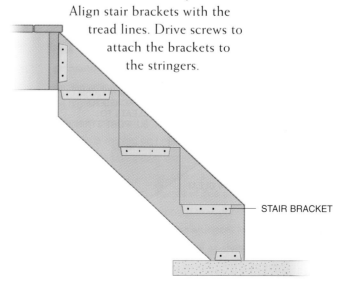

STAIR BRACKET

railing options

ALMOST ALL DECK RAILINGS HAVE THE SAME BASIC COMPONENTS—POSTS, RAILS, and balusters. But there are many potential variations on this basic theme. Don't be afraid to try something a little different; for a modest investment in time and materials, you can build a railing that is definitely a cut above the ordinary.

Railings are typically built out of the same type of wood as the decking, but that is not a rule. Railings that contrast with the decking can be stunning. If you have a great view, alternative materials like metal and acrylic will obstruct it less than a wood railing with closely spaced balusters.

LOWE'S QUICK TIP

The main components of railings are usually vertical members, and for good reason. If you build a railing with horizontal members, it is almost inevitable that children will want to climb it. This situation may actually be less safe than no railing at all.

Right: Safety is a particular concern when the deck is very high. For extra strength, these balusters are anchored firmly to the joist and to the side of the top rail.

Below: This openwork railing extends down to act as skirting as well.

a safe, **approved** railing

Local building codes regarding deck railings range from fairly lenient to tightly restrictive. If your code tends toward the former, do not take that as an excuse to cut corners. A railing should ensure the safety of all people, adults and children alike, on the deck.

A railing may not be required unless your deck surface is 30 inches or more aboveground. But 30 inches is a long way to fall. More safety-conscious codes lower the requirement to 24 or even 15 inches, and you should consider meeting such a requirement even if you don't have to.

Railings are frequently designed to withstand a force of 200 pounds pushing down on or against them, so that a person falling against the railing will

be safe. The instructions on the following pages specify fasteners that will help meet this requirement. Notched posts may or may not be permitted under your code; techniques for installing both solid and notched posts are discussed on pages 152–53.

The minimum height of a railing is usually 36 inches, but many people prefer the railing to be higher. Railing height may be limited by restrictions on the length of 2-by-2 balusters, but adding a middle rail will allow you to use longer balusters and thus create a higher railing.

Spacing between all components of the railing should not be large enough to allow a 4-inch sphere to pass through (some codes say 6 inches). Required to eliminate the chance of a child's head getting stuck, this limitation is well worth obeying.

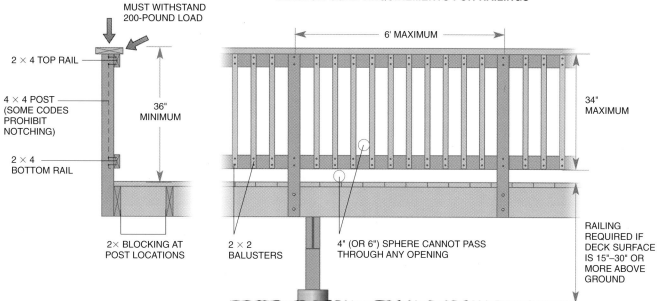

COMMON CODE REQUIREMENTS FOR RAILINGS

MUST WITHSTAND 200-POUND LOAD

2 × 4 TOP RAIL

4 × 4 POST (SOME CODES PROHIBIT NOTCHING)

36" MINIMUM

2 × 4 BOTTOM RAIL

2× BLOCKING AT POST LOCATIONS

2 × 2 BALUSTERS

4" (OR 6") SPHERE CANNOT PASS THROUGH ANY OPENING

6' MAXIMUM

34" MAXIMUM

RAILING REQUIRED IF DECK SURFACE IS 15"–30" OR MORE ABOVE GROUND

wood railings

Wood railings are the traditional choice. They are affordable, easy to build, and time tested. Perhaps the most typical style of wood railing is shown in the diagram above. For variety, the balusters can be attached directly to the rim or end joist as shown at right. This technique uses a minimal amount of lumber but requires that the decking be installed without any overhang. The absence of a gap between the decking and a bottom rail also makes it harder to sweep off debris.

Railings are often built with flat cap rails covering the post tops (below right). An alternate look can be created by building railing sections ladder style (see page 155), installing them between the posts, and then adding a cap rail.

glass and metal

If you want to maximize the view from your deck, it is hard to beat clear-acrylic or tempered-glass panels. Some manufacturers offer a post-and-railing system that accommodates clear panels, matching balusters, or a combination of both. Stainless-steel cable is also great for viewing the scenery,

although some building codes prohibit the use of such horizontal railing systems.

For composite and vinyl railing systems, see pages 158–59.

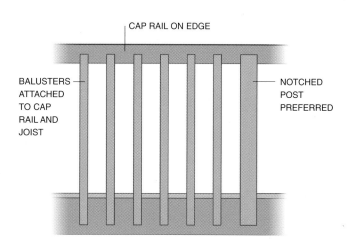

CAP RAIL ON EDGE

BALUSTERS ATTACHED TO CAP RAIL AND JOIST

NOTCHED POST PREFERRED

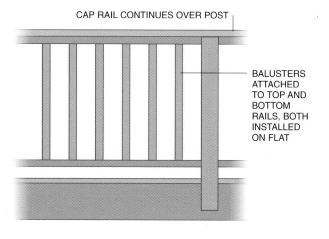

CAP RAIL CONTINUES OVER POST

BALUSTERS ATTACHED TO TOP AND BOTTOM RAILS, BOTH INSTALLED ON FLAT

a chance to be **creative**

Just about every deck railing is made with vertical posts and a pair of horizontal rails. Most railings fill the rectangles between the posts and rails with evenly spaced balusters, but there's no law that says you can't make things more interesting. Of course, if the deck is higher than 3 feet you will need to comply with codes: there should be no openings wider than 4 inches, and the railing should not be climbable by small children.

Above: Clear acrylic panels make for a safe and sturdy railing, yet do not inhibit the view.

Above right: Cedar logs can be purchased to make these posts and rails. The balusters (which do not meet code for a high deck) are made by artfully choosing and debarking cedar branches. Once assembled, the railing receives several generous coats of amber shellac.

Right: Where a bench is incorporated into the railing, the standard code requirements for balusters may be relaxed.

Top left: A home-owner with patience as well as a good jigsaw can cut balusters like these. Use high-quality lumber.

Left: A cottage-style railing calls for careful cutting as well as precise spacing.

Above: Curves are made by cutting boards into thin pieces, bending them into place, and laminating them using polyurethane glue and lots of clamps.

Far left: To create this circle design, install all the balusters except the one in the middle. Cut the circle out of three pieces of 2 by 10 and glue them together. Attach the circle between two balusters, then cut and install the short pieces to fit above and below.

Left: People often lean against the top cap and rest drinks on it, so this one is covered with several coats of sealer.

Above: A baluster section like this decorative one can be assembled as a unit, installed between the posts, and then topped with the cap rail.

Below: At Lowe's you'll find a good selection of post and newel caps. Use post caps for designs in which the post's upper end is visible. Newel caps can be installed on top of a cap rail, giving the illusion of a post that travels up through the cap rail.

planning **posts** and balusters

Some railing posts are the tops of foundation posts. These pages deal with posts that support only the railings.

Railing posts are usually made from 4 by 4s, although you can use 6 by 6s if you prefer a heftier appearance. Space the posts no more than 6 feet apart; a 4- or 5-foot spacing will create an even stronger railing. While working within these guidelines, make an effort to keep the posts equally spaced along each deck edge.

Posts should be bolted, not nailed, to the deck. To create a trimmer profile, you can notch the railing posts to fit over the decking and joist (see pages 152–53). However, because this practice weakens the post connection, it is prohibited by some building codes.

framing for strong posts Railing posts need to be attached to the rim joist and the end joists. There are several ways to do this. A simple connection to the rim joist, if it is within several inches of a perpendicular joist attached to the rim joist (first illustration), can be a strong attachment. However, if the post is attached to an end joist—or to a rim joist in a place where it is not near a perpendicular joist—it will wobble when you push on it. To build firm posts, install blocking in any of the ways shown in the other illustrations at right. If access to the underside of the deck is difficult, install the blocking before you lay the decking.

locating posts Solid posts can be attached most easily to the outside of the joists. This approach allows you to finish the decking before worrying about posts. But many people do not like the appearance of bulky posts on the sides of their deck. With a little more planning, you can install solid posts inside the joists, before laying the decking. Or, if code permits, you can notch the posts, resting the 1½-inch notches against the outside of the joist and on top of the decking, so they stick out less.

turning corners Handling railings at the corners of a deck takes some advance planning. Although it calls for extra posts, a double-post design is generally the easiest to install, especially when you are using continuous rails installed "on edge"—with the wide side vertical. If you prefer the look of a single post at the corner, it is best to install all railing posts inside the joists, with rails set "on flat."

FRAMING FOR STRONG POSTS

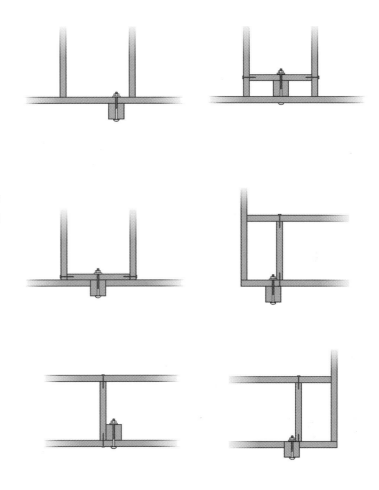

**DOUBLE CORNER POSTS
WITH RAILS ON EDGE**

**SINGLE CORNER POST
WITH RAILS ON FLAT**

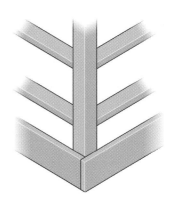

installing railings

THE STRENGTH AND APPEARANCE OF THE RAILING IS DETERMINED FIRST AND foremost by the connection of the posts to the deck frame. If the posts are plumb and evenly spaced, installing the rails and balusters will proceed smoothly. For most railing styles, it is best to attach all the posts before assembling the rest of the railing.

notching posts

1 Cut all posts to the correct length—the desired height of the post above the decking plus the thickness of the decking plus the width of the joists. From the bottom of each cut post, measure up the joist width plus the decking thickness, subtract ½ inch, and make a mark across the post.

2 Set your circular saw to cut exactly 1½ inches deep. Make a series of closely spaced cuts between the line marked in Step 1 and the post bottom. You can also make these cuts on a table saw or radial arm saw.

3 With a hammer, knock out the pieces of cut wood. Use a chisel to clean out each notch. Work carefully to create a notch that is squarely cut and the same depth throughout; avoid gouging out too much wood with the chisel.

4 The exposed bottom edge of the post will look better if it is beveled. Use a power miter saw or a circular saw with the blade tilted to make a 45-degree cut. Apply two or more coats of sealer to all cut areas.

attaching posts

The procedure for attaching posts is similar whether they are notched or solid, or placed on the inside or on the outside of the joists. Be sure to add any blocking that may be needed, as shown in the illustrations on page 151.

1 If your decking overhangs the edge, cut a notch so that the post can rest against the side of the joist. For 4-by-4 posts, cut the notch about 3¾ inches wide, leaving a ⅛-inch gap between the post and the decking on both sides. A jigsaw is the best tool for this job.

2 If you are using notched posts, set each post in place with the top of the notched portion resting on the decking. With solid posts, get a helper to hold the post in place, or use clamps. Use a level or post level to ensure that the post is plumb. Drill a pilot hole for each bolt using a bit the same size as, or just slightly larger than, the bolt diameter. To minimize the chances of splitting the post, do not locate the top bolt directly over the bottom one; instead, set each off center just a bit, as shown in Step 3.

3 Slide carriage bolts through the pilot holes. Reach beneath the deck and behind the joist to place washers on the bolts, then tighten the nuts using a socket wrench or an adjustable wrench.

LOWE'S QUICK TIP

If you plan to coat your deck with paint or solid stain, you may choose to notch the decking 3½ inches rather than 3¾, so the post can fit tightly. Caulk the joints around the post before painting or staining.

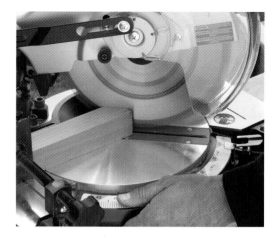

A power miter saw cuts balusters quickly and cleanly.

installing **rails**

The easiest way to install rails is to attach them on edge to the inside faces of the posts. Unless your deck is particularly long, you can probably manage with a single board for each rail. Top and bottom rails installed on edge are sufficient, but you may prefer to add a cap rail, which provides a flat surface along the top of the railing.

Somewhat more involved are rails installed on flat between the posts. Rails can be toenailed to posts or attached with metal brackets designed for the job. Installing rails on flat allows you to create or add decorative post tops; you can also attach milled balusters between the rails. Keep in mind, however, that flat rails are not nearly as secure (when stepped on, for example) as rails set on edge. For a stronger connection for flat rails, place them in dadoes cut into the posts. When rails with balusters are to be installed on flat, it is usually best to build them ladder style, as shown on the facing page.

LOWE'S QUICK TIP

Code may permit you to use only one fastener at each joint, but you will have a stronger railing if you drive two. To prevent splitting, drill a pilot hole before driving a nail or screw less than 2 inches from the end of a baluster.

cutting or buying **balusters**

Balusters are commonly made of 2-by-2 lumber and installed vertically. You can buy precut 2 by 2s or milled balusters in lengths that will fit standard railings. If you want to save a few dollars, you can cut your own balusters from long 2 by 2s. To maximize deck privacy, use wide boards such as 1 by 4s or 1 by 6s and space them closely together.

If you cut your own balusters, make sure they are all the identical length. The most efficient way to do this is to use a power miter saw and construct a simple stop block, as shown in the photograph on the left on page 88.

Balusters can be attached to the sides of rails. If you choose this approach, bevel the baluster ends; the balusters will look much nicer and shed water better. If post bottoms will be visible on the deck, cut matching bevels on the posts and the balusters.

**CONTINUOUS RAILS
ON EDGE**

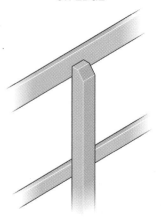

**RAILS ON FLAT
WITH CAP RAIL**

**RAILS ON FLAT
IN DADOES**

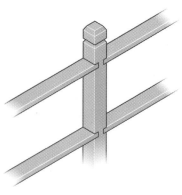

attaching balusters

If perfect symmetry is important to you, take the time to carefully calculate baluster spacing, so that the last space is the same as all the other spaces. To do that you will need to rip a spacer that is precisely the correct width. However, most people are not bothered if the last space is somewhat smaller than the others. If that is your opinion, simply make a spacer that is the correct width to satisfy local codes.

To make a spacer, rip a piece of plywood or 1-by lumber to match the desired space between rails. Make the spacer long enough to span from the top to the bottom rail. Then grasp a baluster and the spacer in one hand. Hold the spacer tight against the post or the neighboring baluster while driving nails or screws.

LADDER-STYLE ASSEMBLY

A railing built ladder style has a more finished appearance than is usual on a deck. With this technique, the railings are assembled in full sections, as you might build a ladder, and the sections are attached as units between the posts. This type of railing takes time to build, and requires posts that are perfectly plumb.

To strengthen the assembly, plan to set the rails into ½-inch-deep dadoes cut into the posts. To make this work, the rails should be cut 1 inch longer than the space between the posts. It's easiest to cut the dadoes before the posts are installed.

To keep the balusters from spinning in place, cut a ½-inch-deep channel along the underside of the top rail just wide enough for the balusters to fit.

When all of the parts have been cut, assemble a railing section on the deck. Position the balusters with a spacer, as described above. Drill a pilot hole at each baluster location, then attach the baluster with 3-inch deck screws driven through the top and bottom rails into the center of the baluster.

Once the balusters have been attached to the rails, lift the railing section into place, sliding the rail ends into the post dadoes. Fasten the assembly by drilling pilot holes and driving 3-inch deck screws at an angle through each rail into the post.

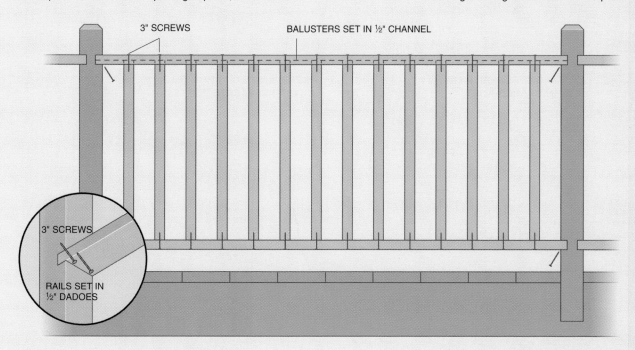

3" SCREWS   BALUSTERS SET IN ½" CHANNEL

3" SCREWS

RAILS SET IN ½" DADOES

finishing with the cap rail

Many railings are topped off with a cap rail, which is laid flat. Since it is so visible, use straight and clean boards, and choose dry lumber that is unlikely to shrink or warp. If possible, use long boards to avoid joints, which are apt to widen over time. And make a special effort to smooth the edges of the cap rail and keep it well protected with sealer.

When cap rails meet at a corner, joining them with miter cuts will hide the end grain. Such miter joints, however, are notorious problem areas. To make the joint more secure, it is a good idea to use a biscuit joiner and polyurethane glue. At the least, carefully drill pilot holes and drive screws to hold the miter tightly together. If you need to make a butt joint on a long run, use a scarf joint (made with two angled cuts) and be sure to locate it over a post.

LOWE'S QUICK TIP

Whenever possible, hide fasteners by driving them through from the bottom. (This will be most successful if you drill pilot holes and drive screws; nails may push the joints apart.) Just be careful that the tips of fasteners do not poke through the top surface.

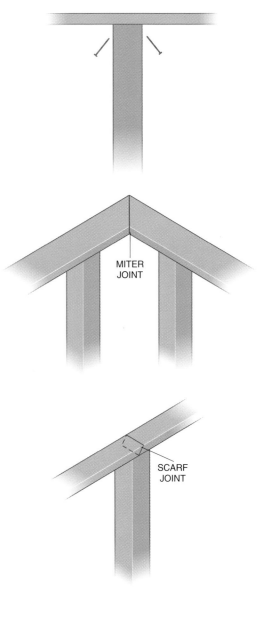

MITER JOINT

SCARF JOINT

stair railings

Stair railings should resemble the decking railing as much as possible, with matching baluster and rail shapes and spacing. For safety, stair railings should have a graspable handrail (facing page). Stairs that are built against the house look fine with a single railing, but stairs in any other location look best when both sides have a railing.

DECK AND STAIR RAILINGS WITH SHARED POST

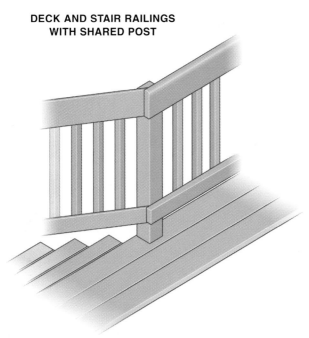

DECK AND STAIR RAILINGS WITH SEPARATE POSTS

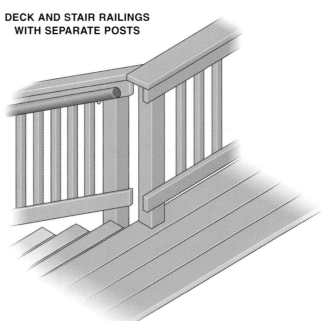

installing the posts With careful planning, you can use deck posts as the top posts on your stairs (facing page). With some railing designs or stair locations, however, it is preferable, or even necessary, to install separate posts for the deck and the stair railings. Start by installing posts a little longer than you need, then measure and cut them to height after they are in place.

Stair railing posts should be bolted to the stringers in the same manner as deck railing posts. You can notch stair railing posts to match notched posts on a deck railing, but the notch will have to be cut at an angle.

installing rails and balusters Lay a 2 by 4 across the treads as shown above right, and clamp it temporarily to the top post. Determine the height of the top rail; building codes allow a range of 30 to 38 inches. Measure straight up from the bottom of the 2 by 4 on the bottom and top posts, as shown above right, and mark the distance on the outside edge of each post.

Depending on your railing style, use the marks to determine where to cut the posts or where to align the upper edge of the top rail. With most stairs, the bottom rail can be installed about 1 inch above the line established by the bottom of the temporary 2 by 4; check your local code. Cut the rails to length and fasten them to the posts. Balusters can then be cut (see tip) and installed as they were on the deck railing.

If you plan to install an on-flat cap rail across the tops of the posts, you will need to cut an angle on the posts to match the top rail. Fasten the cap rail to the stair railing posts in the same way as the cap rail is fastened on the deck railing.

adding a handrail Building codes often require that a handrail be graspable, by which they mean that a person could grip it securely enough to keep from falling. Use a handrail that is small enough to be grasped by children as well as adults. The most sensible width (or diameter) is from 1½ to 2 inches.

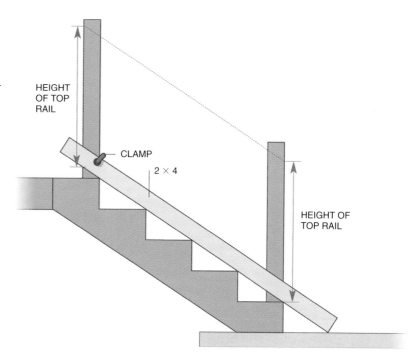

HEIGHT OF TOP RAIL

CLAMP

2 × 4

HEIGHT OF TOP RAIL

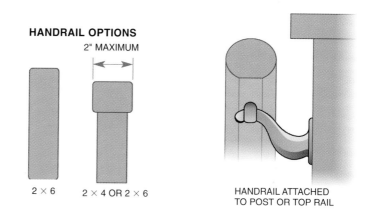

HANDRAIL OPTIONS

2" MAXIMUM

2 × 6

2 × 4 OR 2 × 6

HANDRAIL ATTACHED TO POST OR TOP RAIL

Most people can get a fairly good grip on a 2 by 4 or 2 by 6 on edge. Even better are handrails that allow the fingers to curl around the bottom. These can be made by ripping a board to a 2-inch or smaller width, then fastening it to the top of a 2-by handrail, as shown above left.

Another good choice is to use a standard round handrail, attached to posts with metal brackets. This approach allows you to build the stair railing to look exactly like the deck railing and then attach the handrail, somewhat inconspicuously, to the top rail or the posts.

LOWE'S QUICK TIP

The tops and bottoms of the stair rail balusters will probably need to be cut at an odd angle. To find this angle, first install the top rail (or the rail cap, if there is no top rail). Have a helper hold a board tight to a carpenter's level and hold the board plumb up against the top rail. Use a T bevel (see page 84) to capture the angle at which the balusters should be cut.

composite and vinyl railings

AT LOWE'S YOU WILL FIND AN ASSORT-ment of railing systems manufactured of the same materials as composite or vinyl decking (see pages 79 and 134–37). A composite railing system comes with all the parts you need to build a railing that is both sturdy and attractive, and that will almost certainly satisfy code requirements.

Balusters may resemble straightforward 2 by 2s, or they may be turned for a more stately look. The cap rail may be flat and plain, or it may have a milled appearance that resembles an interior railing. Posts also may be either plain or decorative. Post skirting pieces trim out the post at the bottom; use them to cover imperfect decking cuts.

A composite railing system is easy to assemble. Balusters and posts are precut to the correct length, so you need cut only the cap rail and the top and bottom rails. The balusters fit into channels in the top and bottom rails. Because composite lumber is somewhat flexible, the railing may need to be supported with either posts or support blocks every 2 feet or so.

Install the posts after the framing is finished and before you lay the decking. The posts must be firmly anchored to the joists

LOWE'S QUICK TIP

Somewhat rough-feeling lumber made of plastic combined with wood chips is typically called "composite," while plastic lumber with a smooth, shiny surface is typically called "vinyl." However, some manufacturers call the smoother product "composite" as well.

Above: A straightforward railing mimics the most popular style of wood railing.

Right: Turned balusters are evenly spaced for a finished appearance. On this style, bottom support pieces must be added about every 2 feet.

using special brackets and screws. After installing the decking, slip on the post skirting pieces and slide them down so they rest on the decking, where they will serve as base molding. Cut the rails to fit between the posts. Use a baluster to measure for the correct height for the rails, so that the balusters will fit snugly between the top and bottom rails. Attach the rails using brackets (see below) and screws.

Determine the spacing between the balusters (see page 155). Cut spacer pieces (typically they are the same material as plain 2-by-2 balusters) to fit between the balusters in the top and bottom rails. Slip the spacers and the balusters into the channels of the top and bottom rails, and drive screws to fasten them snugly in place. Install the cap rail and the post caps, and you're done.

Clear acrylic panels are another option. The acrylic is strong enough to keep people from falling through, and it can be cut to fit with a utility knife.

SYSTEM COMPONENTS

Composite pieces must either fit into a manufactured slot, be supported from below, or be attached with screws and angle brackets supplied by the manufacturer. Be sure to purchase the correct brackets for each situation. Some systems use simple angle brackets that are installed so as to be partially hidden. Brackets like those shown at right are meant to be seen. Do not drill pilot holes for the screws or fasten composite pieces by toe-nailing or toe-screwing; the screws will not hold firmly enough. On the far right is a skirting piece, which slides into place to quickly cover all four sides of the post bottom.

adding skirting

VISUALLY SPEAKING, PERHAPS THE WEAKEST LINK ON A DECK IS THE SPACE between the bottom of the deck and the ground. If this view of the deck frame is not to your liking, it is easy to cover it up with skirting. The area can also be put to work as a storage area.

framing for skirting

Unfortunately, most decks are not ready for skirting, because there is no continuous nailing surface for the top, sides, and bottom of the skirting. If the beam rests on top of the posts, you can run 2 by 4s from post to post a few inches above the ground; but that will provide framing for only one side.

A common framing method, shown above right, is to attach 2 by 4s to the inside face of the outside or rim joist, allowing the 2 by 4 to hang down 1½ inches or so. Vertical 2 by 4s and a bottom 2-by-4 rail can then be attached.

Another method, shown at right, is to build a frame of 2 by 4s with their edges, rather than their faces, facing outward. The frame can then be attached at the top to the inside face of the joists.

LOWE'S QUICK TIP

To prevent water damage and allow for air circulation, skirting and the framing for it should be at least 1 inch above the ground whenever possible. In a damp climate, plenty of ventilation is needed, or you may end up with an unpleasant musty odor, not to mention mosquitoes.

Solid vertical skirting, suitable where ventilation is not a concern, makes a seamless transition to the lawn.

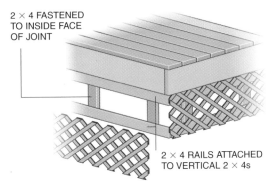

FOR LATTICE

2 × 4 FASTENED TO INSIDE FACE OF JOINT

2 × 4 RAILS ATTACHED TO VERTICAL 2 × 4s

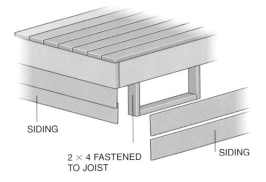

FOR WOOD SIDING

SIDING

2 × 4 FASTENED TO JOIST

SIDING

skirting **options**

Lattice, the most popular material for deck skirting, is inexpensive and easy to install. If you have a choice of wood lattice, select the style composed of pieces that are $\frac{3}{8}$ inch thick, for a total thickness of $\frac{3}{4}$ inch; thinner lattice is easily damaged. Vinyl lattice panels are the sturdiest, and require little maintenance.

If space permits, you can build large, removable lattice panels that permit the space underneath the deck to be used for storage. Attach the lattice to a 1-by-4 frame to give it strength, then use hook-and-eye connectors or other hardware to attach the panels to a suitable frame under the deck.

An alternative to lattice is wood siding or other solid boards. If you like this idea, be sure that the underside of the deck will be adequately ventilated; remember that rainwater will drip down through the decking-board gaps, which could result in a very soggy situation. One option is to install vertical 1 by 4s or 1 by 6s with $\frac{1}{4}$- or $\frac{1}{2}$-inch gaps between the boards.

Lattice is frequently used for skirting (above). Install horizontal 2 by 4s between posts, then attach lattice sections (below right). House sid- ing (below left) requires vertical framing pieces at least every 6 feet.

getting the timing right The ideal weather for applying deck finish is slightly overcast, with no rain in the immediate forecast. Avoid applying finish while the sun is beating down.

Apply a fairly thin layer, let it dry, then apply a second coat soon afterward. Work plenty of finish into exposed end grain and into any joints where water could be trapped.

putting on the finish

1 New lumber often has a slight glaze on the surface. The wood will better absorb finish if you lightly sand it to remove the glaze before applying the first coat. A pole sander, with 120-grit sandpaper, allows you to sand while standing up.

2 Sweep the deck thoroughly with a broom. Use a shop vacuum or a putty knife to clean out sawdust and other debris between boards. If you pick up dust when you run your hand over the wood surface, sweep again.

3 Apply the finish. If you are using a stain, try to minimize the lap marks that occur when you brush new finish over previously applied finish that has already begun to dry. For best results, apply the stain along the full length of a couple of boards at a time. Never let the stain puddle on the surface.

LOWE'S QUICK TIP

In many locales, deck-finishing companies compete for a booming business. Hiring such a company every year or two can save you time and effort and ensure a proper finish.

cleaning and **refinishing**

If left alone, a wood deck will turn driftwood-gray as it weathers. Even if you like this appearance, it is better for the long-term survival of the deck if the wood is regularly cleaned and refinished.

stripping old finish A deck stripper will remove the finish entirely, allowing a deck cleaner to do a more thorough job.

To remove paint, use a water-neutralized paint stripper as directed by the manufacturer. You may need to scrape or sand paint away in some areas.

1 Use a putty knife or a screwdriver to remove debris that has accumulated on joists between deck boards and in other nooks and crannies on the deck. It is tedious to do this cleaning, but it is a vital step: these spots are prime candidates for rot.

2 Some deck cleaners should be diluted with water, others applied full strength. Follow the manufacturer's directions. Apply with a pump sprayer at a time when the deck boards are cool and in shade (cleaners evaporate too quickly under dry, sunny conditions).

3 Let the cleaner sit on the deck for about 15 minutes, then scrub thoroughly with stiff-bristled brushes. Use a large brush for the deck surface; you'll want a smaller one for the railings and stairs. Always brush the wood in the direction of the grain.

4 A pressure washer is ideal for rinsing the deck, but only if you know how to avoid damaging the wood. Use a fan-type nozzle and test on scrap pieces. A spray nozzle on a garden hose is a suitable, and less risky, alternative. Rinse away the cleaner, avoiding garden plants.

5 Let the deck dry for a day or two (but not much longer). Apply the finish as described on the facing page. If you use a roller or a pump sprayer to apply the finish to the deck surface, use a brush to work it between the boards and into other parts of the deck.

LOWE'S QUICK TIP

The underside of the deck is often tormented by moisture, temperature variations, and insects. If at all possible, apply finish to all underside surfaces. A pump sprayer is particularly useful to reach remote sections.

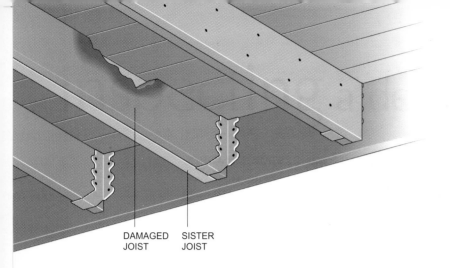

DAMAGED JOIST SISTER JOIST

repairing **joists**

A joist may be rotted at its top, where the decking rests on it, or at its end, where it ties into the ledger or the rim joist. If you detect rot on a joist early enough, the repair is easy to make. Remove the rotted material with a hammer and chisel, then coat the newly exposed wood with a water-repellent preservative. Using the same size lumber, cut a "sister" joist to the same length as the damaged joist, or cut one that extends at least 4 feet in either direction from the damaged area. Position the sister joist into place against the old joist and attach with a pair of 2½-inch deck screws every foot or so. Attach the decking to the sister joist. If the sister runs into the ledger, attach it to the ledger using an angle bracket.

replacing **posts**

Replace a failing deck post as soon as you can. Begin by jacking up the beam. On a low deck, use a hydraulic bottle jack and concrete block along with pieces of wood, as shown below left. For a higher deck, use a telescoping jack. Apply just enough pressure with the jack to lift the beam very slightly off the post. Remove the post and install a new post base if the old one is damaged. Cut the new post to length and set it in place, with a new post cap on top. When it is plumb, lower the beam so that it rests on the post, but keep the jack in place for the moment. Attach the post to the beam, then remove the jack.

For an old post that was buried in concrete, dig out as much of the buried wood as possible, fill up the cavity with fresh concrete, and add a new anchor bolt and a new post base. Then attach the new post to the post base.

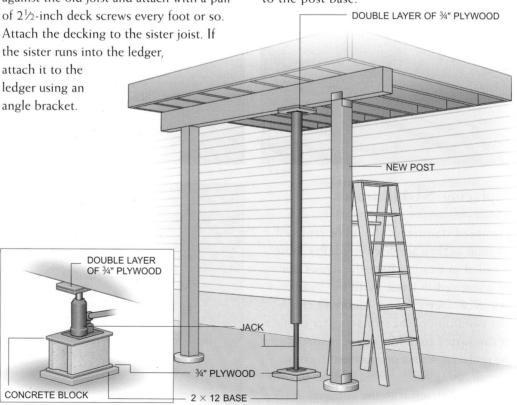

DOUBLE LAYER OF ¾" PLYWOOD

NEW POST

DOUBLE LAYER OF ¾" PLYWOOD

JACK

CONCRETE BLOCK

¾" PLYWOOD

2 × 12 BASE

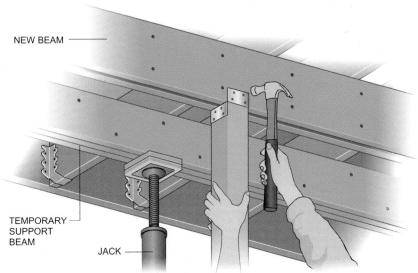

NEW BEAM

TEMPORARY
SUPPORT
BEAM

JACK

replacing a **beam**

A rotted or severely cracked beam
should be replaced. If you inherited
an old deck with a sagging beam, it is
possible that the beam was undersized
when the deck was built, in which
case it should be replaced with a
stronger beam.

Build a temporary replacement
beam by nailing together three 2 by 8s
that are at least as long as the old beam.
Have the new beam ready to install before
you start removing the old one (see pages
108–111 for a full discussion of beams).

Set the temporary beam on top of the
jacks close to the old beam, but leave
enough room to work. Use at least as
many jacks as there are posts supporting
the old beam. Raise the jacks just enough
to release the pressure of the old beam on
the posts. Remove fasteners and hardware
securing the beam to the posts and joists,
then remove the beam. Cut the beam into
smaller sections beforehand if that makes
removal easier.

Set the new beam and new post caps in
place. Make sure the beam spans the full
width of the deck and all the posts are
plumb. Fasten the beam to the joists and
the posts. Then remove the temporary
beam and the jacks.

railing repairs

Individual balusters, rails, and cap pieces
can be replaced with little trouble. Use a
hammer, with medium pressure, and a flat
pry bar to loosen and separate the parts.
You may be able to remove screws using
a drill with a screwdriver attachment, but
often old screws are rusty or stripped and
won't unscrew. Another option is to cut

through nails or screws using a reciprocating saw equipped with a metal-cutting
blade; you can usually slip the blade
between two pieces of wood. Install new
pieces using screws rather than nails, so
you won't shake the structure as you work.

removing a deck

- Cut off power to any electrical fixtures
  on the deck, disconnect the wiring, and
  remove the fixtures. Also remove any
  plumbing.

- Remove overheads, benches, planters,
  or other features.

- Cut the railings into removable sections.

- Snap chalk lines on the decking to
  identify joist locations, then cut
  through and remove the decking on
  each side of each joist.

- Cut and remove the joists, one at a time.

- Remove treads and risers from stairs and
  cut stringers loose from the deck.

- Cut up the beam and then the posts.

- Remove fasteners holding the ledger to
  the house and carefully pry it off.

- Remove old flashing.

patios

AN OUTDOOR FLOOR CAN BE STATELY AND ELEGANT OR
rustic—or it can be both almost magically at the same time. It
can be a tiny sanctuary in a corner or an expansive entertainment
space adjacent to the house. It can be a simple rectangle of interlocking concrete pavers or an elaborate combination of stone,
mortar, pattern, and texture, with planters, benches, and walls.

Whatever your patio preference, the following pages will
help you plan and build it. In addition to information on solving
drainage problems, grading the yard, and building retaining
walls, you'll find an array of choices for paving and edging. The
ambience of your patio will primarily come from these materials.

In most cases, a new patio involves six basic steps. First, lay out
an outline of the future patio and determine its height and slope.
Second, excavate the area to the correct depth. Third, install the
edgings. Fourth, fill the area inside the edgings with gravel and
sand, then screed the sand to the correct height. Fifth, install the
pavers. Sixth, fill the joints with sand or soil.

Installing a large concrete slab is beyond the scope of most
homeowners, but a small one—what you might need for a paved
accent in your yard or for the landing below deck stairs (see page
140)—is not too difficult; instructions appear on pages 228–30.

Before you start, review the safety guidelines
on pages 90–91.

planning a patio

LOWE'S QUICK TIP

Check to see if you need to obtain a permit and to have your patio inspected by your local building department. In many locales, a modest-sized patio with pavers laid in soil or sand does not need to be inspected, whereas a concrete slab or a large patio does.

TYPICALLY, DESIGNING A PATIO—AS OPPOSED TO A DECK—INVOLVES THE DESIGN of the entire yard, or at least a substantial part of it. Because a patio surface is only slightly above grade, it needs to be integrated with the landscaping. Often a patio serves as a transition between the house and the lawn, in the area that receives the most foot traffic. The lawn then becomes an extension of the patio. Neighboring foliage—trees, shrubs, vines, flowerbeds, and crevice plants—integrates the patio with the yard and contributes to its functionality.

For general instructions on planning an outdoor space that is functional and suits your needs, see pages 56–59. A Lowe's sales associate can help you choose your pavers and edging materials; see pages 180–91 for some ideas. Don't be afraid to mix two or more types of pavers—masonry materials almost always complement each other.

planning around trees

If your patio will abut a tree, consult with a nursery to determine whether the patio will damage the tree's root system. Take into account the rate of growth for the tree. In many cases, it is best to keep the patio at least 4 feet from the trunk. If the tree has shallow roots, it may be a good idea to install loose gravel rather than pavers near the tree.

the plan view

Once you have determined the overall contours of your patio, draw a plan, or aerial, view. Be as specific as possible. Measure carefully, and perhaps even draw the patio bricks to scale—that will give you a good sense of the overall appearance. (If you will be using interlocking pavers with odd shapes, you may choose to draw simple rectangles instead, making a note of the actual shape of the pavers.) If the patio slopes, indicate the direction and rate of the slope.

The plan view of this patio would show how the space is divided into various "rooms"; to indicate the level changes, make a detailed elevation drawing.

It may help to draw patio furniture and large planting containers on a separate sheet of graph paper and cut them out. You can then arrange the furniture on the patio drawing to get a realistic idea of spacing. Include foliage in your drawing. For shrubs and trees, estimate what their size will be in two years or so.

This drawing will give you a better idea of the space and will help you estimate the materials that will be needed.

detail views
and materials list

Make detailed elevation, or side-view, drawings showing just how the patio will be installed. As you draw, make a thorough materials list; it will save you time at later stages. You don't need to figure how many pavers you should have, but do indicate

how many square feet will be covered. Calculate the amount of edging, as well as gravel and sand.

If possible, ask a building inspector or landscape designer to check your plans before construction begins. An inspector (and you) will need to know the depth of the excavation, the thickness of the gravel and sand beds, and the length of any reinforcing materials.

LOWE'S QUICK TIP

The word "paver" refers to any masonry unit—such as a brick, tile, or flagstone— that is used to create a floor surface. A "concrete paver" is a specific type of paver manufactured out of concrete (see pages 184–85).

AN ELEVATION DRAWING

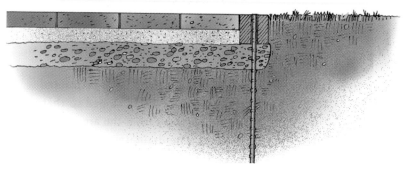

holding back soil

IF YOUR PATIO SITE IS HILLY, YOU MAY need to hold hillside soil in place and prevent it from encroaching on the patio. You may be able to accomplish this by planting shrubs or other plants with strong roots. However, a retaining wall is a more sure solution. Plan to build the wall after you've excavated a fairly level space (slightly sloped away from the house) and before you lay the gravel and sand substrate for the patio.

Retaining walls are typically "battered," meaning they lean back slightly toward the soil that they retain. For added strength, have the stones or blocks that make up a retaining wall interlock in some way.

Where a tall slope must be retained, two or more terraces usually do the job more gracefully than a single high wall.

excavating
for a retaining wall

Digging can be heavy work, especially if the soil is hard or rocky. But be sure to dig deep enough to leave room for drainage gravel, if needed (below right).

There are three basic excavation methods. One is to cut into the entire face of the hillside at approximately the same angle as the wall will batter back. This will mean hauling away plenty of soil. The second option is to build the retaining wall at the bottom of the slope and then fill behind it with gravel and soil. This means hauling in lots of soil. The third option combines the first two, and keeps soil hauling to a minimum: excavate the bottom half of the slope and use the excavated soil to fill in the upper half.

adding **drainage**

Most retaining walls are not made with mortar; therefore, rainwater can seep through their faces. However, if your area usually receives heavy rain or if water often flows down the slope that the wall is being built to retain, you should install drainage as shown below. Excavate a space about 16 inches behind where the wall will be. After laying the first courses, shovel in several inches of gravel. Then set a perforated drainpipe so it slopes at a rate of at least ¼ inch per foot toward the area where you want excess water to flow. Keep adding gravel as you build up the wall.

LOWE'S SAFETY TIP
Most residential retaining walls are modest in size and can be built by a motivated homeowner. However, if you need to build a retaining wall higher than 3 feet or if the soil in your locale is prone to erosion, consult with a landscape contractor or an architect before proceeding; it may be best to have the job done by pros.

These concrete blocks interlock for strength as you stack them, and automatically lean (or batter) back toward the soil being retained. You need adhesive for only the top course.

concrete retaining blocks

Stackable concrete retaining blocks are good looking, strong, and easy to install. You will find a good assortment at Lowe's. Most of these blocks have a lip at the rear bottom that slips over the top back edge of the block below them. Others interlock via grooves or with fiberglass pins.

After excavating, dig a trench 6 inches wider than the blocks and 6 inches deeper than a block's thickness. Fill the trench with 6 inches of compactible gravel so the top of the bottom course of blocks will be at about grade height. Tamp the gravel with a hand tamper or with a 4 by 4. With a straight board, test to be sure that the gravel forms an even surface, though it doesn't need to be perfectly level.

Set the bottom row of blocks upside down and backward, so the lips face up at the front. As you build, check that the blocks form an even surface that does not wobble; adjust as needed by adding or removing gravel underneath them. Lay the second and third courses right side up and fill behind them with gravel or soil.

Continue the stacking and backfilling. When you reach the second-to-last course, apply several beads of construction adhesive with a caulk gun and set the top blocks in the adhesive. Spread heavy-duty landscaping fabric on top of the gravel and fill in behind the top blocks with soil and sod.

setting stones on a slope

A modest hillside can be held stable by dry-stacking boulders and large rocks (see below). However, a retaining wall like this must batter at a fairly steep angle; aim for roughly 45 degrees for maximum strength.

Roughly excavate the slope you want. Dig out any sod, plants, and organic matter. Lay down heavy-duty landscaping fabric and shovel a layer of rough sand or compactable gravel over it. Stack large and medium-size stones so they rest on top of each other without wobbling. Fill in spaces behind the stones with sand or gravel to improve stability. Fill in any gaps between the large stones with small stones and decorative gravel.

LOWE'S SAFETY TIP

See pages 90–91 for guidelines on safe construction methods. Check with utility companies to be sure you will not puncture an electrical, plumbing, phone, cable, or gas line. Work moderately and take breaks to avoid harming your back. Wear heavy work boots, preferably with steel-reinforced toes.

choosing paving materials

A VAST ASSORTMENT OF MATERIALS IS AVAILABLE FOR PATIOS. MANY OF THESE are carried at Lowe's, but if you don't see just what you're looking for, ask if it can be special-ordered.

natural brick

Brick is still made with essentially the same process used by ancient peoples—firing a clay mixture in a kiln. The higher the firing temperature, the stronger the brick. The process results in a building block of rustic charm, at home in any landscape. Brick is not as strong or as weather resistant as concrete pavers (pages 184–85), but if you choose paving bricks (they are sturdier; see below right) and you install them correctly, the resulting patio can last for centuries with little maintenance.

The neat, rectilinear patterns of brick harmonize well with a symmetrical garden and formal patio design.

Especially in an area with freezing winters, many bricks that work for walls will not survive as patio pavers, because in patios they're subject to much more pressure. For a patio, use paving bricks rated SX if your ground freezes; bricks rated MX should be used only in a frost-free climate. Consult with a Lowe's sales associate to be sure the brick you buy will last. Applying a coat or two of sealer will repel moisture and enhance durability, but it will not transform wall bricks into patio bricks.

Even if your choice is restricted to paving bricks, you'll have plenty of options. Bricks may be a single color, speckled, or composed of several slightly different hues. Paving bricks suitable for cold weather are sometimes dark in color with a slightly glossy surface. Some are extra thick for added strength. "Cored" bricks have three or more holes, to

reduce weight and give the mortar greater grabbing power. Such bricks should be used for pavers only in a warm climate. Wire-cut bricks have rough vertical lines; rough facing bricks have the appearance of cracked earth. A fingerprint brick has a number of indentations that look like thumbprints. A "frogged" brick has an old-fashioned indentation bearing the name of the manufacturer; you may want to scatter some of these throughout a patio. Used common bricks are often partially covered with white efflorescence (faux used bricks are actually concrete pavers made to look like old common bricks).

Brick may change in appearance over time. For instance, the surface of a porous brick eventually acquires a patina, giving it a soft, polished look.

Install brick pavers tight against each other on a bed of gravel and sand. Or mortar spaced-apart bricks onto a stable concrete slab and fill the joints with mortar (see pages 236–37). Sometimes paving bricks are set on their sides rather than laid flat. This means buying more bricks, but the patio will be stronger for it.

In an informal garden, brick can meander casually. Efflorescence—a whitish discoloration —gives a nice, slightly aged effect.

The used bricks here, of various sizes and colors, include some imprinted with the manufacturer's name.

Above: Pavers in blue and gray hues tend to settle the mood down.

Below right: A pattern like this is not difficult to install.

concrete pavers

In general, the term "paver" refers to any modular paving unit, such as a brick or an adobe block. A "concrete paver" is a type of paver made of dense, pressure-formed concrete These pavers make an extremely durable paving material that can survive any climate. Because concrete pavers are so precisely manufactured, they fit tightly together to form a surface that is relatively smooth.

Concrete pavers are usually less expensive than brick or stone, making them the obvious choice for many people. Lowe's carries a selection of styles and colors to suit almost any taste.

paver shapes "Interlocking" pavers are shaped so that the pavers fit together like a jigsaw puzzle. However, they aren't necessarily more stable than simple rectangular pavers. Choose interlocking types if you like the pattern.

Non-interlocking pavers can be put together with tight joints for a neat, seam-

less look, or with open joints that sprout grass or crevice plants for a more casual appearance.

Large pavers may be square, round, or hexagonal. Some fit together in groups of four to form a large pattern, and make attractive stepping-stones. Some have an exposed-aggregate surface; others have a slightly raised pattern.

colors Some concrete pavers have a pink-ish hue. Others do a better job imitating natural stone or brick. You can buy a pallet that contains pavers of several different hues; the overall surface will resemble natural cobblestone.

Some pavers come in ensembles—groups of pavers that are designed to form a cohesive grouping. The individual pavers have not only different hues, but different sizes and shapes as well. They form a rich pattern that looks complicated but is actually not difficult to lay out. You don't have to plan the placement of all the pieces—if you maintain a fairly even distribution of the various sizes, you'll achieve an overall sense of balance.

fancy patterns Circular and fan-shaped ensembles are also available. A circular grouping may contain pavers in five or six different sizes and shapes. Follow the man-

Above: Reddish pavers create a more vibrant setting.

Below left: Correctly installed, sand-laid pavers are sturdy enough for a driveway.

Below: Three strips of turf block are set in a mortared flagstone surface.

ufacturer's directions to create a circular or semicircular grouping. A fan pattern (also called an overlapping arc pattern), reminiscent of European walkways, involves five or six different sizes of paver. Of course, if you install a circular or fan-shaped pattern in a rectangular area, you will need to custom-cut quite a few pavers to fit along the edges (see page 195 for instructions on cutting concrete pavers).

turf block This retro-look product is making a modest comeback. Properly installed, turf block provides a surface strong enough to be used as a driveway while allowing grass to grow through.

These large ceramic tiles have the look of natural stone.

ceramic tile

LOWE'S QUICK TIP

You can create a patio with inexpensive, plain pavers and enliven it with a sprinkling of decorative tiles. If field tiles need to be cut to accommodate decoratives, consider asking the tile supplier to do the cutting for you.

If you're looking for splashes of color or for a patio surface as smooth as that of an indoor room, ceramic tile, available in a vast array of colors and shapes, is your best choice. Be sure, however, that the tiles and installation materials you choose will survive your climate (see the tile descriptions that follow). In most cases, ceramic tile must be set in a bed of mortar (usually thinset mortar) atop a solid concrete slab. To fill in the joints between tiles, use latex-reinforced sanded grout, which is durable enough for most outdoor applications, especially if you apply a sealer every year or so. In an area with severe winters, you may want to use epoxy grout instead.

glazed ceramic tile These tiles offer the widest range of color choice, and many can survive even harsh climates if they are properly laid. The

disadvantage of glazed ceramic tile is that a high-gloss glaze is slippery when wet. Some types have a slightly bumpy surface for skid resistance.

saltillos and terra-cotta tile

Mexican Saltillos and terra-cotta tiles have a soft reddish glow that lends warmth to a patio. However, most types are suitable for warm climates only, since they soak up moisture: a hard freeze could cause them to crack. Some Saltillos are unglazed; others have a thin layer of glaze that does not offer good protection against moisture.

quarry tile The name of this type of tile is misleading; quarry tiles are not actually cut from quarry stone, but are made of fired clay. Quarry tiles are unglazed and very hard, so they make for a surface that is skid resistant and often strong enough to survive freezing winters. Colors are generally limited to earth tones and pastels.

porcelain tile Modern methods produce porcelain tiles that are amazingly tough and easy to maintain. And porcelain can be made to resemble almost any type of ceramic or stone tile. While some people regard porcelain tile as an imperfect

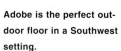

Adobe is the perfect outdoor floor in a Southwest setting.

replica lacking the true texture and natural beauty of stone or ceramic, others swear by how easy it is to clean and by its excellent stain resistance.

mosaic tile

Mosaics are composed of many small tiles joined together, usually over a mesh backing. They are as easy to install as regular tiles, and may be ceramic, stone, or porcelain. The durability of mosaic tile is the same as for full-size tiles of the same materials.

adobe block

Traditional adobe blocks were made by mixing clay with straw, cutting it into slabs, and allowing the slabs to dry in the sun. The resulting blocks could be used only in warm, dry climates. Today, adding asphalt emulsion or Portland cement to the mix improves stability. Blocks made this way can hold up even in cold climates, though they are not widely available outside the Southwest.

Adobe blocks are massive—two common sizes are 4 by 8 by 16 and 4 by 8 by 8. The large, earth-toned slabs look great in generous, open garden spaces. Some types are irregular in shape while others are manufactured with the same precision as bricks or concrete pavers.

Adobe blocks can be installed with tight joints, as you'd install bricks or concrete pavers. Or, they can be set with wide joints that allow grass or crevice plants to grow through.

edging materials

THE MATERIAL THAT RUNS AROUND THE PERIMETER OF A PATIO FRAMES THE PATIO and thus is an important design element. It must also be strong and well anchored, so that it can hold the pavers in place. Edging material may blend or contrast with the pavers.

Be sure to choose an edging product designed for a patio. Landscaping edgings, which are meant to define the border between a lawn and a flowerbed, are not strong enough to keep sand-laid pavers from straying.

Edging installation is covered on pages 204–11.

poundable edgings These edgings can simply be pounded into place, usually via stakes. Some are plastic units that mimic the look of natural stone while others have a scalloped design. Because they are easy to install, poundable edgings can be put in place either before or after the pavers are set. You can easily pick them up and move them, which could save you the trouble of cutting the last row of pavers (see page 220).

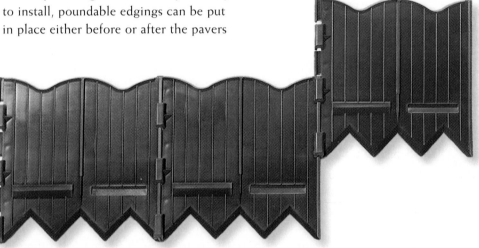

Slabs of cut bluestone make an unusual—and stable—edging.

concrete block edgings Some edging blocks are much like concrete pavers, but are laid on edge for stability. You'll have a choice of plain-looking blocks or blocks that have an interlocking and decorative design.

invisible edgings These edgings are designed to be virtually unseen, giving a patio a clean, classic appearance. Invisible edgings are anchored every foot or so with stakes, which may come with the edging or need to be purchased separately. Most are plastic, and are stronger than you might expect. One type is a straight "board" that can be bent to form gentle curves. Another type can easily be bent to form any curve you desire.

The top of invisible edging is typically slightly lower than the pavers, so you cannot use the edging as a guide for paver height.

wood edgings For a rustic look, edge a patio with landscaping timbers, railroad ties, 6 by 6s, or 4 by 4s. If you want the edging to be less prominent, use 2 by 4s. Whichever edging you choose, make sure it is extremely resistant to rot.

pavers as edging This is a traditional approach that creates an elegant patio perimeter. Use the same materials as you use for the pavers, or use a different material for contrast.

Unless they are mortared onto a concrete slab, edging pavers should be installed standing upright, for strength. "Soldiers" stand upright with their edges (not their faces) facing the patio. This arrangement uses more materials than "sailors," which face the other way, but it is stronger.

concrete edgings A small slab of concrete, typically about 8 inches wide and 6 inches deep, produces a very firm edging. Once it is installed, you can mortar tiles or pavers on top, or you can acid-stain it.

If paver edgers are set as shown here, on their sides rather than upright, they should either be supported with invisible edging (see page 211) or set in a bed of concrete (see page 209).

INVISIBLE EDGING

CONCRETE BLOCK EDGING

Though many mistake it for stone tile, this surface is made of concrete that has been stained and stamped.

decorative concrete

A patio can be made of simple concrete. Generally speaking, this is a big project for which you should hire professionals.

Such a patio may seem a bit bleak, but it need not be plain gray. A number of techniques allow installers to add texture and color to concrete.

If you are having a new slab or walkway poured, see if your contractor can liven things up. Decorative concrete is a booming business these days, so you can probably find someone who is experienced in the following methods.

coloring Concrete can be tinted before it is poured; the concrete company may do this for a fee, or the installer may add the tinting. Standard concrete can be tinted to a wide variety of colors. If the installer uses concrete mixed with white (rather than standard gray) Portland cement, the color can be quite vivid, but this option will be expensive.

Alternatively, colorant can be dusted on just after the concrete has been poured, while it is being worked. This is a two-step process: the colorant is broadcast by hand and the surface is troweled; then more colorant is applied and the surface is finished. If done by an experienced pro, coloring by this method can produce a one-of-a-kind appearance with distinctive mottles or swirls of slightly different hues.

stamping or tooling Using special stamping tools, installers can make a concrete surface resemble tiles, bricks, or

These concrete stairways and patios are tinted a light adobe color and scored to resemble large pavers.

flagstones (see facing page, top). Usually, a stamped surface is colored as well.

adding special finishes Some concrete pros produce stunning effects using standard trowels. A travertine finish, for instance, has a texture that resembles stucco or flagstone. Some installers carve geometric or random patterns into new concrete, to mimic bricks or stones. In a warm climate, rock salt may be sprinkled over freshly troweled concrete to artfully dot the surface with pits.

exposed aggregate This is perhaps the most common decorative effect for newly poured concrete. Pebbles of varying colors are pushed into the wet concrete and the surface is washed at just the right time, so that the stones are fully exposed yet firmly embedded.

For the most part, these methods are best left to the pros. However, if you pour a small concrete slab as described on pages 228–30, you might want to try adding color or giving it an exposed-aggregate finish. See page 231 for instructions.

Above right: Here, concrete with a surface of seeded aggregate is set in a grid made of mortared bricks.

Right: This concrete patio and walkway have been engraved, then expertly stained with mottled hues that pick up the colors in the natural slate of the fireplace.

EFFECTS FOR EXISTING CONCRETE

If an existing slab is strong but ugly, you have a number of options for adding appeal. You can pave over it with tile or pavers (see pages 236–39). You can apply a simple stain yourself (see page 232). Or you can hire a contractor who specializes in beautifying old slabs. Check out the contractor's work by viewing completed projects. Among the contractor's skills should be acid-staining and incised patterns. Acid-staining can produce a solid color, or a mixture of slightly different colors, much like a faux-painted finish on a wall. Installers can also produce geometric or random patterns of different colors. An expert can incise a pleasing pattern using a concrete saw or special engraving tools. Usually, this is done after the concrete has been tinted.

masonry tools

BUY PROFESSIONAL-QUALITY TOOLS LIKE THOSE SHOWN HERE. THE RIGHT TOOL will be comfortable in your hand, will be precisely milled to make your work accurate, and will stand up to the pressures of masonry work. Also have on hand basic carpentry tools such as a circular saw, claw hammer, tape measure, pry bar, and pencils.

excavating tools

shovels and spades Digging tools should have sharp tips and straight blades and be free of encrusted material such as old concrete. Replace a shovel that is not easy to use. A square-bladed one slices fairly straight lines in sod and scoops dirt from the bottom of an excavation. A pointed shovel is useful when the digging is tough.

wrecking bar When you encounter a large root or rock, you'll be glad to own a wrecking bar with a sharp tip. Use it to cut a root or to pry up an obstruction.

garden rake Buy a rake with short, firm prongs—not a lawn rake. You'll find it indispensable for smoothing excavated areas and spreading gravel and sand.

tools for laying out and building a patio

string lines Buy mason's line, which stays taut, rather than regular string. A chalk line marks a perfectly straight line. Red chalk is permanent; blue washes away easily. You can use a chalk line as a plumb bob to line up a spot on the ground with one above.

levels Over a short distance, use a carpenter's level. For a distance of up to 12 feet, set the level on a straight board. For longer distances, use a water level.

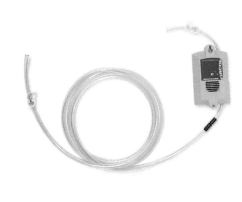

square A carpenter's square lets you quickly check for square over a short distance. For greater accuracy, follow the techniques shown on pages 198–99.

LOWE'S QUICK TIP

The excavation site, gravel layer, and pavers must all be tamped firm as you lay the patio. Use a rented vibrating plate compactor, shown on page 212.

special hammers To drive stakes, a hand sledge usually does the job; if the soil is tough, you may need a full-size maul (not shown). To pound pavers into place without fear of breaking them, use a rubber mallet.

trowels A margin trowel is a great all-around tool for mixing, scooping, and spreading small batches of mortar. You may find a brick trowel comfortable for these purposes as well. Use a notched trowel to spread thinset mortar when paving over a concrete slab. Use a jointer to tool the grout between mortared pavers and a mason's brush to clean the joints.

cutting tools You can roughly cut brick, concrete pavers, and stone using a brick-set chisel, a cold chisel, or a mason's hammer. For precise cuts, rent a masonry saw (see page 196).

tools for **mortar** and concrete

mason's hoe Use a mason's hoe to mix concrete or mortar in a wheelbarrow or a masonry trough (see page 227). It will let you mix faster than a standard hoe or shovel.

concrete smoothing tools Initially, smooth poured concrete using a darby. Then use a magnesium float for a smoother finish. An edger rounds the edges of a slab.

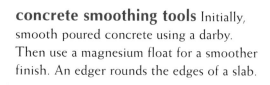

flagstones set in soil

LOWE'S QUICK TIP

Choose flagstones that are fairly consistent in thickness; otherwise, it will be difficult to achieve an even surface. Flagstones are sold by the ton, so you can save plenty of money by buying thin stones—typically, about 1¼ inches thick.

ONE OF THE SIMPLEST PATIOS IS MADE OF FLAGSTONES SET IN SOIL. POTTING soil, sand, and the flagstones themselves are the only materials you need. You don't need to install edging (you could, but then you would have to cut the flagstones to fit around the perimeter) because irregular edges are more in keeping with this informal material.

A flagstone patio, no matter how it is laid, will be relatively rough and uneven, but still smooth enough for most outdoor activities.

Have the stones delivered as close to the site as possible; if they will lie on a lawn, set them on sheets of plywood. Sort the stones into three piles according to size, with a fourth pile for narrow pieces. As you lay the patio, alternate among the piles so that stones of various sizes will be evenly distributed.

preparing the ground

When flagstones are set in soil, you can add the charm of crevice plants growing between them.

The stones will rest directly on the excavated surface. Remove all sod and any roots over half an inch thick. Dig deep enough that the stones will be slightly lower than the lawn, so you can run a lawn mower over them.

A small amount of rainwater will soak into the joints between stones, but to ensure against puddles on the patio during a heavy rain, slope the excavation away from the house. Scrape rather than dig the bottom of the excavation site so you will not loosen the undisturbed soil. Tamp the area with a hand tamper or power tamper, then gently rake to loosen a layer of soil about ½ inch thick.

1 Position the stones in the excavated area and experiment with different arrangements. Aim to achieve joints that are fairly consistent in width—between ½ inch and 1 inch. This will take some time, so be patient. If a stone protrudes beyond the excavated area, you may choose to dig away the sod rather than cut the stone.

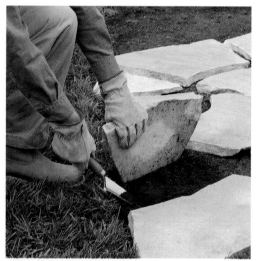

2 You will probably need to cut at least some corners off some stones. See page 197 for cutting techniques. Sandstone will cut easily while limestone will be tough to crack. If you have some very large stones, you may wish to keep them large, and space them regularly for a dramatic effect. Or, score each large stone with lines and break it apart. The resulting pieces can be laid with neat joints.

3 Once you have arranged about 10 square feet of stones, firmly set the stones before moving on to the next section. To set a stone, stand on it or tap it with a rubber mallet to produce an impression in the soil. Tilt the stone up and use a garden trowel to scrape and fill soil as needed. Lay the stone back down, and test for stability. It will probably take several attempts before the stone is free of wobbles and level with its neighbors.

4 Mix some sand with some potting soil to produce a soil that is firm but drains readily. Dampen it slightly, then insert it into the joints between the flagstones using a pointed shovel or a garden trowel. Allow the soil to dry, then gently sweep the stones clean.

5 Set a hose nozzle to produce a fine mist and spray the patio until the joints are soaked. This will compress the soil. Wait for the soil to dry, add more soil as needed, and spray again. If you would like greenery in the joints, sprinkle seeds or embed crevice plants.

LOWE'S QUICK TIP

If chiseling produces artificial-looking edges on your cut stones, you can simply whack the stone with a hand sledge instead of using a chisel. The resulting cut will not be predictable, but it will look natural.

installing edgings

THE NEXT EIGHT PAGES SHOW HOW TO INSTALL ALL THE MOST COMMON TYPES of patio edgings. Any of these edgings will do a good job of keeping your pavers in place, as long as you install them correctly. To tell if your edging is well installed, give it a pretty good kick in the direction that the pavers will be pushing on it. It should remain firm.

poundable edgings

At Lowe's you will find several kinds of edgings that are simply pounded into the ground. They are meant for gardens rather than patios, so are not as strong as other types of edgings. However, if your sod is firmly rooted and you do not have to excavate deeper than 5 inches or so, they will hold the pavers in place. The advantage: you do not have to fill in the excavated space behind the edging with sod.

1 Lay out for the patio (see pages 198–99). Set 2 by 4s on the lawn with their inside edges representing the perimeter of the patio, and drive stakes to hold them in place. Position the poundable edging against the inside edges of the 2 by 4s and drive it into the ground. The type of edging shown comes in pieces that you join; drive one piece only partway in before driving its neighbor.

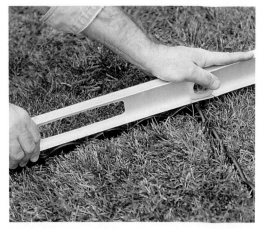

2 Drive the edging down to about the level of the grass. Use a level to check that it is either level or correctly sloped away from the house. If an edging piece is too far down, you can pull it up using pliers.

3 Excavate the interior (see page 212), taking care not to dig so deep that the edging starts to come out. It will be loose but once you install and tamp the gravel and sand and install the pavers, it will be firm again. Remove the 2 by 4s and their stakes.

concrete edgings

Like poundable edgings (facing page), these products are designed for gardens rather than patios, but if your sod is firm they can do a fine job of holding pavers in place.

1 Lay out the patio area (see pages 198–99). Excavate the interior and spread and tamp a gravel base around the perimeter (see page 212). Set the concrete edgers in the gravel base. Check that the edgers are straight and that they are either level or correctly sloped away from the house.

2 Lay straight 2 by 4s against the back side of the edgers, and pound stakes to keep them in place temporarily while you lay the pavers.

3 Once the pavers are laid, remove the 2 by 4s and backfill behind the edging blocks with soil. Tamp the soil firm, and repeat if needed. Cut pieces of sod to fit tightly between the lawn and the edgers.

TURNING A CURVE

Curved concrete edgers are generally available in two shapes, to make either tight or long curves.

Above: The top of your shovel blade may be just the right height to serve as a depth guide.

Below right: A vibrating plate compactor ensures a solid base.

excavating the interior

A patio substrate should rest on undisturbed soil, which is firmer than soil that has been dug up and replaced. So make it your goal to excavate exactly as deep as required, and no farther. To calculate the depth of excavation, add the thickness of the gravel and sand required for your installation plus the thickness of your surface material.

Stretch a grid of mason's lines across the site, attached so the lines lie on top of the edgings or the temporary 2-by-4 guides. Space the lines 4 to 5 feet apart. If the edging is wood, simply drive in nails or screws and tie the lines to them. If the edging is brick, tie the lines to stakes driven a foot or two outside the patio, so that the lines rest on top of the bricks. Pull the lines very taut.

Your shovel blade may be the correct length to use as a depth guide (see above). If not, put a piece of tape on the handle to mark the depth. That way, you can quickly check for depth as you work. Dig first with a pointed shovel, then use a flat shovel to scrape the bottom.

laying a firm gravel bed

Order compactable gravel (also known as aggregate base course or hardcore) made to serve as a patio substrate (to figure out how many cubic yards you need, see page 227). If possible, plan to have the supplier dump the gravel directly into the excavated area. Otherwise, you will need to ferry it in wheelbarrows.

An hour or two before the gravel delivery, rent a vibrating plate compactor. Remove the grid lines and power-tamp the soil. Spread the gravel with shovels, then rake it. Re-install the grid lines and check for depth, keeping in mind that tamping will likely lower the depth by about ½ inch. Remove the lines, power-tamp several times for firmness, and recheck the depth. If necessary, add gravel and power-tamp again.

WP 1550

a gravel patio

A PATIO WHOSE SURFACE IS MADE OF PEBBLES OR LARGE-SIZE GRAVEL IS THE easiest kind to install. You don't need to excavate as deep as for a paver patio; edging does not have to be precisely positioned; and installing the surface is just a matter of spreading and compressing. A patio made with tiny, sharp stones, such as crushed rock or decomposed granite, can form a surface that is surprisingly hard and stable once compacted. This surface provides excellent drainage, and you may enjoy the crunchy sound when you walk

LOWE'S QUICK TIP

You can also use the method described here to create a gravel path.

on it. Gravel or pebbles are also ideal if nearby trees have sent roots near the surface. Rainwater can easily percolate through the pebbles, and if the roots cause waves, you can just rake the surface smooth.

There are drawbacks, however, to this kind of surface: many types of stones can be scattered easily and offer loose footing, and bicycles and wheelbarrows will have trouble rolling over them and will make dents. And the job must be done right. Edging must be installed at the correct height so it effectively contains the loose material but still is low enough for a lawn mower to pass over. The surface material must be firmly tamped to prevent scattering. For the best surface for conditions in your region, check with your Lowe's sales associate.

1 Excavate to a depth of 4 inches, install any type of edging, and tamp the ground firm. Then shovel in a 2-inch base layer of compactable gravel, rake it smooth, and moisten it thoroughly with a fine-mist spray.

2 You can use a vibrating plate compactor or a drum roller to compress the base. It must be firmly compressed so that less attractive stones will not work their way up through the finished surface.

3 Use a rake to spread the finish material, taking care not to disturb the base coat. If the material is small grained, tamp it; do not attempt to tamp large pebbles or stones.

S screeding with pipes as guides

THE METHOD SHOWN ON PAGES 214–15 WORKS TO SCREED THE SAND IF YOUR patio has solid edging that matches the height of the patio. If your patio lacks such a consistent guide along its perimeter, use pipes as screed guides, as shown on these pages.

Excavate and install invisible edging (see page 211). For this method, it is important that the gravel be level or correctly sloped. Depending on local soil conditions, you may choose to first lay landscaping fabric (see page 214) and then lay the pipes on top of it. Check with a contractor or your building department to see whether this is recommended.

LOWE'S QUICK TIP

When tamping and when filling in voids, start near the middle of the patio, close to the house, and walk backward as you work your way toward the perimeter. That way, you can fill in your footprints as you go.

This patio was installed with invisible edging using the pipe-screed method; the decorative stone edging was put in afterward.

1 Use plastic (PVC) pipe, which is inexpensive and light. Pipe is usually sold according to its inside diameter; the outside diameter is larger. For a 1-inch-thick layer of sand, use ¾-inch pipe; for a 1½-inch-thick layer, use 1-inch pipe. Space the pipes about 6 feet apart; pipes parallel to your edging should be about a foot away from it. Cut the pieces to fit within an inch or so. Lay a long straight board across several pipes to make sure they describe a fairly even surface. Check that the patio will be level parallel to the house and sloped down and away from the house at a rate of about ¼ inch per foot. Adjust pipes up or down by adding or removing gravel under them.

Lay
right
so n
betw
the p

Arra
to b
onte
sibl
coa
san
layr
bag
the
pav

2 Pour sand into the area and roughly smooth it with a garden rake so it is slightly higher than the pipes at most points.

3 Lay a straight 2 by 4 across two or three of the pipes. Press the board firmly onto the pipes and pull or push it across the patio to screed a smooth surface. Fill in any low spots, moisten, and repeat.

4 If the sand dries out at any point, set the nozzle on a garden hose to mist and spray the sand until it is damp.

5 Use a power tamper to press the sand firmly into place. Fill in any footprints or low spots and screed one more time.

6 Remove the pipes, taking care not to disturb the surface. Fill the resulting voids with sand and pat the surface smooth.

setting rectangular pavers

THE NEXT THREE PAGES SHOW HOW TO INSTALL A BASIC paver surface with rectangular pavers and tight joints. To install other shapes, or to install with large joints or a wood grid, refer to pages 221–25.

choosing a pattern

Don't compromise when it comes to the paver pattern. Laying the pattern you like best may add time, but probably not more than an extra day—small potatoes compared to all that work you put into excavating and laying a bed of gravel and sand.

To make the patterns shown below, the pavers must be factory-produced to precise dimensions and must be modular—half as wide as they are long.

Jack-on-jack is the easiest pattern to install, but only by a small margin. Half-basketweave and basketweave (which can be installed with or without a grid of 2 by 4s) are nearly as easy. None of these patterns requires a lot of cutting; if you arrange to move two sides of the edging after the pavers are installed, you can get away with no cuts at all.

For the pinwheel pattern, every fifth paver must be half-sized. The 90-degree herringbone pattern and the running bond pattern also call for plenty of half-sized pavers. If half-sized pavers are not available precut, you can mass-produce them using a wet masonry saw. The 45-degree herringbone pattern requires lots of 45-degree cuts of various sizes. When you're installing a running bond, start by cutting plenty of half-pavers; you'll need them for every other paver along one side.

A patio can be divided into a grid of squares or rectangles using 2 by 4s. The sections can be filled with pavers in most any pattern (see page 222).

These bricks set in a basketweave pattern have joints filled with dark stone dust, for an enhanced geometric effect.

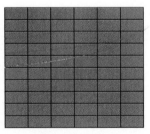

JACK-ON-JACK

HALF-BASKETWEAVE

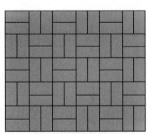

BASKETWEAVE

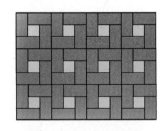

PINWHEEL

90-DEGREE HERRINGBONE

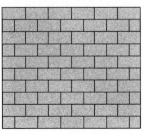

RUNNING BOND

45-DEGREE HERRINGBONE

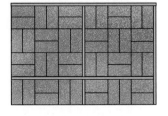

BASKETWEAVE WITH 2-BY-4 GRID

laying the pavers

Here we show how to install a 90-degree herringbone pattern. The jack-on-jack and running bond patterns are simpler. For other patterns, see pages 222–23.

LOWE'S QUICK TIP

Usually, the joints between pavers are filled with fine sand (page 220, Step 5), which has a neutral color that blends with most pavers. To emphasize the joints and achieve a more geometric look, spend a little more for dark-colored stone dust, which is finer than the sand.

1 Starting in one corner, set several pavers to abut the edging. Use a level or straightedge to check that the pavers are at the desired height; if they are not, adjust the screed and screed again. Set each paver straight down onto the bed, gently scraping the side of the edging or an already-laid paver as you lower it; if you slide a paver more than ¼ inch or so, you will create waves in the sand and the surface will not be level. Install all pavers so they fit snugly against each other.

2 After you have set 10 or 12 pavers, place a beaterboard—a flat 2 by 4 or 2 by 6 about 2 feet long—on top, then tap with a hammer or rubber mallet. If a paver is noticeably higher than its neighbor, tap it directly with the mallet.

3 As you install more pavers across the surface, move the guideline with you every 2 feet or so. Until they are all locked in place by edging, bricks can easily push out of position, so if you need to kneel on top of the patio, first put down a piece of plywood, large enough to support your toes as well as your knees, to evenly distribute your weight.

PROJECT CONTINUES ➡

4 If you installed a temporary screed guide, work up to it, then remove it, taking care not to disturb the pavers or screeded sand. If the size of your patio requires it, install the guide for a new section. Spread sand in the next section. To screed, rest one end of the screed on the patio surface and the other end on the edging. Continue laying pavers.

5 Scatter the fine filling sand over the pavers and use a soft-bristled broom to sweep the sand into the joints. If the sand is wet, allow it to dry and sweep again.

LOWE'S QUICK TIP

It's usually a good idea to install all the full-size pavers and then rent a wet-cutting masonry saw to cut all the partial pieces at once. See pages 194–95 for measuring and cutting techniques.

6 Run a vibrating plate compactor over the surface. This will cause the fine sand to settle into the joints. Sweep more sand into the joints and compact again. Alternatively, moisten the patio by spraying it with a mist of water; this also will cause the sand to settle.

ADJUSTING EDGING TO MINIMIZE PAVER CUTS

You may be able to avoid cutting some pavers at one edge of the patio by adjusting the edging. Install pavers until you're near the end of the patio, then move the edging to abut them. In the case of 2-by edging (as shown), push the edging up against the pavers and drive stakes and screws to secure it. Use a handsaw or reciprocating saw to cut the other piece of edging flush. In the situation shown, you will, of course, still have to cut the half bricks.

installing a small paver patio

INSTALLATION OF A SMALL PATIO IS BASICALLY THE SAME AS FOR A LARGE ONE; follow the basic steps for patio installation starting on page 198. However, if your patio is 50 square feet or smaller, you may want to simplify the installation as follows.

■ Instead of installing a layer of gravel followed by a layer of sand, install a single layer of "paver base," sold in bags at Lowe's. This product contains gravel, so it compacts well for strength. It also contains enough sand that you can screed it quite easily and smoothly.

■ In laying out the patio, skip batterboards and string lines. Instead, measure out a perimeter and dig a trench around it. Set edging in place—2 by 4s are the easiest—check it for square and correct height, and stake it in place. If you make any mistakes, you can correct the edging while installing the pavers.

■ Rather than renting a vibrating plate compactor, use a 2 by 4 about 7 feet long to tamp the soil, then the paver base. It will take time, but not as much time as two trips to the rental store. If the soil is already fairly stiff and you tamp assiduously, the results will be nearly as firm as those achieved by a power tamper.

■ Use dry runs to figure the layout ahead of time (Step 1 at right), so you can minimize cutting.

■ On a small patio you may have only 20 or so pavers to cut, so consider buying a masonry blade for your circular saw rather than renting a masonry saw. The cutting will be only slightly slower.

1 Set the pavers in a dry run to figure out where you need to make your cuts. Ideally, you should only have to cut every other paver on two sides. When installing "keystone" pavers like these, you can use special perimeter pieces for two of the edges.

2 Excavate a somewhat larger area than you need, and cut the edging boards longer than needed. Set the pavers in a dry run and mark for cutting the edging so you will have minimal cutting to do.

3 Spread the paver base, tamp and screed it, and set the pavers. Sweep sand into the joints.

setting pavers in a **grid**

With this method, you first build a wooden grid, then install pavers inside the sectors. Each grid sector must be perfectly square (or rectangular) and must be just the right size to hold a certain number of full-sized pavers. You may choose to determine the overall size of the patio ahead of time, counting on very careful measurements. A safer course is to estimate the overall size and cut the outer edging boards slightly larger than needed, then cut them to fit precisely once you construct the grid. Use pressure-treated or other very rot-resistant lumber.

Pavers of two different sizes can also be used to create a grid effect.

LOWE'S QUICK TIP

If you are making your grid out of soft, good-looking wood, such as redwood, cover the tops of the boards with masking tape before you screed and install the pavers. This will prevent you from scratching the surface.

1 Install wood or timber edging and lay a bed of well-tamped gravel 4 inches below the top of the edging. Then build a grid from 2 by 4s. When measuring for the grid, lay pavers in dry runs as shown; use ¼-inch plywood spacers to make certain there will be ample room for the pavers. Install a series of 2 by 4s that run the entire length of the patio first, then install short boards between them. Fasten the boards by driving 2½-inch deck screws.

2 Construct a short screed that will fit into an individual grid section. Pour and screed sand in each section. This is painstaking work, because you must add or subtract the exact amount of sand for each section. Lay the pavers in the pattern of your choice and fill the joints with sand (see pages 219–20).

pinwheel pattern

The half-pavers in a pinwheel pattern can be of a different material as long as they are the right size: they must be the same thickness as, and no wider than, the other pavers. It's alright if they are a bit smaller; the joints can be easily filled with sand.

Set one square—composed of four full pavers and one half-paver—and then move on to the next square.

angled herringbone pattern

This technique is for creating a herringbone pattern at a 45-degree angle. Before you screed the patio, measure and mark the exact center of the edging on opposite sides of the patio.

If the edging and paver installations are very accurate, you will end up with a large number of cuts that are exactly 45 degrees However, it is likely that things will go slightly out of alignment, so make sure the rented saw comes with an adjustable saw guide, which will enable you to tinker with the cutting angles.

1 Tack a small nail at one of the marks (usually, where the patio abuts the house) and hook the clip of a chalk line to the nail. Unroll the chalk line and put it out of the way, taking care not to jostle the chalk. After you have screeded, pull the chalk line taut between the two marks and snap a line in the sand.

2 Carefully, with painstaking precision, install a V-shaped row of pavers along the line for about 6 feet. The paver corners should just touch the chalk line, as shown. Use an angle square to check the angle; you are establishing the alignment for the whole patio. For succeeding rows, just install pavers tight against each other, ignoring the line.

LOWE'S QUICK TIP

Installing a pinwheel, half-basketweave, or basketweave pattern is largely a matter of sustained attention. Every 15 minutes or so, stand back and examine the installation to make sure you haven't made any mistakes.

Uncut pavers form this circular design; a center piece of another material spices things up.

LOWE'S QUICK TIP

Circular and fan-shaped patterns can be created with a purchased ensemble of various-sized and -shaped concrete pavers. See pages 184–85 for examples.

paving a **circle**

An informal circular patio can be built using only standard-sized pavers, though you may want a special stone or several cut stones at the very center. Place the pavers in a circle, then adjust as necessary to achieve consistent joint widths. Once the pavers have been laid out, slip invisible plastic edging (see page 189) under the outermost pavers. Measure from the center outward at numerous points to check that you have formed a fairly precise circle, then drive spikes into the edging to hold the patio firmly together. Near the center, joints may be too wide to simply fill with sand, so mix a batch of wet mortar and pour it into the joints. Wipe away any mortar that spills on the bricks (see page 241). Once the mortar has hardened, brush sand into the rest of the joints.

MAKING A CURVED PATH

A paver path is essentially a long, narrow patio: you have the same options for edgings and paving materials and use similar building techniques. The path can be as narrow as 2 feet if it is used rarely, but for most situations it should be at least 40 inches wide.

1 Plan the width so you can use all full-sized pavers; it would be tedious to cut pavers all along one side. To install the edgings, set out a row of pavers that is the desired width of the path. Cut a 2-by-4 spacer ½ inch longer than the paver row (to accommodate minor discrepancies in size). Position the edgings in their approximate locations. Use the 2 by 4 as shown to establish correct spacing between the edgings; every 3 feet or so, drive stakes on either side to secure the edgings.

2 A crowned walk sheds water quickly and ensures against puddles. Make a screed as described on page 215. Cut a curve in the plywood piece, as shown; at the highest point, in the middle, it should be 1 to 1½ inches higher than the ends. Screed the sand and install the pavers as for a patio. Fill a gap of ½ inch or less between paver and edging with fine sand. If the gap is greater, pull up some stakes, move the edging closer to the pavers, and re-install the stakes.

blocks with **wide joints**

Large adobe concrete paver blocks or cut stones can be set with joints that are ¾ inch to 2 inches wide. The joints can be filled with compactable gravel or rough sand, but a classic look is achieved by fill-ing them with soil and adding crevice plants. The larger the paving units, the more lush the crevice plants can be.

Pavers set this far apart may become wobbly in time, especially if the crevice plants have strong roots. However, you can easily reset a paver.

1 Lay out, excavate, and install a gravel bed as for a standard patio (see pages 198–212). Enclose the patio with either invisible edging or massive timbers; narrow edging will look out of place. Dry-fit the pavers with the desired joints; if necessary, adjust joint widths rather than cut pavers. If the pavers are factory-made to precise sizes, use spacers, such as scraps of 2 by 4, to position them. If the pavers are irregular in shape, place a group of them, forming a square of 3 to 4 feet, spaced as you desire. On the edging, mea-sure and mark the center point of every second or third joint. Remove the pavers, add sand, and screed (see pages 214–17).

LOWE'S QUICK TIP

With bricks and small pavers, wide joints may make the installa-tion look sloppy rather than charming. For these materials, use joints no wider than ¾ inch, a gap that will still provide plenty of room for your favorite crevice plants.

2 Using the marks made in Step 1, tack small nails and stretch mason's line to form a grid of equal-sized squares. Double-check the sizes. Place pavers in one grid and fine-tune the placement to achieve joints that are relatively consistent in width. If you need to move a paver, pick it up and set it back down; don't slide it. Use a straight board to check that the pavers are even with each other. If a paver is wobbly, pick it up and add or remove sand underneath.

3 Use a square shovel or a garden trowel to fill the joints with soil that is appropriate for the crevice plants you have chosen. Because this soil gets tightly compacted, it is often best to mix some sand in with potting soil to produce a soil that is firm but able to drain.

4 Sweep the surface using light strokes. Gently tamp the joints using a board that is slightly thinner than the joints. Fill and sweep again. Sow seeds or add plants to the joints.

concrete slabs

POURING AND FINISHING A LARGE SLAB ARE PROBABLY JOBS BEST LEFT TO PROS; at the least, you should enlist the aid of someone who is experienced in moving, placing, and finishing concrete. The next six pages describe the elements of a solid concrete slab, then show how to pour a small one. Pages 232–39 describe how to beautify an existing slab that is in good condition.

Concrete can be purchased from a ready-mix company, or you can mix your own. For a small job, consider dry-mix bags, to which you need to add only water. For larger jobs, you may choose to mix the dry ingredients yourself.

what makes a solid slab

A well-constructed slab uses strong concrete that is reinforced with metal and poured into a properly prepared form.

a good mix Concrete is composed of Portland cement, sand, gravel (also called aggregate), and water. The more cement, the stronger the concrete. A standard "six-bag mix" contains six bags of cement per cubic yard of concrete, making it strong enough for most residential purposes.

The mix should contain enough water that you can easily pour and work it, but no more; too much water weakens the concrete and causes cracks. An inspector may test the concrete for "slump" using a special testing cone. A sag of about 4 or 5 inches indicates the right consistency for most jobs—not too soupy and not too dry (see Step 3, page 229).

In an area with freezing winters, a large slab should be made with air-entrained concrete, which contains tiny bubbles. The bubbles lend a bit of flexibility so the concrete is less likely to crack when it freezes. Air-entrained concrete is available only from a ready-mix company.

metal reinforcement Building departments have specific requirements for steel reinforcement. Wire mesh embedded in a slab keeps the slab together if it cracks during or after curing. Reinforcing bar (rebar) is used to make walls and footings stronger.

the right installation To remain free of cracks, a concrete slab must rest on a stable subsurface—typically a 4- or 5-inch-thick layer of compactable gravel that has been compressed with a vibrating plate compactor (see page 212). In addition to meeting local codes for strength, the concrete should be at least 3 inches thick for a patio. At all exposed edges, the concrete should be rounded off with an edging tool to prevent chipping.

LOWE'S QUICK TIP

In most areas, you need a permit to pour more than a very small concrete slab. Check with your building department; it has very specific requirements, and you'll achieve a better result if you follow them to the letter.

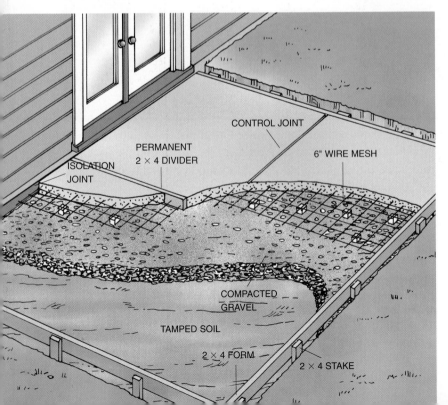

ISOLATION JOINT

PERMANENT 2 × 4 DIVIDER

CONTROL JOINT

6" WIRE MESH

COMPACTED GRAVEL

TAMPED SOIL

2 × 4 FORM

2 × 4 STAKE

calculating concrete

Ready-mix concrete is typically sold by the cubic yard, also just called a yard. A yard of concrete (or sand or gravel) fills an area 3 feet by 3 feet by 3 feet. If you are mixing concrete yourself, you may choose to measure cubic footage instead. A 60-pound bag of dry-mix concrete produces ½ cubic foot; a 90-pound bag yields ⅔ cubic foot. Fourteen 60-pound bags of dry mix will yield ¼ yard. (See page 103 to calculate how much concrete you'll need for a cylindrical footing.)

Take careful measurements of the area to be filled. Measure for thickness in a number of spots to obtain a reliable average; a discrepancy of ½ inch can make a big difference in the amount of concrete you need. A supplier can quickly do the calculations for you, but it's a good idea for you to double-check them. Using a calculator, this is easy to do.

For a rectangular slab or footing, multiply the width in feet by the length in feet; multiply the result by the thickness in inches. Divide the result by 12 to get the number of cubic feet. Divide that number by 27 to get the number of cubic yards.

For example, if a slab measures 6 feet by 8 feet and is 3½ inches thick:

$$6 \times 8 \times 3.5 = 168$$
$$168 \div 12 = 14 \text{ cubic feet}$$
$$14 \div 27 = 0.52 \text{ cubic yards}$$

Adding about 10 percent for waste, you'll need about .6 (or ⅗) of a yard.

If a slab is circular, it is actually a shallow cylinder. Measure the radius in feet and square that figure; multiply the result by pi (3.14); multiply that result by the thickness in inches. As with a rectangle, divide that number by 12 to get the number of cubic feet and divide that number by 27 to get the number of cubic yards.

mixing it yourself If you live in a remote area or want to mix concrete in small batches, you might consider renting an electric- or gas-powered concrete mixer to mix separate ingredients. This method allows you to add special ingredients, such as colorant. Consult with your inspector for the code-approved ratio of ingredients and have the rental company instruct you in the use of the machine. A typical mix consists of one part Portland cement, two parts sand, and three parts gravel.

LOWE'S QUICK TIP

The method for calculating concrete can also be utilized to figure how much gravel or sand you need for a patio substrate.

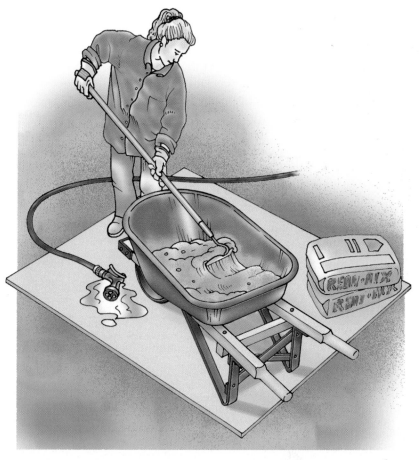

pouring a small concrete slab

THIS IS AN AMBITIOUS UNDERTAKING—THE LARGER THE SLAB, THE MORE AMBI-tious. The work is physically demanding; more important, everything must be done in a timely manner, before the concrete hardens. However, if you plan carefully and follow the steps in order, you can achieve a modest slab that is sturdy and long lasting.

The project depicted on the next three pages is a good size for a beginner. Dividing the slab with permanent wood dividers makes the job more manageable: you can mix, pour, and finish one small section at a time.

If you want a very smooth surface, hire a professional finisher. It takes months of practice to learn how to produce a "hard-trowel" finish. For a do-it-yourselfer, a broom finish is fairly easy to achieve. Somewhat rough, it provides traction so the concrete won't be slippery when it rains.

LOWE'S QUICK TIP

Spend some time practicing finishing concrete: make a rough 4-by-6-foot frame out of 2-by-2 boards and attach it on top of a piece of plywood. Mix a 60-pound bag of concrete and pour it into the frame. Screed and finish the concrete following the steps on pages 229–30.

casting the slab

Use batterboards to lay out the site, then remove any sod (see pages 198–201).

If the slab will abut the house (or any other structure), attach an isolation joint to the house at the same height as the concrete will be. The isolation joint will keep the new concrete from adhering to the side of the house.

Plan how you will get the concrete to the form. If you are mixing your own, try to set up right next to the form. For con-crete delivered in a ready-mix truck, try to have the truck drive close enough so its chute reaches into the form. If neither of these is possible, you will need to take the concrete to the formed area in wheelbar-rows. Make paths out of 2-by-12 planks and do a test run to make sure you can easily negotiate the route.

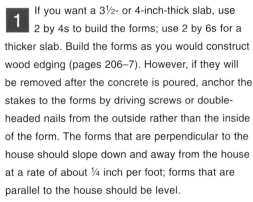

1 If you want a 3½- or 4-inch-thick slab, use 2 by 4s to build the forms; use 2 by 6s for a thicker slab. Build the forms as you would construct wood edging (pages 206–7). However, if they will be removed after the concrete is poured, anchor the stakes to the forms by driving screws or double-headed nails from the outside rather than the inside of the form. The forms that are perpendicular to the house should slope down and away from the house at a rate of about ¼ inch per foot; forms that are parallel to the house should be level.

Stretch a grid of string lines and excavate the area following the directions on page 212. Pour in a gravel base and tamp it firm.

If you are installing permanent wood dividers, use pressure-treated 2 by 4s. Check them for square and for even spacing and attach them to the outside frame with 3-inch deck screws or 16d nails. Apply masking tape to the top edges of the boards to protect them while you are screeding and finishing the concrete.

2 Purchase wire reinforcing mesh or rebar that meets local codes. Cut pieces of rebar (as shown) and tie them together in a grid using rebar wire or the wires attached to a dobie. Or install 6-inch wire mesh. Cut the metal to come within 1 inch of the form boards. The metal should end up in the middle of the concrete's thickness.

3 Have the concrete delivered or, if you are doing it yourself, mix it. Properly mixed concrete is completely wet, so it does not crumble but it is not soupy. It should hold its basic shape yet be liquid enough to pour. If you pick some up (wearing gloves) and squeeze, it should roughly hold its shape and liquid should not drip through your fingers.

Wheel the concrete to the formed area and pour it out, starting in a far corner.

LOWE'S QUICK TIP

It's easy to tip over a wheelbarrow full of concrete if you are not practiced at handling one. If you start to lose control, don't try to right it. Instead, push down on the handles with both hands to firmly plant the legs on the ground. Then pick up the handles and start again.

4 The first step in smoothing the concrete is screeding. Use a straight 2 by 4 as the screed. Position it so the ends rest on the forms. Using a sawing back-and-forth motion, draw the screed across the surface to flatten the concrete to the same height as the forms (if the area to be screeded is wider than 5 feet, have a helper hold the other end of the screed). If there are voids (low spots), fill them by shoveling in more concrete and screed again. Screeding will cause water to rise to the surface.

5 As soon as the water has evaporated, run a magnesium or wood float over the surface. (Easier to use, a magnesium float is definitely recommended for beginners.) Hold the tool so that the leading edge is slightly raised and press down very gently as you work. Avoid overworking the concrete, which can weaken it; stop using the float when the surface is covered with water again.

PROJECT CONTINUES ➡

LOWE'S QUICK TIP

If you cannot reach across a slab, place a piece of plywood about 3 feet by 4 feet on the far corner of the concrete and kneel on it. Move backward as you work so you do not kneel on just-floated concrete.

6 Slip a brick trowel between the inside of the forms and the concrete and slice all along the perimeter of the slab. This will fill in pockets of air that can weaken the concrete. Tap the forms with a hammer every foot or so to help the concrete settle snugly against the form boards.

7 Run an edging tool along the outside edges and along both sides of any permanent wood dividers as well. The tool has a "toboggan" edge on its front and rear so you can easily run it back and forth. It will take two or three passes to create a smooth edge.

8 Wait for the water to disappear. Then create a broom finish by gently dragging a push broom across the surface of the concrete, pulling the broom rather than pushing it. Work carefully and aim to produce a consistent look with straight lines. Avoid overlapping the strokes; they should be right next to each other. The stiffer the broom bristles, the more pronounced the texturing will be. If the bristles are not digging in and producing the surface you like, try wetting the broom.

If the forms are temporary, wait an hour or so and then carefully pry them away. Smooth any exposed rough edges using an edger or a magnesium trowel.

9 The more slowly concrete cures, the stronger it will be. Once you have achieved the right finish, make sure that the concrete will remain damp for at least a week. Cover it with plastic sheeting to hold in moisture; weigh the sheeting down with boards to keep it from blowing away. Alternatively, spray a fine mist on the concrete about twice a day, depending on the humidity.

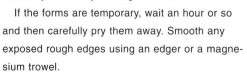

special effects for concrete

THE PHOTOS ON PAGES 190–91 SHOW DECORATIVE CONCRETE EFFECTS THAT can be produced by professional installers. Below are the directions for producing two fairly simple effects yourself.

tinting

The most reliable way to achieve a consistent color is to tint the concrete while it's being mixed. A ready-mix concrete company may do this for you, or you can do it yourself if you are mixing your own concrete.

Typically, a ready-mix company dumps an entire bag of colorant into the top of the mixer. Make it clear that the driver should not put in additional water after you have started pouring because it will change the color (drivers sometimes add water if the concrete starts to move sluggishly). It is likely there will be an extra fee for cleaning out the mixer.

To color your own concrete, purchase a liquid or powdered coloring agent and follow the manufacturer's directions. If you mix the concrete from dry ingredients, take care to measure the ingredients precisely to attain consistent color.

seeded aggregate

Seeded aggregate, made specifically for spreading on the surface of a slab, is available in bags; colors usually run from brown to light tan. Always buy more aggregate than you think you will need; it's easy to return leftovers, but you'll really be stuck if you run short.

LOWE'S QUICK TIP

Applying seeded aggregate takes longer than producing a standard broom finish. To give you extra time to work, avoid pouring the concrete while the sun is shining on the slab. If you are ordering ready-mix from a truck, arrange for a retarder to be added to the concrete. When you mix your own concrete, purchase small bags of retarder with your other materials to add yourself.

1 Pour and screed the concrete; you do not need to float it, but make sure all voids are filled and the surface is flat and even. As soon as the water has disappeared, use a shovel to scatter the aggregate over the entire surface; aim for a single layer. You may choose to sprinkle the area with colorful stones as well, and perhaps even install several decorative accent stones.

2 Use a flat board to gently press the stones into the concrete. If the slab is large or if it is a hot, dry day, cover the slab with plastic to keep it wet, uncovering it section by section as you work. Work the surface with a magnesium float so that a thin layer of cement (but none of the concrete's gravel) barely covers the aggregate stones. Avoid overworking. Use an edger to round off the perimeter.

3 When the concrete begins to harden, spray it with a fine mist; use a broom or a mason's brush to expose the tops of the stones. Wait for the concrete to harden more if stones start coming loose. After a few hours, spray the surface harder to fully expose the stones. Allow the slab to cure slowly. If a haze is present, wash the surface with a mild muriatic acid solution (see page 241).

applying finishes
to an existing slab

IF YOU HAVE AN EXISTING CONCRETE slab that could stand some refurbishing, you have several choices. A slab that is in good condition can be acid-stained (see below); if it is damaged, you may be able to repair it (see pages 242–43), but any large patches will likely turn a different hue when the stain is applied. Or, for a solid color, apply two-part epoxy paint made for concrete surfaces. Typically, you mix the two parts, apply a thin coat, wait a day or two, then apply a second coat.

You can also apply a resurfacing product (facing page) or flagstones, pavers, or tile (see pages 234–39).

acid-staining

Acid stain penetrates beneath the surface of cured concrete for a finish that is extremely durable. The effect is pleasantly mottled, often with marble-like veins. In fact, this look is so attractive that some people are removing interior floor surfaces and staining the underlying concrete.

A new slab can be stained after it has cured, which usually takes two or three weeks. Many decorative, even artistic, effects are possible using stencils, stamps, or tape to create geometric patterns. Here we show a basic application.

1 The concrete should be completely clean and dry. Fill a bucket halfway with the stain. Position it so any drips can be quickly brushed; otherwise, they will show as blotches. Dip a large brush in the stain and brush it onto the concrete, using sweeping or figure-eight strokes. It is important to keep the edges wet as you work; brushing wet stain over dried stain will produce a darker color. Work methodically so all areas receive the same amount of stain.

3 Wait a day or two for the stain to cure. To provide added protection to the surface, apply acrylic concrete sealer using a large paintbrush, a pump sprayer, or a paint roller.

2 After several hours, dry-wipe the area with rags to remove any residue. If a rag becomes damp with stain, flip it over or replace it so you are always soaking up, rather than spreading, residue. Rinse the surface with a spray of water.

LOWE'S SAFETY TIP
Wear long sleeves and heavy-duty rubber gloves throughout the process of acid-staining. Be sure the area is well ventilated or wear a respirator. Read and follow the manufacturer's directions.

the importance of cleaning

Unfortunately, many people approach acid-staining casually, and often end up with disappointing results that cannot be erased. To achieve an attractive surface, the concrete must first be cleaned thoroughly; see page 241 for cleaning techniques.

applying the stain For a professional-looking result, you'll need to plan carefully and work systematically. You'll be able to choose among a generous selection of available colors. Be aware that over a large area a color may look darker than it looks in a small sample. Purchase a rinsing agent along with the stain and have plenty of rags on hand.

resurfacing concrete

At Lowe's you will find several products that will let you put a new surface on an old concrete slab. The most common is Quikrete's Concrete Resurfacer. A concrete resurfacer comes as a bag of dry ingredients that is mixed with water; the resulting paste-like substance is spread over the slab to cover imperfections and achieve the look of freshly poured concrete. Though only ¼ to ⅜ inch thick, the finished surface is more attractive than old concrete, and is quite strong.

Resurfacing products can be colored using standard concrete colorant. Just be careful to keep the recipe exactly the same for all batches so you end up with even color.

Clean the old concrete and patch any cracks (see pages 242–43). At the edges of the slab, make simple forms by butting 2 by 2s or 2 by 4s against the sides of the slab and staking them slightly higher than the slab. Do the work when the sun is not shining directly on the surface. Mix the resurfacer with water to produce a paste that is barely pourable. Working fairly quickly with a magnesium float or a broom-handled squeegee, spread the paste at a uniform thickness.

Top: Stained concrete of most any color usually takes on a surprisingly natural hue that complements brick.

Above: New resurfacing products are easy to apply and very durable.

Smoother than most, these flagstones are installed carefully so chairs will rest and scoot easily.

mortaring **flagstones** onto concrete

A mortared flagstone surface is easier to keep clean than soil-laid flagstone, and also more permanent. You can create a slab for mortaring flagstone, but you can also use an existing one—and upgrade it nicely in the process. The slab should be in sound condition; see page 242. Mortaring the stones on top of the slab will give it some additional strength.

If you want to install edging for this project, you will need to cut most of the stones around the perimeter, which is unnecessary work. It's fine to leave ragged edges on the stones that overhang the slab, and they'll have a natural appeal.

getting ready See pages 202–3 for tips on selecting, cutting, and arranging flagstones. Sort the stones into several piles according to size. When you arrange the flagstones, alternate among the piles so that you end up with an even distribution of large, medium, and small stones.

Clean the concrete to eliminate oily residue that could inhibit bonding. Then, following the manufacturer's instructions, brush liquid concrete bonding agent onto the concrete. Usually, you will need to wait for the bonding agent to dry at least partially.

In a wheelbarrow or trough, dump a bag of Type N mortar. Slowly add water and mix with a mason's hoe. You want the mortar to be stiff enough to hold up a stone yet wet enough that it will cling for a second or two to a trowel held vertically.

LOWE'S QUICK TIP

Limestone or other strong flagstone can overhang the concrete by as much as 6 inches, if at least two thirds of the stone rests on concrete. Weaker materials such as sandstone should overhang by less than 3 inches. You can strengthen the overhangs by stuffing soil under them after the mortar has cured.

1 On a small surface, you can skip this step. If you have a large one, to provide a reference point for height and to help ensure an even distribution of large stones, start by setting one stone. Shovel some mortar near the middle of an area that is about 6 feet square. Set a large, thick stone in the mortar, checking it for level.

2 Around the set stone, fill in a 6-foot-square area with dry-laid stones. Aim for joints that are roughly uniform in width; avoid having stones touch each other. You'll probably need to shuffle and re-orient stones many times to get the right look. If a stone needs to be cut, hold it in place and mark it.

3 Every 10 minutes or so, stir the mortar. If it starts to stiffen, add a little more water—but do this only once. If the mortar stays stiff, throw it out and make a new batch.

Pick up one large or several small dry-laid stones and set them to the side, oriented so you can easily replace them in the correct positions. Shovel some mortar onto the concrete and use a trowel to roughly even it out. If a stone is thin, apply a thicker layer of mortar where it will sit.

4 Set the stones in the mortar. With practice, you can produce a stone surface that is reasonably level. Set the stones one at a time, and check that each is close to level and about the same height as its neighbors. Make any needed adjustments immediately, before the mortar starts to set; if you feel a definite resistance when you reposition a stone, pick the stone up, scrape away the stiffening mortar, and apply new mortar. If a stone is low, remove it, apply more mortar, and reset. If a stone is too high, tap it down and scrape away the excess mortar that oozes out.

5 To fill the joints with mortar, carefully use a mason's trowel or a grout bag (see page 237). Gently scrape with a small piece of wood to fill evenly. After it has started to dry, lightly brush away crumbs. For a more natural look, sweep in fine, crushed stone, as shown; it will become nearly as hard as mortar.

6 If you applied mortar to the joints, wait several hours for it to harden, then scrub the stones with water and a stiff bristle brush and/or a rag. If you swept in gravel, set a garden hose nozzle to mist and spray the entire surface. Allow the surface to dry, then sweep in more crushed stone to fill any gaps and mist again.

Here, bricks of various hues are mortared onto a slab in a basketweave pattern.

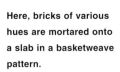
LOWE'S QUICK TIP

Setting and filling the joints between pavers is time consuming, so work when the sun is not shining on the patio—otherwise, the mortar will likely harden too quickly. Covering exposed mortar with plastic will retard the drying process.

setting pavers on concrete

You can use this technique to install either paving bricks or concrete pavers. See page 218 for paver patterns. You can install permanent edging and use it as a screed guide, as shown on these pages, or install temporary 2-by-4 forms and remove them after the mortar has dried.

The existing slab should be basically stable (see page 242), though this installation will help keep cracks from growing and will add a measure of solidity as well.

1 The edging or forms should be higher than the slab by the thickness of a paver plus ½ inch. Make a screed out of a 2 by 4 and a piece of plywood (see page 215); the plywood should extend downward ¼ inch less than the thickness of a paver.

In a wheelbarrow or mixing trough, combine a bag of mortar mix with a shovelful of Portland cement and mix with water to achieve a mortar that is barely pourable and clings to a trowel held vertically. Shovel the mortar onto the slab and smooth it with the screed guide.

2 Using scraps of ½- or ⅜-inch plywood as spacers, set the pavers in the mortar. (The pavers will settle ¼ inch or so into the mortar when you install them.) Lay a flat board on top and tap with a hammer to bed the pavers and produce a flat surface.

LOWE'S QUICK TIP

Applying mortar with a grout bag is a skill that takes time to learn. Set some bricks on a scrap piece of plywood and practice Steps 3 and 4 (on this page) until you feel confident that you can apply mortar without excessive smearing.

3 The next day, mix a small batch of mortar. It should be fairly stiff, so it will not ooze out and smear the pavers. Fill a grout bag with the mortar and squeeze the bag to squirt mortar into the joints.

4 Once you have completed a 5-foot-square section, use a jointer to finish the joints. Tool the long joints first, then the short ones. If the mortar is too thin, wait a few minutes for it to partially harden, then try again.

Mortaring anchors each brick firmly, so you make free-form designs more easily than with a sand-laid patio, which must be contained with edging.

5 When the mortar is fairly dry, brush it lightly with a masonry brush. Take care that you don't brush any wet mortar or you will smear it. After several hours, clean the surface using a masonry brush and water.

attaching to masonry

LAG SCREWS
AND SHIELDS

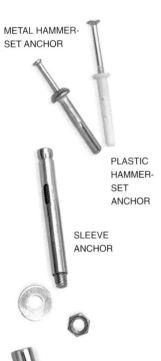

METAL HAMMER-
SET ANCHOR

PLASTIC
HAMMER-
SET
ANCHOR

SLEEVE
ANCHOR

DROP-IN
ANCHOR WITH
SETTING TOOL

FOR A VARIETY OF REASONS—TO ADD AN OVERHEAD, FOR INSTANCE—YOU MAY want to make a secure attachment to a concrete, brick, or concrete paver patio. If you are pouring a concrete slab, you can embed an anchor bolt (J-bolt) in the wet concrete, as shown on page 105. However, if you are dealing with an existing patio, you need to use a technique for attaching to cured concrete or to pavers. There are a number of strong options, which follow; check with your building department to see which are approved by local codes.

masonry anchors

Lag screws and shields (see top left) take some time to install but are very strong. Position the board or bracket where you want it and mark the masonry surface for holes. Remove the board or bracket and, using a masonry bit, drill holes of the correct size for the shields you will use. The holes will be fairly large and may take some time to drill, especially if you are attaching to concrete. Tap a shield into each hole so that it comes flush with the masonry surface. Set the board or bracket back in place and drive the lag screws using a ratchet and socket.

To install **sleeve anchors** (see left), follow the same procedure for drilling a hole, above. Insert the anchor and screw in the threaded rod, slip the bracket or board over the threaded rod, and add a washer and nut. As you tighten the nut onto the rod, the anchor expands to grip the masonry.

Hammer-set anchors (see above left) install the quickest; metal anchors are somewhat stronger than plastic. Drill a hole, insert the anchor, position the bracket or board, and pound the nail head with a hammer. Insert a **drop-in anchor** (see bottom left) into the hole, then tap it using a special driving tool that comes with the anchors so that it expands to become firm. Then you can thread a bolt of any length into the anchor.

injectable epoxy

This fairly new product produces a very strong attachment. However, you do have to wait a day for the epoxy to cure.

1 Put the board or bracket to be anchored in position and mark the masonry surface for holes. Using a masonry bit, drill each hole slightly wider than the bolt to be anchored. Vacuum out the holes, then blow out all remaining dust using a can of compressed air. Snip off the end of the epoxy syringe and squirt epoxy into the holes.

2 Immediately insert a threaded rod to the desired depth in each hole. See that this assembly is undisturbed for a day so the epoxy can set rock-solid. Then slip on the bracket or board, add washers, and tighten the nuts.

cleaning concrete

LOWE'S QUICK TIP

A rented pressure washer offers plenty of power, but an inexpensive model purchased at a home center may supply all the pressure you need. A nozzle that directs a single stream can actually dent a brick or block surface; use a fan nozzle instead.

CONCRETE, BRICKS, PAVERS, AND NATURAL STONE ARE ALL POROUS AND THEREfore vulnerable to stains that can soak in deep. Prevent stains by applying a coat of acrylic masonry sealer, and if a staining substance spills onto the surface, wipe it up immediately. Have a bag of oil-soaking garage-floor cleaner on hand to quickly soak up oil spills.

There are three strategies for cleaning concrete, brick, or block. In ascending order of powerfulness: (1) Apply a detergent solution or a product made for cleaning masonry and scrub with a stiff bristle brush; rinse well and allow to dry. (2) If the spot or discoloration remains, try using a pressure washer. (3) If that does not solve the problem, try a muriatic acid solution (see below).

common cleaning problems and **solutions**

- A white powdery film called efflorescence is caused when a masonry surface stays moist for prolonged periods, bringing minerals to the surface. To prevent it, keep the surface dry or make sure it dries out quickly after a rain. To remove it, scrape and wire-brush the area, then clean with a detergent or a pressure washer.

- Smeared mortar may come off with scraping and wire-brushing. If the mortar is old, clean it with acid.

- Mortar haze, a general light discoloration of a large area of mortar, is typically caused by insufficient wiping during grouting. Try eliminating the haze with a detergent solution first, then acid if needed.

- Reddish-brown iron stains can be lightened using household bleach or a solution of oxalic acid.

- Ivy actually does not damage brick or block. If you don't like the way it looks and want to remove it, do not simply pull it off; small chunks of brick may come off as well. First cut the vine near the ground and wait a few months for it to dry out. Then pull it off.

cleaning with **muriatic acid**

Muriatic acid can damage clothing and cause serious discomfort if it gets on skin. Wear long clothing and heavy-duty rubber gloves. If you are working on a slab, wear kneepads to keep your knees dry. Be sure the area is well ventilated or wear a respirator. Also be sure that the acid will flow to a safe place when you rinse it. A strong acid solution will likely damage the roots of nearby plants.

First clean the surface with a pressure washer or a detergent solution and rinse away any detergent. Wet the surface lightly so it is damp but has no puddles.

Mix ten parts water to one part muriatic acid. Always add acid to the water—never water to acid. Carefully pour or wipe the acid solution onto the surface and gently scrub with a brush. A light bubbling indicates that the acid is at work. Once the bubbling has stopped, rinse off the surface thoroughly.

If this mild solution does not do the trick, use progressively stronger solutions.

concrete repairs

BEFORE ATTEMPTING A CONCRETE REPAIR, FIRST DETERMINE WHETHER THE DAMage is structural or only cosmetic. Most structural problems cannot be easily fixed; usually, it is best to demolish the slab and start again. However, as long as a slab is basically stable, almost any damage can be repaired.

■ An occasional crack does not mean structural damage as long as both sides of the crack are at the same height. If a crack is ¼ inch wide or narrower, just fill it with concrete repair caulk. Repair a wider crack as shown at right.

■ A pattern of medium to large cracks indicates a more serious problem, especially if one side of a crack is higher than the other. Consult with a pro; you probably need to replace the slab.

■ If one section of a slab has sunk lower than an adjoining section but the slab itself has few cracks, then the slab is in good shape but the base beneath it has sunk. A concrete-raising contractor (check the Yellow Pages) may be able to raise the section up and resupport it.

■ Three problems can occur due to poor finishing during slab installation: a web of hairline cracks, called crazing; bubble-like deterioration or flaking of the surface, called spalling or scaling; and a scattering of small holes, called popouts. All three occur only on the surface, but if left untreated can cause the top of the slab to crumble. Apply concrete sealer to keep any of these problems from worsening. Or if only a specific area is cracked or suffers from spalling, cut around the area and apply a patch (see facing page).

LOWE'S QUICK TIP

Experiment on a scrap of plywood or in an unobtrusive location to see how closely the color of patch material matches the existing concrete. Allow the patch a full day to cure; it will likely get lighter in color. You may choose to add a bit of concrete colorant while mixing the mortar to achieve a less obvious-looking patch.

caulking small cracks

Caulk made specifically for repairing concrete is stronger and longer lasting than standard caulk. It's also quick and easy to apply and will seal out moisture, preventing further damage. However, it will probably need to be renewed every year or two.

filling larger cracks

You can fill a wide crack with vinyl- or latex-reinforced patching cement.

1 Use a hammer and cold chisel to "key" a crack—chisel it at an angle so the bottom of the crack is wider than the top. Clean out all loose material using a wire brush and a vacuum.

2 Paint the crack with latex concrete bonding agent. Then mix a small batch of concrete patching compound and use a brick trowel to stuff the compound into the crack. Scrape the surface so the patch is at the same height as the slab.

patching a damaged area

Use this method to repair an area less than 2 feet square; for larger areas, consider resurfacing (page 233).

1 Draw a geometric shape around the damaged area. Using a grinder or a circular saw equipped with a masonry blade, cut the lines about ½ inch deep. Chisel out the area inside the cut lines. Using a wire brush, clean away all loose material.

2 Paint the damaged area with latex bonding agent. Mix a batch of concrete patch and, with a trowel, apply it to the damaged area.

3 Use a magnesium or wood float to smooth the surface and bring it level with the surrounding concrete. Use a broom or steel trowel to match the finish of the surrounding concrete.

repairing
a damaged corner

If there is a small amount of damage to a corner, you can fix it with a simple form by attaching two pieces of wood with tape.

1 Cut around the damaged area using a circular saw or grinder equipped with a masonry blade. Angle the blade to "key" the cut, making the bottom wider than the top. Using a wire brush, clean away all debris. If the cut is deeper than 3 inches, partially drive several masonry screws into the concrete so their heads stick up somewhat. This will give the patching concrete a firmer hold.

2 Build a simple form by screwing together two pieces of 2-by lumber and hold them in place around the damaged area with something heavy, such as concrete blocks. Fill the cut-out area with patching concrete and trowel the surface to smooth it. Remove the boards as soon as the patch has started to harden and smooth the surface again.

LOWE'S QUICK TIP

If a corner chips in one piece, you can simply reattach the piece. Paint the surfaces to be joined with a concrete bonding agent. Apply a small amount of concrete patch to the edge and press the chip back into place. Use duct tape to hold the chip firm while the patch sets. Alternatively, use polyurethane glue.

finishing touches

The ideas and projects in this chapter will allow you to personal-ize your outdoor room. Consider the particular qualities of your site, your family's interests and activities, and the functions you want the outdoor space to serve. You may want to add lighting so you can use the patio in the evening, or an overhead that makes it pleasant to be outdoors even in heavy summer heat. Perhaps you'd like a built-in grill for family meals. Or you might build a trellis or pergola so you can be surrounded by the color and fragrance of climbing roses.

Enhancements such as stairs, stepping-stones, overheads, benches, and planters add beauty, comfort, and convenience to your outdoor space. Such projects often call for only a modest investment in time and money, but have a big visual impact. Other added touches—built-in benches and standard-voltage lighting with underground cable, for instance—require careful forethought and are best installed either before or while you are building your patio or deck.

Most projects, however, can be added with little difficulty after your outdoor space has been installed. For example, ready-made arbors and trellises can be pounded into place in less than an hour. New patio furniture can make a big splash with no in-stallation time at all. Homemade stepping-stones can be strewn across the lawn whenever you wish, providing a charming touch and forming a visual bridge between patio and yard.

Use this chapter to customize your deck or patio, making it the ideal space you've dreamed of.

installing stepping-stones

LOWE'S QUICK TIP

After a year or two, a stepping-stone may become wobbly. Simply tilt it up and scrape or fill in soil beneath it as needed.

STEPPING-STONES LET YOU EASILY CREATE A DECORATIVE PATH TO AND FROM a deck or patio. They're best used in a light-traffic area. If you will be including bushy crevice plants, the steppers may get partially covered, so choose larger stones. On a manicured lawn, smaller steppers are fine.

On the facing page, we show how to install irregularly shaped natural flagstones. You can also use this technique to install any of the precast concrete stepping-stones that are available at Lowe's. There are a number of shapes; surfaces may be smooth or made of exposed aggregate.

positioning the steppers

The goal here is to set out one stepping-stone per typical adult step. Stretch mason's line to lay out a straight path, or use two hoses about 2 feet apart to outline a curved path. Place the stones in the space, alternating right and left. Have family members walk on the stones to determine the most comfortable arrangement.

setting the steppers

Stepping-stones can simply be set in tamped soil, but adding a bit of sand makes the installation easier.

1 If you have some time, leave the stones on the lawn for a week or so; when you pick them up, the yellowed grass will show you where to cut. Or, as shown here, set each stone in place and use a shovel or garden trowel to slice a line through the sod all around it.

2 Dig up and remove the sod under the stone. Remove all organic material, including any roots. Dig deep enough so that after adding ½ inch of sand the stone will be just below grade—low enough so you can run a lawn mower over it. Tamp the soil firm using a 2 by 4.

3 Add about ½ inch of damp sand and spread it. If you are installing a flagstone that is uneven in thickness, roughly mirror the stone's contours with the sand. Set the stone in place. If it is too high, dig the hole deeper. Tap the stone with a rubber mallet or step on it.

4 Tilt the stone up to reveal any voids and high spots. Scrape the high spots and fill the voids with sand, then replace the stone. Test by walking on the stone. If it wobbles even slightly, pick it up and add or scrape sand where needed.

making your OWN stepping-stones

HERE IS AN ENJOYABLE WAY TO CREATE ONE-OF-A-KIND FEATURES FOR YOUR YARD that are practical as well as charming. Making homemade stepping-stones can be a fun family project: the adults can do the serious work of making the form and casting the concrete, and youngsters can add patterns of decorative elements. If the kids first lay out their patterns in a dry run, you can monitor the designs.

Tile or glass shards are easy to arrange in patterns and set into the concrete.

Among the possibilities for homemade stepping-stones are imprints of leaves (see page 250).

buying or **making** forms

Lowe's carries plastic forms to use for making stepping-stones (see page 251). Fill and finish these forms as shown on page 251.

You can also build your own forms out of 1 by 2s. To make it easy to create a rounded top on the stepping-stones, use a power saw or plane to bevel the top edges of the 1 by 2s. When constructing a pentagonal form, as shown, cut both ends of each piece at 72-degree angles. Install a strap hinge at one corner and a hook and eye on an adjacent corner; screw the other corners together. This will make it easy to release the form. Place each form on a piece of plywood and coat all surfaces that will touch concrete with oil (spray cooking oil works well).

getting **ready**

For each stepping-stone, arrange the decorative elements on a piece of plywood or cardboard so you can quickly transfer the pattern to the wet concrete. The next two pages show some design options, but don't hesitate to use your imagination.

molding, decorating, and finishing

Purchase ready-mix bags of concrete. You may want to get the kind that has fiber reinforcement, which will ensure against cracking. If you wish to tint the concrete, purchase bottles of liquid concrete colorant and follow the manufacturer's instructions for achieving the color of your choice. Be sure to measure both the colorant and the dry-mix concrete carefully so you can exactly duplicate the recipe for each subsequent batch of concrete.

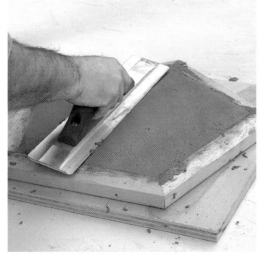

1 Mix the concrete to a fairly stiff consistency so it nearly holds a ball shape when you squeeze it. Pour it into a form, overfilling the form slightly. Using the beveled edges of the form as a guide, smooth the stepping-stone with a magnesium float. Avoid overworking it; stop when the surface is smooth and water has appeared.

2 Add decorative elements soon after the water has disappeared. If the concrete is too mushy, remove the decorative elements, retool the surface, and wait 10 minutes or so before trying again. Once the designs are in place, unfasten the eye hook and use a trowel or putty knife to separate the form from the concrete.

3 Remove the form. Use a paintbrush to round the edges, further embed the decorative elements, and finish shaping the stepping-stone. Brushing will probably cover the decorations with a thin watery coat that will dry to a haze. Once the concrete has hardened, gently rub off the haze with a damp rag.

LOWE'S QUICK TIP
Cover the steppers for a day or two with plastic so the concrete can cure slowly. A day after removing the plastic, brush the stones with a coating of acrylic concrete sealer to protect them from freezing water and to make them cleanable.

The technique of creating mosaics by embedding colorful fragments in the concrete can also be applied to slabs poured in small sections.

design possibilities

A craft store will carry tile shards, pieces of colored glass, and other items meant for embedding in stepping-stones. Feel free to use almost anything as long as it can survive winters without cracking.

To make a leaf imprint, select leaves that have large, prominent veins. Carefully press each leaf fairly deep into the concrete, so its outline breaks the surface. You can either peel the leaves away immediately to see what the impression looks like or leave them in place and allow them to decompose after a week or two. You may choose to carefully paint the impressions before applying acrylic sealer to the stone.

If pebbles or stones are dry and porous, soak them in water briefly before placing them. To ensure that stones are solidly embedded, press them into the concrete slightly deeper than you want them; you can brush away some surface concrete once it begins to harden.

Children will naturally want to press their hands into the concrete. Coach them to press straight down, without wiggling, and then to lift their hands straight out. They can also scratch in their initials or names using a small stick. For a more polished appearance, have them practice using a jointer tool or the rounded handle of a screwdriver or butter knife.

using a patio mold

Lowe's carries plastic molds for forming concrete into attractive shapes that resemble bricks (see right) or flagstones (see below). These molds make it easy to form the shapes, but you will have to spend time smoothing rough edges. You may choose to add liquid concrete colorant to the concrete as you mix it; follow the manufacturer's instructions.

To ensure against cracking, excavate the soil, spread compactable gravel, and power-tamp the gravel (see page 212). You don't need to add edging or a layer of screeded sand as you would for a patio; the concrete will settle down and mold itself to the gravel. The excavated area should be big enough to accommodate full-size formed sections.

1 Set the mold on the gravel and press it down so concrete cannot seep out the sides. Mix a fairly stiff batch of concrete; it should be barely wet enough to pour. Shovel the concrete into the mold, taking care to fill each cavity.

2 Use a magnesium float or a trowel to level the surface, moving across the form in at least two directions and pressing down to fill in any voids. You may need to add a bit more concrete and use the trowel again. The trowel should slightly scrape the plastic mold as you work.

3 Once the water on the surface has disappeared, carefully lift the mold straight up; you may have to gently shake it as you lift. If one of the stepping-stones starts to crack and fall apart as you lift the mold, press it back down into place and wait 10 minutes or so before trying again. Smooth rough edges using a mason's brush or a paintbrush. The resulting "joints" can be left as is, or you can fill them with sand or mortar. Once the concrete has dried, apply a coat or two of acrylic masonry sealer.

adding stairs

TO GET TO AND FROM YOUR DECK OR PATIO, YOU MAY NEED TO NEGOTIATE A slope. If the slope is gentle, stair construction can be casual: perhaps excavate a few level spots and position large stone slabs on them. However, a stairway of three or more steps should be carefully planned so that all steps are consistent and of a comfortable height.

The stairway shown here is essentially a set of small patios. See pages 214–21 for instructions and installation options for this kind of "patio."

planning and **excavating**

All the steps in the stairway must have the same rise (the height of the step) and the same run (the depth of the tread) to prevent tripping. For complete instructions on figuring stair rises and runs, see pages 138–41.

With 4-by-6 timbers, all steps will have 5½-inch rises. Try to plan the run and width of the steps so you don't need to cut any pavers. For comfort, the run should be 12 to 12½ inches. Three feet is a common width, and 4 feet will allow people to walk abreast. Steps should be slightly sloped downward or to the side so rainwater can easily run off.

To calculate the number of steps, position a long, straight board at the level where you want the top of the stairs and place a level on top. Measure down from its bottom side to find the stairway's total rise. Divide the total rise by the desired height for each step—here, 5½ inches—to find out how many steps you need. Then multiply the number of steps by the run for each—in this case, 12 to 12½ inches—to find the total run, or length, of the stairway.

For the initial excavation, create an even slope that's approximately the right depth for the front edge of each step plus 2 to 3 inches for the gravel bed that will underlie the steps. As you install each step, you'll dig out a rectangular shape to accommodate the back of the timber frame.

Measure and mark off the area with mason's line and stakes. Start your excavation at the top, digging down 5½ inches to accommodate the first riser. Continue down the slope. Excavate the ground at the landing to a depth of 2 to 3 inches.

1 Purchase straight pieces of 4-by-6 pressure-treated lumber that are not deeply cracked. On a flat surface, lay pavers (in whatever pattern you wish) in a dry run; this will let you check the inside dimensions of the frame you planned to assure that you won't need to cut any pavers. Measure for the frame pieces. One timber should cross the entire front of each step; the side timbers should butt into it. Fit the rear timber between the sides.

To mark for a cut on a 4 by 6, use a square to draw a line all around the timber. Cut with a circular saw or a 12-inch power miter saw. Working on a flat surface, assemble the pieces of the frame. At each joint, drill two pilot holes using a long bit, tap a 7-inch lag screw with washer partway into each hole, and use a socket wrench to tighten the screws.

2 Start at the bottom. Place 2 to 3 inches of compactable gravel at the bottom of the stairway, bringing the surface to 5½ inches below the calculated level for the first step. Tamp with a hand tamper or a 2 by 4. Set the frame for the first step on the tamped gravel and check that it is level or sloped in the desired direction. Set up the long board with a level (facing page) again to make sure the bottom step is at the correct level.

3 Add succeeding frames one at a time, checking each for correct slope. The front timber of an upper step should rest on the rear timber of the step below it. Excavate, making sure each frame will be at the correct height, then add 2 to 3 inches of gravel and tamp. Anchor each frame with at least four pieces of reinforcing bar, two in the front timber and one on each side. Whether the frame piece rests on gravel or on another 4 by 6, drill a hole for each anchor through the frame and drive a piece of rebar 2 to 3 feet long, depending on soil conditions. Driving the rebar should take some effort, but should not be a struggle.

4 When all the frames have been installed, check that they are stable. In each, measure below the top edge one paver thickness plus 1½ inches; mark. Pour compactable gravel to these marks and tamp with a 2 by 4. Shovel in sand and use a scrap piece of wood to screed so the sand is a paver thickness below the top of the frame.

5 Set the pavers into the frames. Place a board over the pavers and tap with a hammer or rubber mallet. Check with a straight board to see that the pavers are all at the same height. Sweep in fine sand to fill the joints, spray with a fine mist, and repeat the process once or twice until the sand no longer sinks down when you spray it.

choosing outdoor furniture

EVEN IF YOU BUILD FIXED BENCHES LIKE those shown on page 278, you will probably also appreciate the convenience of movable furniture on your deck or patio.

Pieces that spend a lifetime outdoors should be exceptionally durable. When you consider the array of chairs, tables, and benches available, check to be sure they are not only comfortable and beautiful but will stand up to your climate.

Wood furniture has a timeless appeal. It can last for decades if made of a durable species such as teak or oak, protected by yearly coats of sealer, and stored indoors during winter.

Inexpensive wicker and rattan furniture will probably not last long out-of-doors, but high-end products may well be durable. However, even these pieces should be stored indoors during winter.

Patio furniture made of roble wood has a mellow color and needs only an occasional application of clear sealer.

If classic wicker furniture is painted regularly, it can last for a long time.

LOWE'S QUICK TIP

Folding furniture tends to be less durable than most of the products shown here, but may be a good choice if you will use it only occasionally and store it in a dry place.

254

Aluminum patio furniture is strong and rust proof and stands up well to years of harsh weather. In recent years, a wider selection of finishes has made aluminum more versatile than ever. Hand-forged wrought-aluminum frames and vinyl strap seating create furniture that is not only durable but also very comfortable.

Classic wrought-iron furniture offers a distinctive, formal look that has long been a patio favorite. Every year or so, touch up any chipped paint to prevent rust from forming.

Resin (or plastic) furniture is by far the least costly choice. Now available in an array of styles, it stays cool in the sun and requires little maintenance. Chairs often nest for convenient off-season storage. However, long exposure to intense sun can cause the color of plastic furniture to fade, so keep pieces covered or in the shade when they are not in use.

Padded seat cushions add comfort and color. Newer synthetic fabrics have the feel of cloth rather than plastic, yet are weather resistant. Still, it's a good idea to store them in a bin when not in use, especially if they would otherwise be exposed to intense sunlight.

Top: This powder-finished aluminum furniture is easy to move around.

Left: The least expensive option, resin furniture, is available in many styles and colors.

Above: Wrought-iron chairs and tables look both airy and solid at the same time.

LOWE'S QUICK TIP

A "powder" finish on aluminum furniture is more durable than a finish that is anodized or simply painted on.

ready-made trellises

A TRELLIS IS ANY SORT OF GRIDWORK THAT ALLOWS PLANTS to cling and climb. It may stand alone or be a part of a larger structure such as an arbor or a pergola. Trellises have many virtues: they can add gardening space in a small yard, link disparate elements in a landscape, define an outdoor retreat, or provide privacy.

Pages 258–61 show how to build a trellis, but at Lowe's you may find just the one you want—already built. Most come ready to install: just push or pound the feet into soil beside a wall or in a planter box, plant a vine, and wrap the stems around the supports (use plant ties if needed). A few trellises need minor assembly, and some must be anchored to a wall.

If a trellis is attached to a wall, the climbing plant will likely trap moisture against the house. Make sure the house siding is amply covered with paint, then install the trellis so that its slats are held about an inch away from the house. Some trellises come with special hardware or have small "legs" that separate the slats from the house automatically.

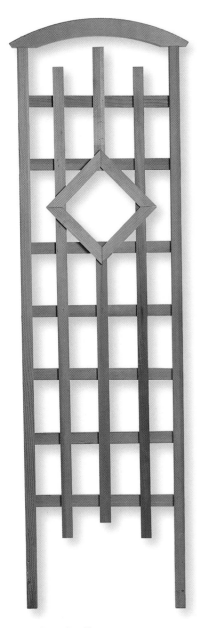

Lowe's variety of trellises can be either attached to a wall or anchored in the ground.

To firmly set a trellis in the ground, drive 1-by-2 stakes, leaving about a foot above the ground. Attach the trellis's feet to the stakes by drilling pilot holes and driving two deck screws into each stake.

ATTACHING TO A WALL

If your trellis does not come with hold-away hardware, cut a length of ½-inch copper pipe into a number of 1-inch-long pieces. At each attachment point, hold a piece of pipe behind the trellis and drive a deck screw through the trellis, through the pipe, and into the siding. The copper will turn a pleasant shade of green when it weathers.

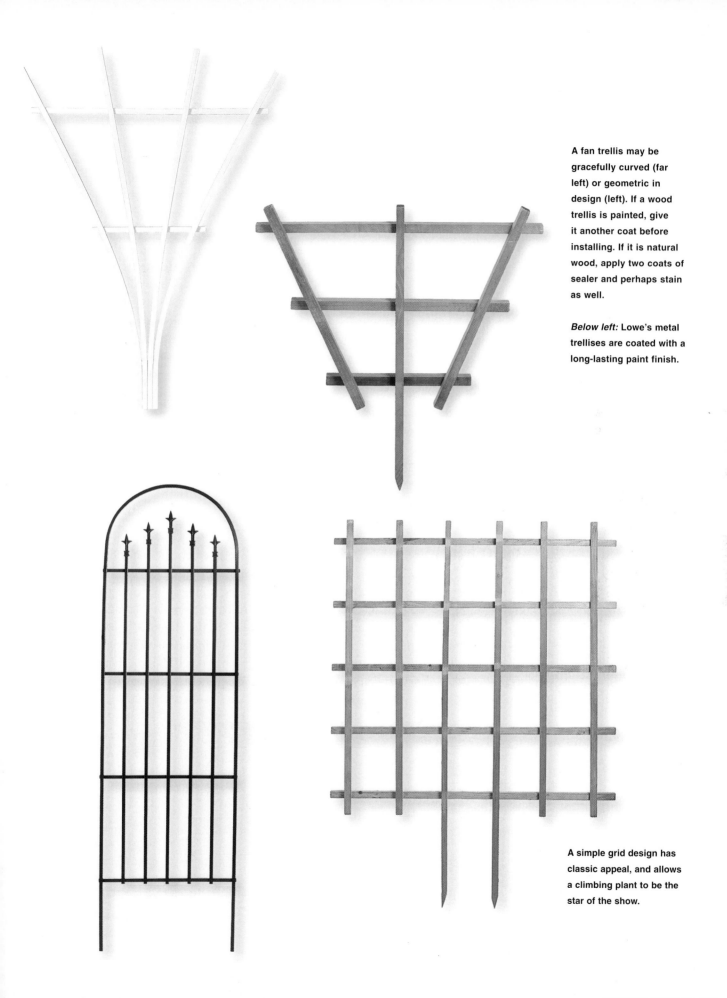

A fan trellis may be gracefully curved (far left) or geometric in design (left). If a wood trellis is painted, give it another coat before installing. If it is natural wood, apply two coats of sealer and perhaps stain as well.

Below left: Lowe's metal trellises are coated with a long-lasting paint finish.

A simple grid design has classic appeal, and allows a climbing plant to be the star of the show.

building a wooden trellis

A TRADITIONAL WOODEN TRELLIS GIVES PLANTS A GOOD FOOTHOLD, ALLOWS air to circulate, and is durable despite being made of thin, narrow pieces. The size of the trellis should suit its setting: a 3-foot-high grid may overpower a small patio container, while a 7-foot-tall tower may look small in the center of a large, open space. The trellis design and finish should also suit the setting. A formal landscape may call for a trellis that's sanded, filled, rounded over, and painted to match the house trim; in more casual surroundings, a rough cedar cage or a frame of lashed-together branches may be right at home.

choosing materials

Use decay-resistant wood, such as the dark heartwood of cedar or redwood, or else pressure-treated lumber. If you choose to paint the trellis, carefully apply at least two coats, because it may be difficult to repaint around plants later.

Most trellis pieces are lightweight. Sometimes standard 1 by 2s or 2 by 2s are appropriate, but often you will want narrower and thinner pieces, perhaps ½ by 1½ inches or ¾ inch by ¾ inch. If such small-dimensioned lumber is not available in rot-resistant wood, ask a lumberyard to rip-cut pieces for you.

To join the pieces, stainless-steel screws and nails are the best choice; you can also use deck screws and galvanized nails. Polyurethane glue is highly recommended because it makes a very strong and weather-resistant joint.

a basic trellis

The method here is largely a matter of crisscrossing uprights and crosspieces; no special joinery is required. The grid uses ⅝-by-1½-inch redwood pieces on 8-inch centers. You may choose to space the crosspieces more closely for delicate climbing plants or farther apart for particularly bushy plants. The instructions that follow show how to build a trellis with legs so that it can be freestanding. Alternatively, you may choose to build a simple rectangle that can be attached to the side of a house. (See pages 256–57 for instructions on how to anchor both types.) The top framing piece can be cut in the decorative shape of your choice.

LOWE'S QUICK TIP

Make sure the trellis is suited to the kind of plants you have chosen. Large bushy plants grow best with a grid of widely spaced crosspieces; more delicate plants need crosspieces closer together.

1 Lay the uprights on a flat surface, face down, then lay out crosspieces one at a time. Once you are sure of the layout, attach the pieces, drilling pilot holes first to prevent splitting the ends of the crosspieces. At each joint, add a dab of polyurethane glue, then drive a nail or screw.

2 If you need only a simple trellis that will be attached to a structure, you can stop here. To add a frame that will make the trellis freestanding, carefully measure the grid. Cut top and bottom rails to the exact width of the grid. For this design, we used a 2 by 8 for the top piece and gave it a decorative jigsaw cut. The remaining frame pieces are 2 by 2s. The side pieces should be at least 16 inches longer than the grid; you can cut them to exact length after the unit is constructed. Join the top and side pieces by drilling pilot holes, adding glue, and driving deck screws.

3 Slide the trellis grid inside the three-sided frame, then snug the bottom 2-by-2 rail up against the grid's bottom edge. The grid is not as thick as the frame; line the backs up, leaving a reveal at the front. Screw and glue the bottom rail in place. Finally, drill pilot holes and drive screws through the side pieces and into the grid.

making a **larger** grid

For a more graphic, architectural look and a stouter carrying capacity, scale up to more heavy-duty trellis materials such as 2-by-2 or 2-by-4 verticals and 2-by-2 crosspieces. Fasten the pieces by drilling pilot holes, adding a dab of polyurethane glue, and driving deck screws. The gridwork trellis shown at right has a decorative top piece in a traditional shape; it's cut with a jigsaw from a piece of 2-by-8 lumber. In constructing the grid, you can simply fasten these layers on top of each other or, for a sleeker grid that's joined in a single thickness, you can cut lap joints where the members cross, as shown above right.

MAKING A LAP JOINT

To make a full lap joint, use two boards of equal thickness and cut each notch half as deep as the board's thickness. Use a scrap piece of wood to measure and mark the outside edges of each notch. Set a circular saw or table saw to cut exactly half as deep as the board's thickness; test on a scrap piece to be sure you have the correct depth. Make cuts for the outside edges of each notch, then make a series of closely spaced cuts between the edges. Use a chisel to remove the waste and to smooth the joint's bottom.

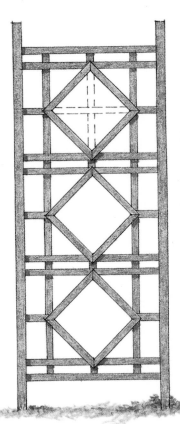

getting **fancy**

Once you have mastered the basics of making trellises, you can design your own. Either draw the patterns on a piece of grid paper or experiment with actual crosspieces until you find a configuration that pleases.

A standard size for a stand-alone or house-attached trellis is about 6 feet tall by 2 feet wide, but feel free to alter the dimensions to suit your needs.

Generally, these grids are constructed in layers, in crisscross fashion, as shown on pages 258–59. Lay the vertical crosspieces on a flat surface, then place horizontals on top. Openings in the grid of 6 to 8 inches are the norm, but it's fine to make some of them bigger. If your boards are large, you may choose to make lap joints for extra strength (see page 259). Otherwise, fasten each joint with a nail or screw that is just barely less than the combined thickness of the two parts; for extra strength, add a dab of polyurethane glue to the joint.

A curved piece at the top can have a big visual impact. If you're planning to paint the trellis, curved members can be fashioned from ¾-inch pressure-treated plywood or wider pieces of 1-by lumber. Make a cardboard template, cut it out, and trace it onto the wood. Cut the shape out with a jigsaw.

To create a "window" in a trellis, assemble and attach all the pieces, then cut out one or two pieces to make an opening.

fan trellis

To make vertical trellis pieces that are bendable, have a lumberyard rip-cut a 1-by board into strips that are about ½ inch thick to produce pieces that are ¾ inch by ½ inch. (If you have a table saw, this is easy to do yourself.) Make sure the lumber is clear (free of knots) or it will be prone to snap.

First, lay the verticals side by side, face down. Clamp them together at the bottom. Drill two holes and fasten the pieces together with carriage bolts, as shown at far right. Then, spread the fan (you may need some help) and nail on the top crosspiece. Add the other crosspieces.

For a freestanding fan, fasten the long center vertical piece to a stake driven into the ground.

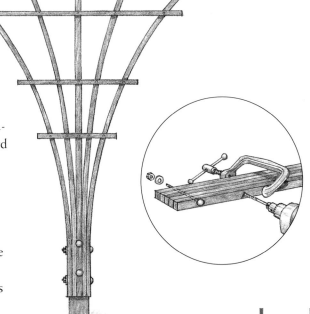

wire-fastened bamboo trellis

Bamboo is surprisingly durable, especially if you apply two coats of clear sealer to the pieces before letting plants grow onto them. Poles come in ½- to 4-inch diameters and in lengths from 4 to 12 feet. Use whole bamboo; "split" bamboo will not last long.

Where poles cross, clasp or clamp the two pieces together and drill a ¼-inch hole through both pieces. Bind the pieces together with 14-gauge copper or aluminum wire, feeding the wire through the holes, then twisting the ends together with a pair of lineman's pliers. Wear gloves to protect your hands. For a traditional effect, cover the wire with a decorative wrapping of black hemp twine or with strips of split bamboo. Either may need to be replaced every year or two.

Because bamboo may rot when its ends are buried, attach the trellis to a structure aboveground. Or, if the bamboo is thick enough, slip each vertical piece over a pipe or a piece of concrete reinforcing bar (rebar). The bamboo's solid internodes will keep the pole from sliding down the pipe into the soil. Alternatively, drive stakes into the ground and attach the trellis to the stakes via pipe clamps.

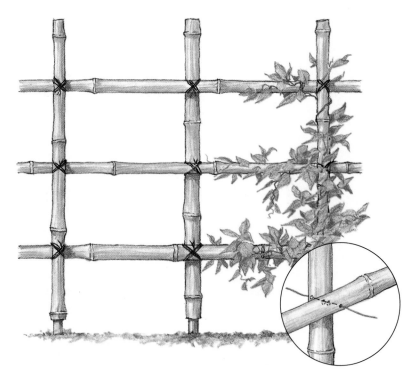

arbor with facing benches

HERE'S AN ADMIRABLE PORTAL TO ANY backyard destination. Tucked behind the flowering plants is a pair of 28-inch-long benches that flanks the 36-inch-wide passageway. The structure is built almost entirely of 1-by lumber, which lends an airy feeling yet makes it plenty strong.

MATERIALS LIST

▪ 2-by-4 pressure-treated sills	▪ Galvanized nails and deck screws
▪ 1-by-2 trellis stock	▪ Metal angle brackets and screws
▪ 1 by 3s	
▪ 1 by 10s	▪ Wood stakes
▪ 2 by 3s	▪ Sanding and finishing supplies
▪ ¼-inch plywood or cardboard for template	▪ Paint or stain

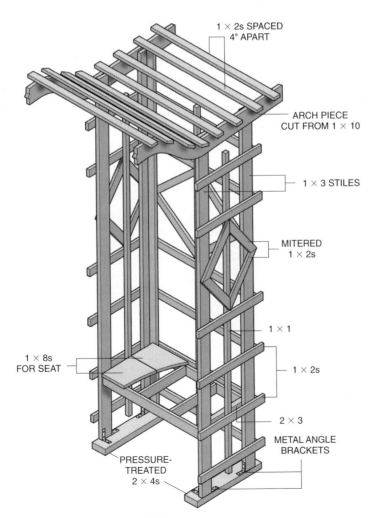

1 × 2s SPACED 4" APART

ARCH PIECE CUT FROM 1 × 10

1 × 3 STILES

MITERED 1 × 2s

1 × 1

1 × 8s FOR SEAT

1 × 2s

2 × 3

METAL ANGLE BRACKETS

PRESSURE-TREATED 2 × 4s

1 Cut all the 1 by 2s except for the diamonds: twenty-four at 18 inches, twelve at 29 inches, four at 12 inches, and fifteen at 35 inches. Cut the 1 by 3s: twelve at 83 inches, four at 29 inches, and eight at 12 inches. Cut four 1 by 1s at 73 inches.

2 Cut the arch pieces. To make sure that the left and right portions of each arch are mirror images, cut a template 41½ inches long, for half the pieces, out of ¼-inch plywood or a large piece of cardboard. Make the template 4 inches wide, rising 4 inches in the center and 1 inch at each end. Trace around the template onto your stock, then flip the template over to mark the other half. Use this arch as a template for the second one.

3 Construct four identical ladder trellises as shown, omitting the diamonds for now. Set the 1-by-3 stiles on a flat surface, lay the 18-inch 1-by-2 rungs in place, and check for square; correct the layout if needed. At each joint, apply a dab of polyurethane glue and drive a 1¼-inch deck screw. Attach the 1 by 1s to the center of the rungs using 4d casing nails.

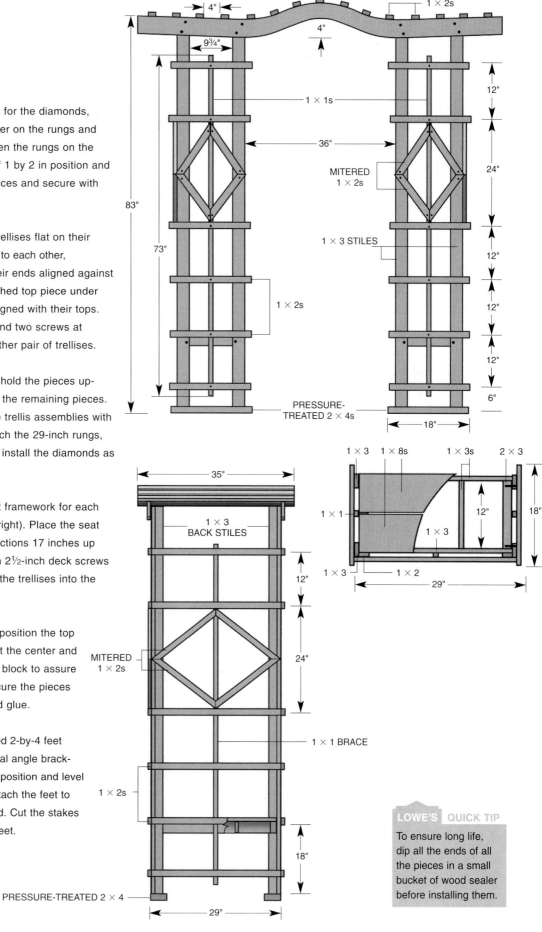

4 To determine the cuts for the diamonds, mark the vertical center on the rungs and the horizontal center between the rungs on the stiles. Then hold a length of 1 by 2 in position and mark the angles. Cut 16 pieces and secure with screws and glue.

5 Lay a pair of ladder trellises flat on their outside faces, parallel to each other, 36 inches apart and with their ends aligned against a straightedge. Slide an arched top piece under the trellises, its top edge aligned with their tops. Secure the arch with glue and two screws at each joint. Repeat for the other pair of trellises.

6 Have a helper or two hold the pieces upright while you attach the remaining pieces. Attach the back stiles to the trellis assemblies with screws every 8 inches. Attach the 29-inch rungs, omitting the diamond. Then install the diamonds as instructed in Step 4.

7 Assemble the support framework for each bench as shown (far right). Place the seat framework into the trellis sections 17 inches up from the base. Attach it with 2½-inch deck screws driven through the faces of the trellises into the ends of the framework.

8 Working on a ladder, position the top 1-by-2 pieces. Start at the center and work outward using a wood block to assure uniform 4-inch spacing. Secure the pieces with 2-inch deck screws and glue.

9 Attach pressure-treated 2-by-4 feet onto the legs with metal angle brackets. Set the trellis in its final position and level the ground as necessary. Attach the feet to stakes driven into the ground. Cut the stakes off flush with the top of the feet.

LOWE'S QUICK TIP

To ensure long life, dip all the ends of all the pieces in a small bucket of wood sealer before installing them.

overheads

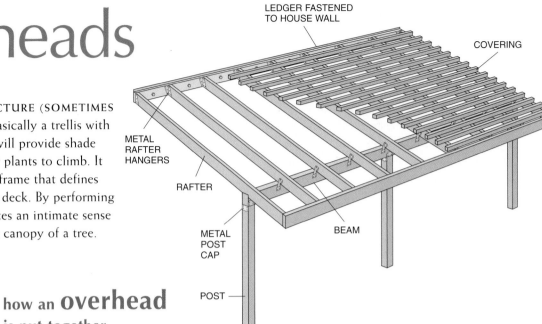

LEDGER FASTENED TO HOUSE WALL

COVERING

METAL RAFTER HANGERS

RAFTER

METAL POST CAP

BEAM

POST

AN OVERHEAD STRUCTURE (SOMETIMES called a pergola, and basically a trellis with an overhead element) will provide shade and perhaps a place for plants to climb. It also can act as a visual frame that defines all or part of a patio or deck. By performing these functions, it creates an intimate sense of space, much like the canopy of a tree.

how an **overhead** is put together

LOWE'S QUICK TIP

For your overhead, use lumber that is stable and resistant not only to rot but to warping as well. Daily exposure to sunlight will cause low-quality boards to twist and crack.

An overhead may be freestanding, as shown below, or it may be attached to the house with a ledger, as shown above. In either case, it is supported by posts. These can be continuations of deck posts or they might be separate pieces resting on concrete piers, paving, or footings. To add lateral strength, posts also can be set in postholes that are then filled with concrete. If you're adding an overhead to an existing deck, screw post

anchors to the decking or bolt the posts to existing railing posts.

In a freestanding arrangement, the posts support beams on either side; the rafters rest on top of the beams. For an overhead attached to the house, the rafters rest on a beam at one end and tie into a ledger at the other end. Often, the rafters are topped with evenly spaced top pieces (sometimes called lath); see facing page for other possible roofing materials.

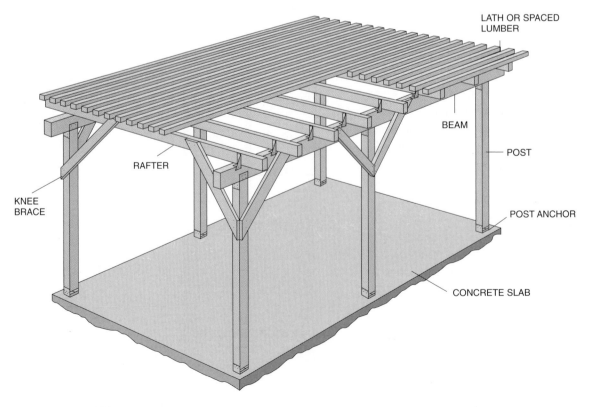

LATH OR SPACED LUMBER

BEAM

POST

POST ANCHOR

CONCRETE SLAB

RAFTER

KNEE BRACE

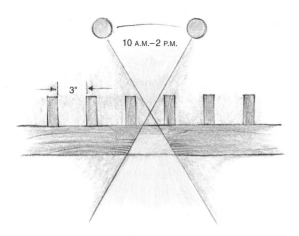

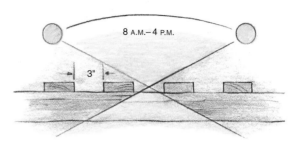

planning for shade

To increase or decrease the amount of shade the structure provides, vary the width and spacing of the top pieces. The direction in which you run the top pieces depends on the time of day you need the most shade. If you want midday shade, run the pieces east to west; for more shade in morning and early evening, run the pieces north to south. (Of course, changing the orientation of the top pieces means changing the orientation of the beams and rafters as well.)

Top pieces laid on edge diffuse early-morning and late-afternoon sun but let in plenty of light at midday (see above left). The same pieces laid flat (see above right) allow in more sun in the early morning and late afternoon but block more sun midday.

You can experiment with the width, spacing, and direction of overhead members by temporarily screwing some top pieces in different configurations to the rafters and observing the amount and kind of shade produced for a few days.

overhead covers

The most common way to top off an overhead is with small-dimensioned pieces of wood. However, there are other options.

Corrugated fiberglass panels let in filtered light and protect from the rain. Use special corrugated molding at the front and rear edges, and attach with aluminum gasket nails. You'll need to caulk some joints carefully if you really want to keep the rain out.

A variety of shade cloths are available. Depending on the weave, these cloths provide 20 to 90 percent shade.

A simple egg-crate design typically uses a grid of 2 by 4s. The overhead is open to the sky but provides a sheltered feeling.

SHADE CLOTH

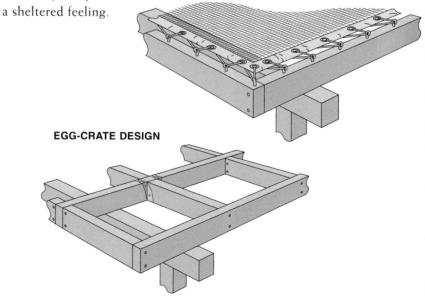

CORRUGATED PANEL

EGG-CRATE DESIGN

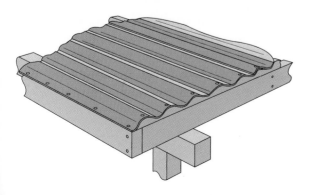

basic overhead
construction

Here's a brief overview of the process for building an overhead. You'll find more detail in the descriptions of specific overheads on pages 270–75.

If you will be attaching your overhead to a deck or patio that is reasonably level (or consistently sloped), cut all the posts to the same length. Otherwise, install the posts longer than they need to be and cut them to the same height later in the building process.

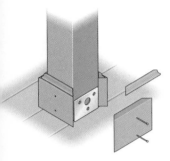

You can cover ugly anchoring hardware with two-part base molding.

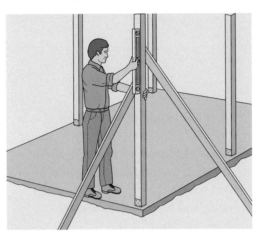

1 Set the posts in post anchors that elevate them slightly, so they won't rest in rainwater. Plumb each post in both directions; a post level makes this easy (see page 107). Secure each post with temporary wood braces nailed to wood stakes driven into the ground.

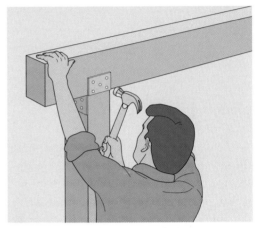

2 It usually looks best to have the beam overhang the posts by at least a few inches on each side. See pages 108–11 for instructions for building and attaching beams. Set the beam on top of the posts and check that the beam is level; you may need to slip shims between the post and beam at one or two places. Secure the beam to the posts via post caps or by drilling angled pilot holes and driving nails or screws.

An attractive beam can be made by screwing or bolting a 2-by board to either side of a post. This arrangement allows you to install attractive 4-by-4 bracing.

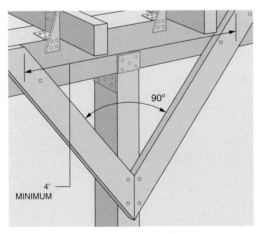

3 Cut rafters to overhang the beams by at least a few inches. Set and space the rafters on top of the beams and secure them with seismic straps or by drilling angled pilot holes and driving nails or screws. To improve wind resistance, nail or screw 1-by-4 or 1-by-6 braces that are at least 3 feet long, with the ends cut at 45 degrees, between the beams and posts.

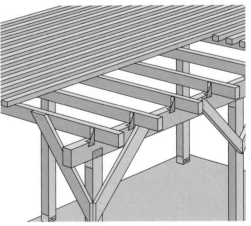

4 Top the structure with 1 by 2s or other small-dimensioned lumber, spaced to achieve the desired amount of shading. If you wish, you can dress up the post bottoms by attaching miter-cut pieces of 1 by 6s that are topped with pieces of cove molding, as shown at top left.

attaching to the house

Rafters for an overhead can be attached to a ledger much as you would attach a ledger and joists for a deck (see pages 94–97, and below). The overhead structure need not be as strong as deck framing, but the ledger should be firmly attached to the house. Be sure to drive screws or bolts into the house's framing, not just the siding.

Often, the best place to mount a ledger is on the wall under the eaves. If there is no rim joist behind the siding, use an electronic stud finder or drill test holes to find the studs. Then fasten the ledger with screws driven into the studs.

On a two-story house, you can usually find the rim joist for the second floor by measuring down from a window (see right).

Fasten the ledger so it is level. Local building codes will tell you if you can attach it tight to the siding or if you need to cut out a section of siding or use the hold-off method. You may need to install flashing as well; see pages 95–97 for information on all of these techniques.

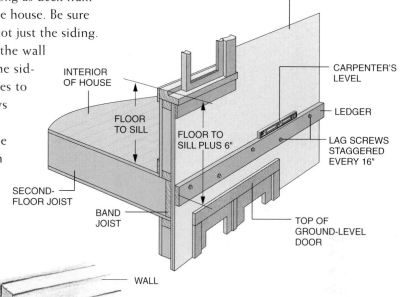

EXTERIOR WALL

INTERIOR OF HOUSE

FLOOR TO SILL

FLOOR TO SILL PLUS 6"

CARPENTER'S LEVEL

LEDGER

LAG SCREWS STAGGERED EVERY 16"

SECOND-FLOOR JOIST

BAND JOIST

TOP OF GROUND-LEVEL DOOR

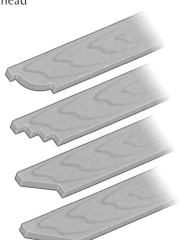

WALL

LEDGER

dressing up posts and rafters

To make posts look less leggy, add trim and molding at the bottom (see facing page, top left). You can also dress up the tops of posts: run the posts a foot or two above the rafters and add decorative post caps like those shown on page 150. The overhead designs on pages 270–75 show two ways to trim out posts.

Overhanging rafter and beam ends are highly visible features. One simple way to give the structure its own look is to cut the ends in a decorative pattern. Some popular examples are shown here, but you can easily come up with your own. Once you settle on a pattern, make a cardboard or plywood template and use it to trace the pattern onto the boards before cutting them.

crisscrossed square

THIS HANDSOME 8-FOOT-SQUARE OVERHEAD, FLOORED WITH FLAGSTONE AND furnished with comfortable chairs, provides an inviting place to relax and enjoy the view.

design **features**

Posts that are made of pressure-treated lumber, though ideal for durability (especially below grade), inevitably crack. Although minor cracking does not affect strength, it is particularly unsightly when the wood is painted. Wrapping posts with 1-by-8 fascia boards gives this structure the benefits of both types of wood. In addition, the fascia provides a ledge for the 2-by-8 beams to rest on, eliminating the need for bolted connections. Be sure to soak all board ends in sealer before you install them. If you intend to paint the structure, also prime all the pieces before installing them.

LOWE'S QUICK TIP

The architectural details visible at the ends of the front and rear beams can be tailored to blend with design elements of your home. Before cutting the beams, experiment by holding up shaped plywood patterns tacked onto the ends of uncut 2-by boards.

GANG-CUTTING NOTCHES FOR LAP JOINTS

To efficiently cut a series of notches in a group of boards, cut the boards to length and clamp them together with the ends perfectly flush. Use a square to draw lines for the notches. Set a circular saw to the correct depth and test-cut a scrap piece to make sure it is correct. First cut the outside lines, then make a series of closely spaced cuts in the inside of the notch. Use a chisel to clean out and square up the notches (see page 259).

MATERIALS LIST

- Concrete, #4 rebar, and form lumber for footings
- Gravel
- 6-by-6 pressure-treated posts
- 2-by-8 beams
- 2-by-4 trellis stock
- 1-by-8 trim
- Galvanized nails and deck screws
- Sanding and finishing supplies
- Paint, stain, or wood preservative

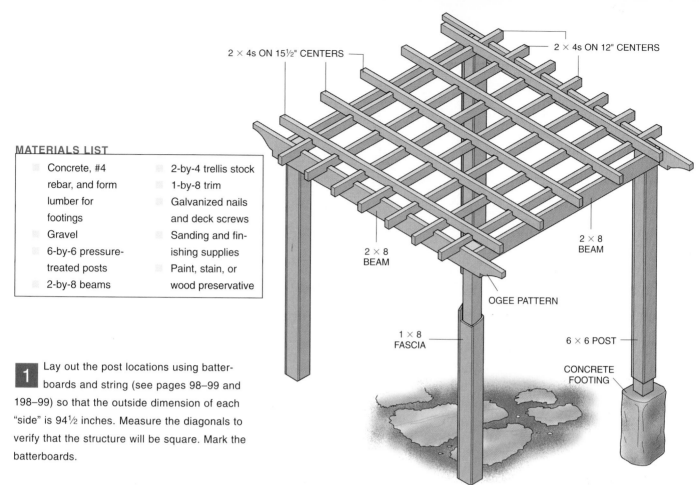

2 × 4s ON 15½" CENTERS

2 × 4s ON 12" CENTERS

2 × 8 BEAM

2 × 8 BEAM

OGEE PATTERN

1 × 8 FASCIA

6 × 6 POST

CONCRETE FOOTING

1 Lay out the post locations using batter-boards and string (see pages 98–99 and 198–99) so that the outside dimension of each "side" is 94½ inches. Measure the diagonals to verify that the structure will be square. Mark the batterboards.

2 Dig holes for the footings and put about 3 inches of gravel at the bottom of each hole. Set the posts in place; hold them plumb with two temporary braces attached to stakes driven into the ground. Pour the footings (see pages 100–105 for detailed instructions).

3 Using a level set atop an 8-foot-long straight board, or a water level, mark the tops of the posts level with each other, at least 8 feet 2½ inches above the ground. Use a square to draw a line around each post; cut with a circular saw.

4 Cut the two long beams to length, cutting the ends in a decorative pattern (make a cardboard or plywood template for the pattern and clamp it onto each beam to mark for cutting). Mark the tops of the beams for the 2-by-4 rafters, 12 inches on center. Secure the beams flush with the tops of the posts using exterior nails or deck screws.

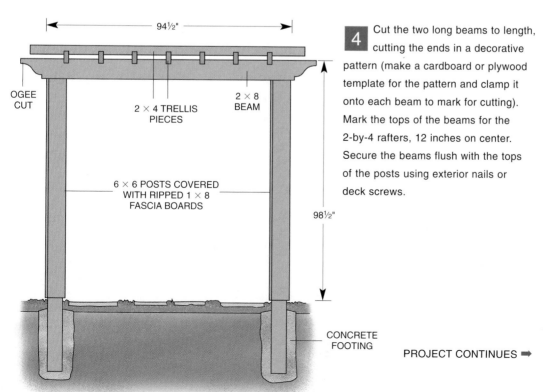

94½"

OGEE CUT

2 × 4 TRELLIS PIECES

2 × 8 BEAM

6 × 6 POSTS COVERED WITH RIPPED 1 × 8 FASCIA BOARDS

98½"

CONCRETE FOOTING

LOWE'S QUICK TIP

To trim the post tops, you'll need to work on a ladder with a circular saw. Check that the ladder is stable before you climb it, and have a helper hold the ladder firm while you work.

PROJECT CONTINUES ➡

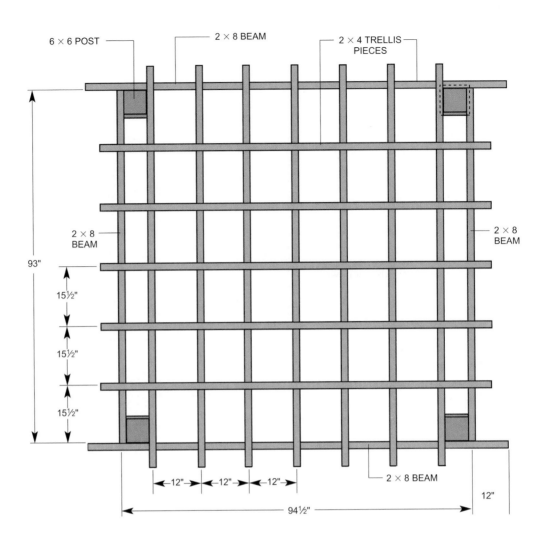

6 × 6 POST

2 × 8 BEAM

2 × 4 TRELLIS PIECES

2 × 8 BEAM

2 × 8 BEAM

2 × 8 BEAM

93"

15½"

15½"

15½"

←12"→←12"→←12"→

12"

←————— 94½" —————→

5 Cut the two side beams to fit between the long beams and secure them flush with the post tops with nails or screws.

6 For each post, cut four fascia boards exactly as long as the post. Rip-cut two boards about ⅛ inch wider than the posts and two 1½ inches wider than those. Butt one narrow board against one wide one to make an outside-corner post covering; nail together and secure to the post.

7 For each post, cut a ¾-by-7¼-inch notch in the top side edge of the other narrow fascia board so it will fit around the beam. Fasten it to the other wide board to create the inside-corner covering; secure it to the post.

8 Cut the 2-by-4 rafters to length, overhanging the beams by 6 inches on either side. Lay one rafter across the long beams, center it for an equal overhang on each end, and mark the

1½-inch-wide notches where the rafter crosses the two beams. Set your circular saw to cut 1 inch deep, and gang-cut notches in all the rafters, as shown on page 270.

9 Cut the 2-by-4 top pieces to length, overhanging the side beams by 6 inches on either side. (If the posts were laid out accurately, the top pieces will be the same length as the rafters.) Mark and cut the notches in the bottoms of these as you did for the rafters. Drill pilot holes, then toenail the boards onto the tops of the 2-by-4 rafters.

10 Sand the fascia and round the corners to eliminate any splinters. Touch up the primer as needed and top-coat the entire structure with 100 percent acrylic-latex paint.

attached pergola

THIS DESIGN IS STRAIGHTFORWARD, BUT TWO SUBTLE FEATURES—PAIRED RAFTERS
and decorated post tops—give it interest. Painted white, the boards' crisp lines create a
contemporary look. If the pergola were stained or allowed to turn gray, the effect would
be more casual.

design features

As shown, the overhead extends over two
deck levels and part of the yard; the design
could be easily adapted to form other
shapes. Paired rafters are not structurally
necessary, but add a nice touch. Nailing
blocks between rafter pairs allow very solid
connections without joist hangers.

See pages 266–69 for the basic overhead construction techniques needed to
build this structure. Enlist the aid of at
least one helper, and have two sturdy
stepladders available. Soak all ends of
boards in sealer before you install them.

If you will be painting the structure, also
prime all the pieces before installing them.

MATERIALS LIST

- Concrete and #4 rebar for footing
- 4-by-4 posts
- 2-by-6 rafters and ledger
- 2-by-2 top pieces
- Galvanized nails and deck screws
- Galvanized lag screws and washers
- Metal post anchors
- Sanding and fin-ishing supplies
- Wood preservative
- Exterior primer
- Acrylic-latex exterior paint

LOWE'S QUICK TIP

If you will be painting
the overhead, choose
high-quality boards
that are unlikely to
crack, especially for
the posts. For the
paint, premium-quality
100 percent acrylic-
latex exterior is an
excellent choice.

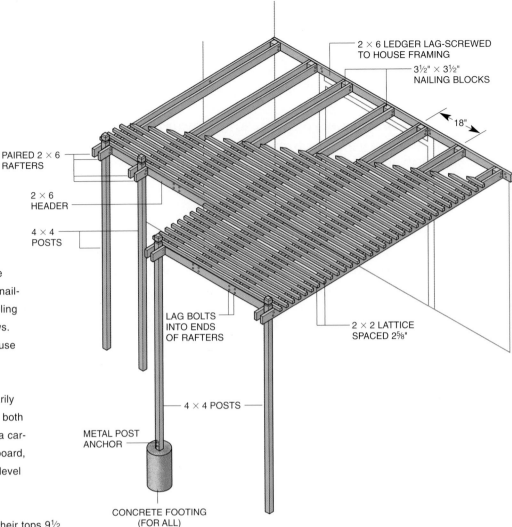

2 × 6 LEDGER LAG-SCREWED TO HOUSE FRAMING

3½" × 3½" NAILING BLOCKS

18"

PAIRED 2 × 6 RAFTERS

2 × 6 HEADER

4 × 4 POSTS

LAG BOLTS INTO ENDS OF RAFTERS

2 × 2 LATTICE SPACED 2⅝"

4 × 4 POSTS

METAL POST ANCHOR

CONCRETE FOOTING (FOR ALL)

1 Lay out the post positions (see pages 98–99 and 198–99). Attach post anchors directly onto decking or a patio surface or dig holes and pour footings (see pages 100–105).

2 Cut the ledger and mark the rafter locations. Cut 2-by-4 nailing blocks and attach them by drilling pilot holes and driving deck screws. Firmly attach the ledger to the house (see pages 269 and 94–99).

3 Position the posts. Temporarily brace each so it is plumb in both directions. Using a water level or a carpenter's level set atop a straight board, mark a point on each post that is level with the bottom of the ledger.

4 Remove the posts and cut their tops 9½ inches above the marks. Four inches down from the top of the post, use a square to draw a line around the post. Use a circular saw or a router to cut a ½-by-½-inch groove around each post on the line. One inch down from the top, draw another line around the post. Set a circular saw to cut at a 45-degree angle and cut to the line to create a chamfered top.

LOWE'S QUICK TIP

Rather than cutting post-top details yourself, you may choose to fasten a decorative newel cap atop each post; see page 150.

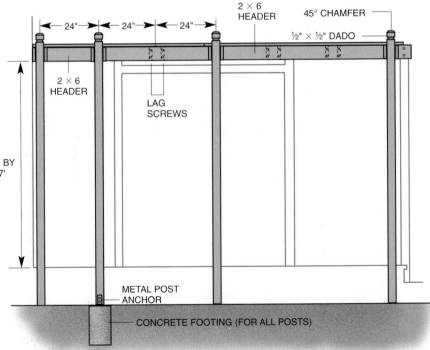

24"   **24"**   **24"**

2 × 6 HEADER

45° CHAMFER

½" × ½" DADO

2 × 6 HEADER

LAG SCREWS

HEIGHT DETERMINED BY LOCATION (MINIMUM 7' FROM SURFACE)

METAL POST ANCHOR

CONCRETE FOOTING (FOR ALL POSTS)

5 Cut the rafters that attach to the posts; they run past the posts by 3½ inches. At the ledger, attach the rafters to the nailing blocks by drilling pilot holes and driving deck screws. At the other end, attach the rafters to the posts with ⁵⁄₁₆-by-6½-inch carriage bolts, washers, and nuts.

6 Cut the headers to fit between the installed rafters. Attach each header to the rafters with deck screws (you will have to drive them at a slight angle).

7 Measure and cut the remaining rafters, which fit between the ledger and the headers. Attach them to the nailing blocks by drilling pilot holes and driving deck screws. At the other end, drive pilot holes through the header and into rafter ends, then drive 3-inch lag screws with washers.

8 Cut 2-by-2 top pieces to length, letting them overhang the rafters by 3½ inches on either side. Starting at the farthest point from the house, snap a string line across the tops of the rafters to establish a straight line for the first top piece; install it by driving a 3-inch deck screw at each joint. Use a spacer board to maintain even spacing for the remaining top pieces. Every sixth piece or so, check for straightness with a string line. As you near the house, measure the remaining space to make sure the boards will end up parallel to the house. You may need to make minor adjustments in the spacing of the final boards to avoid having the last one fall either too close or too far from where you want it.

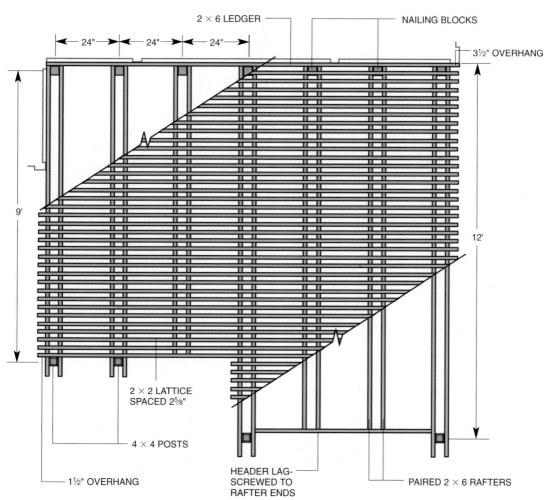

2 × 6 LEDGER — NAILING BLOCKS

3½" OVERHANG

24" 24" 24"

9'

12'

2 × 2 LATTICE SPACED 2⅝"

4 × 4 POSTS

1½" OVERHANG

HEADER LAG-SCREWED TO RAFTER ENDS

PAIRED 2 × 6 RAFTERS

gazebo kits

FEW OUTDOOR STRUCTURES RIVAL THE CHARM OF A GAZEBO. However, building one from scratch is beyond the capabilities of most do-it-yourselfers: cutting compound angles, shaping wood, and making difficult joints can be challenging. What you can do, though, is order a gazebo kit. Lowe's carries a number of options. With one of these, the difficult work is already done. You provide the spot, assemble the parts, and admire the results.

This top-of-the-line gazebo kit features serpentine balusters for the railings and arched "gingerbread" sections for each of its eight sides. The gazebo and the furniture inside are made of clear cedar that is stained and sealed to maintain a like-new appearance.

Left: Precut lattice sections and sheets of metal roofing give this gazebo a rich look, yet also make it quick to build.

Below: Gazebo kits have all the parts needed to build the structure, cut to the right size so they fit snugly together.

Kits come with complete instructions for assembly; be sure to follow them to the letter. With most, components are numbered or coded to correspond with diagrams and assembly directions. Kits include screws, bolts, nails, and all the hardware you need. Foundation materials are not included.

Because some of the components are heavy or awkward to handle, you'll need at least one helper—two would be better—and at least two sturdy stepladders.

Before you begin assembly, you'll probably need to cast a concrete foundation according to the manufacturer's directions. In most cases, this means pouring a series of concrete footings and piers using techniques described on pages 100–105. The framing rests on the footings, so all the footings need to be at the same height.

A gazebo may rest on a series of piers (below left) or on a continuous concrete slab (below right). Typically, all the eight flooring and roofing sections are the same size and shape.

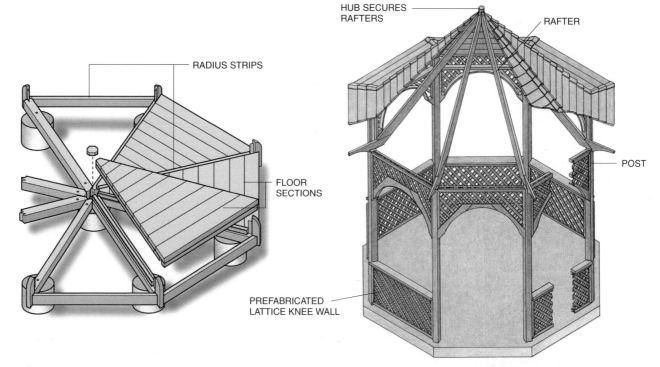

RADIUS STRIPS

FLOOR SECTIONS

PREFABRICATED LATTICE KNEE WALL

HUB SECURES RAFTERS

RAFTER

POST

benches

DECKS AND PATIOS NEED SEATING. OUTDOOR FURNITURE (SEE PAGES 254–55) meets this need, but you may want to augment it with benches, either built in or free-standing. You can show off your skills by building the benches yourself. Choose materials that match the deck or other elements in your yard.

Here we show two relatively easy projects. The first, installed on a deck, must be started before the decking is laid. You can create the freestanding bench any time.

A gently curved bench can be built using standard lumber.

BENCH PARALLEL TO JOISTS

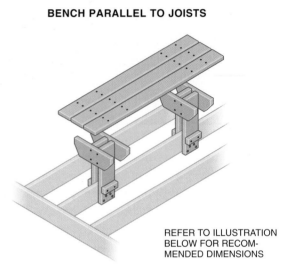

REFER TO ILLUSTRATION BELOW FOR RECOMMENDED DIMENSIONS

built-in bench for a deck

This simple but attractive bench is solidly supported by four 2-by-8 legs bolted to the joist framing. At 5 feet long, it can comfortably seat three. The basic design can be adapted to run either perpendicular or parallel to the joists. You can make a longer bench if it runs perpendicular to the joists. Install additional supports spaced no more than 4 feet apart. Lengthening is not a good idea if all the weight rests on a single joist.

Before you lay the decking, construct the seat supports. Assemble them by drilling pilot holes and driving deck screws. Install them an equal distance from the end of the deck using deck screws and carriage bolts. Install the decking, then attach the seat pieces.

BENCH PERPENDICULAR TO JOISTS

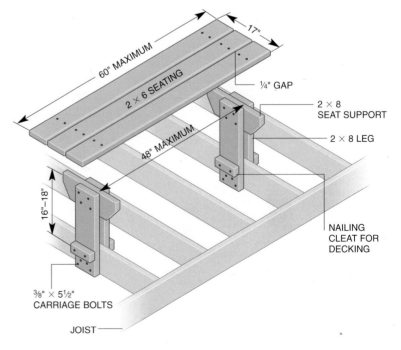

60" MAXIMUM

17"

2 × 6 SEATING

¼" GAP

2 × 8 SEAT SUPPORT

2 × 8 LEG

48" MAXIMUM

16"–18"

NAILING CLEAT FOR DECKING

⅜" × 5½" CARRIAGE BOLTS

JOIST

freestanding bench

This bench is equally at home on a deck or a patio. The 4-by-4 legs make it stable. Take extra care to cut all the leg pieces precisely square, and clamp them together so they are aligned before you drill pilot holes and drive deck screws. Fasten the 2-by-4 seating pieces to the supports, then add the edging pieces.

Left: **This bench is made of logs cut with a chain saw. The rough surface created by the chain saw may be left, or it can be smoothed using a belt sander or a power planer.**

Below: **Pieces of 1-by-2 interspersed with 2-by-2s create a slatted bench seat.**

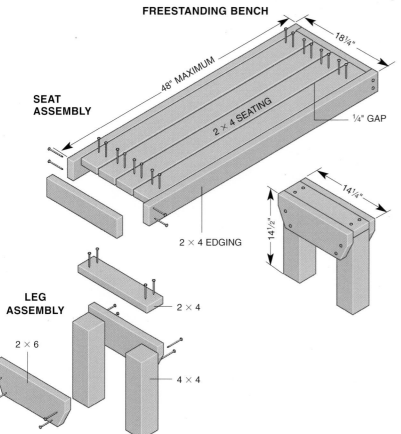

FREESTANDING BENCH

18¼"

48" MAXIMUM

SEAT ASSEMBLY

2 × 4 SEATING

¼" GAP

2 × 4 EDGING

14¼"

14½"

LEG ASSEMBLY

2 × 4

2 × 6

4 × 4

slatted seating

Another popular seating design uses numerous spaced slats that are 1½ inches wide. If the supports are less than 2½ feet apart, you can use 2 by 2s for the slats. Otherwise, use 2 by 4s set on edge. A pleasing look is easily achieved by "self-spacing" the slats—installing them 1½ inches apart.

planter bench

THIS BENCH HAS TWO LITTLE GARDENS BUILT RIGHT IN, SO YOU CAN SIT NESTLED between plants. The planters are deep enough to hold very large pots. If you prefer to fill the planters with potting soil, use pressure-treated lumber rated for ground contact.

For all attachments, drill pilot holes, add polyurethane glue, and drive galvanized nails or deck screws.

To make each container base, cut four 2 by 8s and fasten them together. Cut a piece of pressure-treated plywood to fit on top of the assembly and attach it. Drill drain holes in the plywood.

Cut the container sides, fronts, and backs. Mark the side pieces with the locations of the ¼-inch rods and the ¼-inch lag screws (see below left). Counterbore ¾-inch-wide, ⁵⁄₁₆-inch-deep holes for the washers, nuts, and bolt heads. In the center of each counterbore, drill a ¼-inch hole for the bolts and rods.

For each container, cut and assemble three open squares, each made of four 2 by 8s set on edge, to fit around the base. Set the bottom square over the base and use scrap pieces of 2-by lumber to hold it 1½ inches above the ground. Stack the other two squares on top. Cut four 2-by-4 cleats for each container and fasten them to the insides of the side pieces. Drill holes through the cleats. Cut and insert the threaded rods, add washers and nuts on either side, and tighten.

Cut the 2-by-6 bench supports and attach them. Cut bench slats to fit and set them in place, spacing them evenly, then fasten them to the supports. Add the 2-by-6 bench faces.

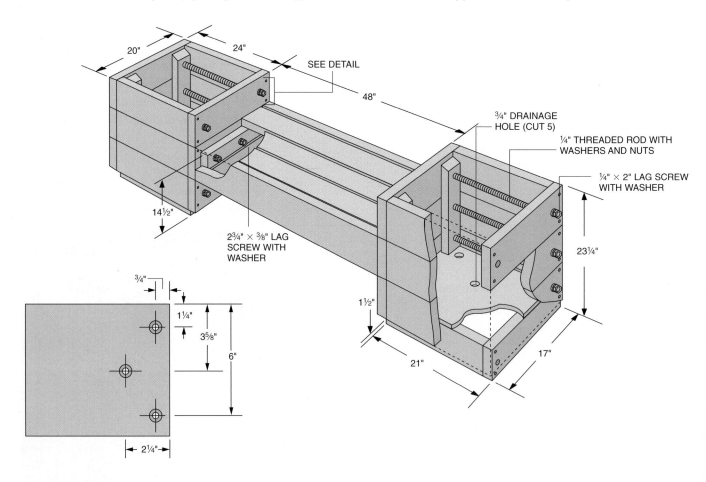

planter

AT ITS MOST BASIC, A PLANTER IS A box made of decay-resistant material with drainage holes in the bottom. The outside of the planter can be dressed up any way you want.

If you will be setting flowerpots in the planter, its sides do not need to be very rot resistant. However, if you will fill the planter with soil, a galvanized or an aluminum liner is recommended. Build the planter first, then have a sheet-metal shop make the liner to fit.

First, build a basic box using 1-by lumber or pressure-treated plywood. Join the corners with screws and polyurethane glue. Bore drainage holes in the bottom, or leave space between the bottom boards to allow for drainage. Finally, attach trim boards to the corners, and perhaps add decorative trim as well.

Planters like these can be filled with soil and plants, or they can act as decorative containers for flowerpots.

3" WOODEN NEWEL CAP

1 × 4 CAP

2 × 3 TRIM

¾" EXTERIOR PLYWOOD WITH INSIDE SURFACES WATERPROOFED

2 × 6

2 × 3 FRAME

¾" EXTERIOR PLYWOOD BASE

1 × 2s MITERED TO COVER CORNER

1 × 2s CROSS LAPPED AT JOINT

3" WOODEN NEWEL CAP

1 × 4 CAP

2 × 3 TRIM

1 × 2 TRIM

1 × 2 TRIM

2 × 6 BASE

2' 6"

2'

2 × 3 FRAME

DRAIN HOLE

¾" EXTERIOR PLYWOOD WATERPROOFED ON INSIDE

installing low-voltage lighting on a deck

IN MOST CASES, IT IS EASY TO CONNECT WITH THE HOUSEHOLD WIRING. SEE pages 286–87 for general instructions on connecting low-voltage systems.

available products

Many of the lights that come in standard landscaping light kits can be easily attached to a deck's posts or fascia. However, there are products made specifically for attaching to wood structures, and these will probably look and perform better.

A riser light is installed in the riser of a step, where it will shine down at just the right angle to illuminate the step below.

A wall-mounted decorative spotlight is easily screwed to any vertical surface such as a post. Some can be mounted overhead. For the best appearance, the wiring must be run through the wood.

A post cap light does double duty as a decorative post cap (or newel cap).

Above: Uplights at the bases of the trees here animate the landscape around the deck. Simple candles can also be part of the lighting scheme.

Right: Available fixtures include lights that can be attached to the top of a post, a vertical surface, the underside of a horizontal surface, or a riser.

installation methods

As long as you can get there without too much difficulty, the underside of a deck is an ideal location for a lighting transformer (see right). Then the wires can be run along the joists and either up through the decking or out through an end or header joist.

Install a riser light (see center right) after the risers have been installed and before you install the treads. Draw the outline of the hole using the manufacturer's template. Drill a hole near one corner, then cut the outlined shape using a jigsaw. Insert the light's box, make the connections, and screw on the cover. Test the light before you install the treads.

Where possible, hide the cable by running it under the decking, through holes drilled in framing, or through channels routed in posts or rails. (You can cover the channel with a decorative piece of trim.) Railing systems that are made from extruded composite materials provide ideal runways for cable, as do railings that are made with tubing.

Fasten wires with wire staples that are made for exterior use (see above left). Pull the wires fairly taut and position them neatly before you fasten them.

To install a post cap light (see above right), bore a hole through the post using a long drill bit or a drill bit extension. Alternatively, cut a channel in the side of the post and cover it later with a piece of trim. Thread the wire, make the connections, slip the light over the post, and drive small nails or screws to hold the light in place.

building an outdoor kitchen

AN OUTDOOR COUNTER PROVIDES
space for food preparation and cuts down on trips to the kitchen, making grilling more of a pleasure and less of a chore. It also provides ample storage area for charcoal, plates, and other supplies, keeping them handy and protected from the elements.

This unit has a built-in charcoal grill. You could easily install a propane unit instead; there is plenty of room for a tank in the cabinet below. A full-scale outdoor kitchen might include a sink with running water, electrical receptacles, and perhaps a natural-gas hookup.

An outdoor counter made of heavy masonry materials (see page 293) must rest on a solid concrete footing. This project uses steel studs and concrete backerboard instead—just as fire resistant as concrete block but much lighter, so the unit can rest on a deck or an unreinforced patio.

The next three pages show how to build the cabinet, which can then be covered with the countertop of your choice. Pages 294–95 show how to build a concrete countertop for this cabinet.

Purchase your doors and the grill unit or get ahold of the specs so you know the rough openings required. Make a detailed drawing, including every framing member. Studs and top cross braces should be spaced no farther than 16 inches apart.

Top: Doors and grill units are available in both black and stainless steel. Either contrasts handsomely with masonry materials.

Above: Steel framing makes this counter light enough for a deck or unreinforced patio. To avoid mistakes, make a detailed drawing of the framing before you build.

MATERIALS LIST

- Steel studs and channels
- Self-tapping screws made for metal studs
- Concrete backerboard
- Backerboard screws
- Slate tiles or other tiles
- Plastic tile spacers
- Latex-fortified thinset mortar
- Latex-fortified sanded grout
- Steel doors made for outdoor counters
- Drop-in grill unit

1 Measure and cut the framing pieces. Working with metal framing is not difficult. There are two basic components: U-shaped channels and the studs that fit into the channels. When measuring to cut a stud, take into account the thickness of the channels—⅛ inch on either end. Cut a channel or stud using metal snips.

2 Cut a rectangle of channels for the frame bottom. Using tin snips, cut flaps on pieces for attaching as needed. Frame the back and sides: cut the upper channels, then cut studs to fit between them. Join the studs to the channels by driving self-tapping screws made for metal studs.

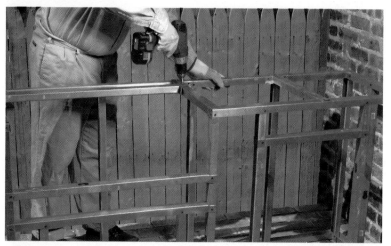

3 Build framing for the front, which has three openings—two for the doors and one for the grill unit. To make cross braces to support the countertop, cut studs 3 inches longer than the opening, then snip the ends to make three tabs that screw to the upper channels. The framing will be unstable as you work; it will all tie together and become solid once you attach the backerboard (Step 5). Continually check for square using a framing square.

4 To make sure the openings are the correct size, set each door and the grill unit in place. When testing the grill, take into account the thickness of the countertop you have chosen. If the openings are slightly large, you can add backerboard to overhang the framing by as much as an inch. There should be at least ¼ inch clearance between the framing and the grill's sides and bottom so the framing will not heat up excessively when you cook.

PROJECT CONTINUES ➡

5 Cover the framing with ½-inch-thick concrete backerboard. When you measure, subtract ¼ inch (that is, cut the backerboard a little short), because the edges tend to be ragged. Use a drywall square or a straightedge to guide your cuts. To cut, score one side several times with a backerboard knife or a utility knife, snap the piece into a fold, then score the opposite side and snap the piece off. To make a cutout, use a reciprocating saw or a jigsaw equipped with a rough-cutting blade to cut one or two sides, then cut the remaining side using a knife. Check the framing for square, then attach by driving concrete backerboard screws every 4 inches or so into studs and channels. Check again that the doors and the grill unit will fit.

6 Plan the tile layout, avoiding thin slivers if possible. Be clear which tiles will overlap at the outside corners. Cut at least some tiles before you mix the mortar. See pages 238–39 for general tiling instructions. Mix a batch of latex-fortified thin-set mortar; apply it using a square-notched trowel. Set the tiles in the mortar using plastic spacers to maintain consistent joints. Where a tile is not supported by a tile below, use pieces of tape, as shown, to hold it in place until the mortar sets.

7 Allow the mortar to cure for a day or so. Pry out the plastic spacers. Mix a batch of latex-fortified grout and apply it using a laminated grout float. First press the grout firmly into the joints by holding the float nearly flat and moving it in several directions. Then tilt the float up and scrape away most of the thinset mortar. Use a damp sponge to wipe the surface and tool the joints to a consistent depth. Wipe several times, each time rinsing with clean water. Allow the grout to dry, then buff the surface with a dry cloth. If a haze persists, clean the tiles with a mild solution of muriatic acid (see page 241).

8 The cabinet doors come prehung on jambs. Set a door in place and lightly mark around its casing with a pencil. Remove the door, lay a bead of silicone caulk inside the pencil line, and press the door in place; the caulk should seal at all points. Drive screws through the holes in the jamb to secure the door to the studs on either side. Either wipe away the caulk immediately using a rag dampened with mineral spirits or wait for it to dry and cut it away with a utility knife.

building a **masonry** counter

A masonry counter is rock solid, but building one is a major undertaking. Unless you have some experience building masonry walls, you will probably want to hire a pro to construct a unit like this.

Because it is so heavy, the counter must rest on a thick slab of reinforced concrete. Typically, the slab's footing (which runs around its perimeter) is 24 inches deep, and the rest of the slab is 4 inches deep.

Once the concrete has cured, a concrete block wall is built. The wall is then faced with bricks or tiles.

The top is made by building a temporary form and pouring metal-reinforced concrete at least 2 inches thick. The concrete can be covered with brick, as shown, or with ceramic or stone tile.

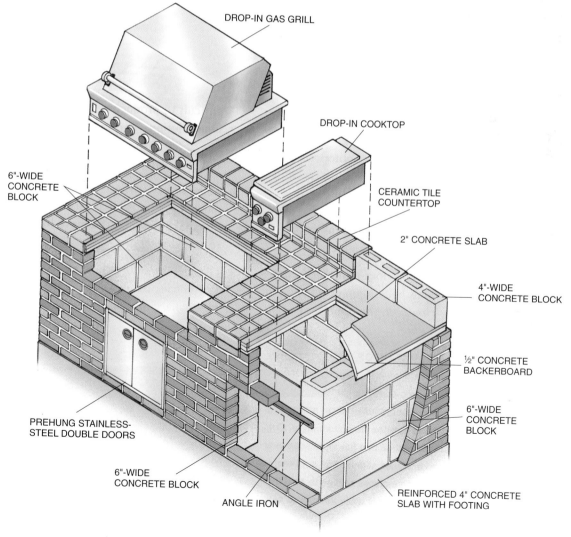

DROP-IN GAS GRILL

DROP-IN COOKTOP

6"-WIDE CONCRETE BLOCK

CERAMIC TILE COUNTERTOP

2" CONCRETE SLAB

4"-WIDE CONCRETE BLOCK

½" CONCRETE BACKERBOARD

6"-WIDE CONCRETE BLOCK

PREHUNG STAINLESS-STEEL DOUBLE DOORS

6"-WIDE CONCRETE BLOCK

ANGLE IRON

REINFORCED 4" CONCRETE SLAB WITH FOOTING

5 Use a board or a magnesium float to move and spread the concrete so it is about half as thick as the countertop will be; be sure it fills in above the 2 by 4s to make an overhang with no voids or bubbles. Set the reinforcing metal on top and add more concrete. Spread the concrete, pushing downward to prevent voids and bubbles. If the forms bulge, straighten them by tightening the clamps.

6 Continue filling with concrete, pushing it firmly against the form. Spread with a magnesium float, then use a piece of 2 by 4 to screed the top so it is level with the tops of the form boards. Lightly tap with a hammer on the sides of the form to remove small air pockets.

7 As soon as any water disappears from the surface, run a magnesium float across the surface to begin the smoothing process. Press just hard enough to bring up a little water.

8 Run a concrete edger along the perimeter two or three times, until the surface is smooth. As soon as the water disappears again, run a magnesium trowel over the surface.

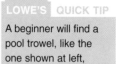

LOWE'S QUICK TIP

A beginner will find a pool trowel, like the one shown at left, easier to use than a square-cornered one.

9 Slowly release the clamps. If the concrete forces the form outward, retighten them; wait five minutes or so. Once you remove the clamps, unscrew the boards and gently pull them away.

10 Use a magnesium float, then a steel trowel, to smooth the edges of the slab. If any large gaps are present, fill them by hand and run the trowel over them again.

LOWE'S QUICK TIP

Avoid overworking the surface of the concrete. Stop when water appears; if you bring up too much water, the surface will be prone to cracking. If troweling starts to make the concrete tougher rather than smoother, it is definitely time to stop working it.

11 Use a small piece of plastic to smooth and round the corners.

12 Taking care to keep the leading edge slightly raised, go over the surface with a steel trowel. Avoid overworking the surface; stop if the trowel starts to roughen rather than smooth.

credits

PHOTOGRAPHY

Jean Allsopp: 248 center and bottom left; **Brian Baer:** 45 top; **Ernest Braun:** 273; **Ernest Braun, California Redwood Association:** 5 center left, 149 top right; **Marion Brenner:** 12, 31 top, 38 bottom, 56, 180, 218; **Gay Bumgarner:** 5 right, 41 bottom; **Gay Bumgarner/Positive Images:** 138, 160; **Karen Bussolini:** 17 bottom, 40 bottom, 42 bottom, 43 bottom, 55, 178, 181 bottom right, 184 bottom, 185 bottom left, 188 bottom, 206 top left, 216 bottom left, 223 center left, 250 top left; **Wayne Cable:** 234 bottom, 235, 238, 239 top and center; **David Cavagnaro:** 184 top left; **Philip Clayton-Thompson:** 30 bottom; **Gary Conaughton:** 191 bottom; **Crandall & Crandall:** 26 bottom, 50 top, 185 bottom right; **Dalton Pavilions, Inc.:** 277 left; **Danuser Machine Co.:** 101 center; **Ben Davidson:** 72, 74; **R. Todd Davis:** 176, 246 left; **F. Didillon/M.A.P.:** 38 top; **Ken Druse:** 28, 30 top, 42 top, 122, 146, 172; **Catriona Tudor Erler:** 121; **Cheryl Fenton:** 71, 78 top left, 79 bottom left, 82, 83, 84 post level, 85 nail set, hand sander, and flat pry bar, 87 magnetic sleeve, 88 top right, 89 bottom, 128, 133, 150 bottom, 162 bottom, 163 bottom, 184 top right, 188 top, 189 center and bottom, 204, 205, 221, 228–230, 245, 247 bottom right, 251 top right, 256, 257, 270 bottom, 283 bottom, 287, 288 bottom left, 289 bottom left and right; **courtesy of Fiber Composites, LLC:** 148 top left, 159; **Bob Firth:** 118, 119; **Scott Fitzgerrell:** 61, 78 bottom, 79 top right and bottom right, 82, 83, 84 except water level and post level, 85 except upper right, 87 drills, 129, 130 center; **Frank Gaglione:** 7 bottom, 84 water level, 91, 171, 177 top, 179 top, 181 bottom left, 182 top, 183 top, 186 bottom, 187 center and bottom, 192 except wrecking bar, 193–201, 202 right, 203, 206 center and bottom, 207–210, 211 center and bottom, 212–215, 216 top, bottom right, 217, 219, 220, 222 bottom, 223 top and bottom, 224, 225, 231, 232, 233 bottom, 236 bottom, 237 top right and left, bottom left, 242, 243 top, 246 right, 247 top and bottom left, 252, 253; **Tria Giovan:** 16 bottom, 17 top, 18–20, 31 bottom, 43 top, 44 bottom, 150 top; **Jay Graham:** 27; **John Granen:** 11 top, 24, 116, 127; **Steven Gunther:** 23; **Hadco Lighting:** 288 bottom right; **Marcus Harpur:** 25 bottom; **Philip Harvey:** 32, 82, 85 posthole digger, 270 top, 276, 293; **David Hewitt/Anne Garrison:** 34, 36 right; **Vixen Hill:** 277 right; **Saxon Holt:** 11 bottom left; 25 top, 48 right, 59 bottom, 181 top, 182 bottom, 191 top, 202 left, 211 top, 233 top, 234 top; **James Frederick Housel:** 148 bottom; **William Howard:** 47 bottom; **Dennis Krukowski:** 189 top; **David Duncan Livingston:** 22 bottom; **Lowe s:** 51 bottom, 254 top, 255, 262; **Peter Malinowski/In Site:** 35, 284; **Allan Mandell:** 5 center right, 9, 11 bottom right, 40 top, 45 bottom, 46 top, 48 top and bottom left, 52 top, 53 right, 58 top, 222 top left; **Robert Millman:** 51 top; **Sharron Milstein/Spindrift Photographics:** 29 bottom left; **Terrence Moore:** 187 top; **Richard Nicol:** 76; **Russell J. Nirella/Thermal Industries:** 79 center right, 136 bottom; **Jerry Pavia:** 41 top, 44 top, 53 left, 64, 177 bottom, 179 bottom; **D. Petku/H. Armstrong Roberts:** 161 top; **Norm Plate:** 39 top left, 237 bottom right; **Norman A. Plate:** 258, 259, 263; **Kenneth Rice:** 283 top, 288 top; **Susan A. Roth:** 68, 185 top; **courtesy of Rubbermaid:** 50 bottom; **Mark Rutherford:** 86, 87 top right, 88 center and bottom, 89 top and center, 90, 100, 101 top and bottom, 102–105, 107, 110–115, 117, 124 bottom, 126, 130 top right and left, 131, 132 bottom left and right, 134 bottom, 135, 136 top and center, 137 bottom, 142–145, 152–155, 161 bottom, 164–167, 289 top and center; **Douglas A. Salin:** 10 bottom; **Richard Shiell:** 282 bottom; **Phil Schofield:** 149 top left; **Marv Sloben:** 132 top; **Joe Sohn/Unicorn Photos:** 124 top; **Thomas J. Story:** 21, 22 top, 33 bottom, 39 center right and bottom, 59 top, 192 wrecking bar; **Dan Stultz:** 239 bottom, 240, 241, 243 bottom, 248 top left and right, bottom right, 249, 250 center and bottom, 251 center and bottom, 290–292, 294–297; **Michael S. Thompson:** 29 top, 190 top, 264, 282 top; **E. Spencer Toy:** 190 bottom; **courtesy of Trex:** 134 top; **Mark Turner:** 13–15, 16 top, 26 top, 33 top left and right, 46 bottom, 47 top, 54, 57 bottom, 120, 149 bottom left; **Brian Vanden Brink:** 5 left, 6, 7 top, 58 bottom, 148 top right, 149 center and bottom right, 254 bottom, 278, 279 top, 281; **Dominique Vorillon:** 36 left; **David Wakely:** 57 top; **Jessie Walker:** 279 bottom; **Deidra Walpole:** 10 top, 51 center, 52 bottom, 162 top, 163 top, 183 bottom, 186 top, 236 top; **courtesy of Weyerhaeuser:** 137 top, 158; **judywhite/ GardenPhoto.com:** 29 bottom right

DESIGN

Adams Design Associates: 36 right, 191 bottom; **Tibor Ambrus:** 72; **Henry Angeli:** 273; **Jeff Bale:** 11 bottom right, 53 right; **Shari Bashin-Sullivan:** 182 bottom; **Bellevue Botanical Garden:** 33 top right; **BEM Design Group:** 236 top; **Berghoff Design Group:** 284; **Big Red Sun:** 181 bottom right; **Stephen Blatt Architects:** 149 bottom right; **Brigitte M. Burke:** 189 top; **Pamela Burton:** 5 center right, 52 top; **Bob Carlson:** 24, 127; **Theresa Clark Studio:** 21; **Connie Cross:** 185 top; **Gary Cushenberry:** 5 center left, 149 top right; **Dalton Pavilions, Inc.:** 276; **Ernest Delto:** 51 top; **Enchanting Planting:** 234 top; **Bob Feasey:** 278; **Konrad Gauder:** 40 top, 181 top; **Michael Glassman and Associates:** 27, 45 top; **Nancy Goslee:** 218 top; **The Green Scene Design:** 51 center; **Guthrie + Buresh Architecture:** 47 bottom; **Milare Hare:** 46 top; **Heartwood Log Homes:** 7 top; **Heliotrope Garden Design:** 43 bottom, 206 top left; **David Helm:** 13 top, 14 bottom, 54, 149 bottom left; **Henning/Anderson:** 237 bottom right; **Horiuchi & Solien:** 5 left, 281; **Huettl-Thuilot Associates:** 48 right; **Johnsen Landscapes & Pools:** 178; **Kane Design and Associates:** 39 bottom; **Judy and Rick Keith:** 14 top; **KenMark Landscaping:** 17 bottom, 55 top; **John Kenyon, Sundance Landscaping:** 11 top; **Kichler Lighting:** 288 top; **Robert Knight:** 124; **Helen Koontz:** 52 bottom; **Rick LaFrentz:** 33 bottom; **Elizabeth Lair:** 264; **Lankford Associates/Landscape Architects:** 76, 270; **Terry Lehmann:** 16 top; **Mike Lervick and Vicki Mandin:** 148 bottom; **Eric Logan, Carney**

Architects: 116; **Ron Lutsko Associates:** 28; **Robert Marien:** 162 top; **Randolf Marshall:** 42 bottom; **Terry Martin:** 22 top; **Stephanie Mathews, ASID:** 34; **Clark Matschek:** 48 bottom; **Eleanor McKinney:** 40 bottom; **John Montgomery, Landgraphics, Inc.:** 32; **Eryl Morton:** 58 top; **Fran and Jim Murray:** 35; **New Leaf Garden Design:** 183 bottom; **Marietta and Ernie O Byrne:** 48 top; **Per Olaf Odman:** 42 top, 172; **Jason Payne:** 25 bottom; **Putman Construction and Landscaping:** 23; **Ransohoff, Blanchfield, Jones, Inc.:** 293; **Bill Remick, Remick Associates:** 74; **Sarah and Lance Robertson:** 29 top; **Ruby Begonia Fine Gardens:** 10 top, 163 top; **Michael Schultz:** 45 bottom, 222 top (with Will Goodman); **Bob and Sandy Snyder:** 68; **Addison Strong:** 22 bottom; **Bud Stuckey:** 59 top; **Irving Tamura, Pat Sunseri, Peter O. Whiteley:** 190 bottom; **Paul Tennant, AIA:** 13 bottom; **Michael Thilgen:** 202 left; **Tramontano & Rowe Landscape Architects:** 223 center left; **Gregory Trutza:** 36 left; **Turnbull Griffin Haesloop Architects:** 57 top; **Van Atta Design Associates:** 186 top; **The Village of Arts & Humanities:** 250 top; **William John Wallis, ASLA:** 146 bottom; **Sally Weston:** 254 bottom; **Randall Whitehead, lighting design:** 283 top; **Rob Whitten:** 148 top right, 279 top; **David Yakish:** 25 top, 211 top, 233 top; **Michael Yandle:** 10 bottom; **Zischke Studios:** 39 top left

ILLUSTRATION

Anthony Davis: 286; **Jim Kopp:** 62–169, 178, 268 top and bottom left, 269 bottom, 278, 279; **Bill Oetinger:** 173–176, 198, 201, 218, 226, 227, 252, 264–266, 268 top center and right, bottom center and right, 269 top, 271, 272, 274, 275, 277 left, 293; **Mark Pechenik:** 259–261

THANKS TO

The Coleman Co., Inc; DekBrands; Handy Home Products; Fred Kilby and John Kelly; Ian Reid and Kathy Niles; Andy and Maxine Oh; Weyerhaeuser

index